W9-CKH-033

JUL 5 – 1985

Cataloging
GOVERNMENT
DOCUMENTS

Cataloging

GOVERNMENT

DOCUMENTS

A Manual of Interpretation for AACR2

DOCUMENTS CATALOGING MANUAL COMMITTEE
GOVERNMENT DOCUMENTS ROUND TABLE
AMERICAN LIBRARY ASSOCIATION
BERNADINE ABBOTT HODUSKI, editor

AMERICAN LIBRARY ASSOCIATION
Chicago 1984

Designed by Vladimir Reichl

Composed by Automated Office Systems, Inc.
in Times Roman on a Text Ed/VIP
phototypesetting system

Printed on 50-pound Glatfelter,
a pH-neutral stock,
by Malloy Lithographing, Inc.,
and bound in Kivar 6 cover stock
by John H. Dekker & Sons

Library of Congress Cataloging in Publication Data
Main entry under title:

Cataloging government documents.

    Includes index.
    1. Cataloging of government publications—Handbooks,
manuals, etc.   2. Anglo-American cataloging rules—
Handbooks, manuals, etc.   3. Descriptive cataloging—Rules
—Handbooks, manuals, etc.   I. Hoduski, Bernadine A.
(Bernadine Abbott)   II. American Library Association.
Government Documents Round Table. Documents Cataloging
Committee.
Z695.1.G7C26   1984   025.3′434   84-6499
ISBN 0-8389-3304-1

AMERICAN LIBRARY ASSOCIATION
GOVERNMENT DOCUMENTS ROUND TABLE
DOCUMENTS CATALOGING MANUAL COMMITTEE
1978–1983

Bernadine Abbott Hoduski
  Coordinator (GODORT)
  U.S. Congress Joint Committee
  on Printing
  1978– 83
Jaffry Aronson (NTIS)
  National Technical Information Service
  1979– 81
John Byrum (LC)
  Library of Congress
  Descriptive Cataloging
  1978– 83
Marion Carroll (GODORT)
  Illinois State University Library
  1978– 81
Elwynda Chapmon (FLC)
  Census Bureau Library
  1982– 83
Nora S. Copeland (GODORT)
  Colorado State University Library
  1980– 83
Mary Feldman (FLC)
  Department of Transportation Library
  1978– 81
Richard Fox (LC—Geography & Map)
  Library of Congress
  Geography & Map Division
  1979– 83
Shirley Glazener (GODORT)
  George Mason University Library
  1978– 79

Stuart Greenburg (GPO)
  Government Printing Office Library
  Editor, *Monthly Catalog of U.S.*
  Government Publications
  1978– 83
Sylvia Hsieh (GODORT)
  Rutgers University Library
  1978– 79
Barbra Buckner Higginbotham (GODORT)
  Columbia University Libraries
  1978– 83
Irene Itina (GODORT)
  New York Public Library
  1978– 80
Asta Kane (NTIS)
  National Technical Information Service
  1982– 83
Edna Kanely (GODORT)
  Government Printing Office Library
  (retired)
  Editor, *Monthly Catalog of U.S.*
  Government Publications
  1978– 80
Paul Klinefelter (DTIC)
  U.S. Defense Technical Information
  Center
  1978– 81
Tae Moon Lee (GODORT)
  State University of New York
  at Albany Library
  1978– 82

(Dates included above indicate years served on the committee.)

Documents Cataloging Manual Committee

Daniel Lester
  University of New Mexico Library
  1978
Margaret Lane (GODORT)
  Louisiana. Secretary of State Office
  (retired)
  1978– 81
Suzanne Liggett (LC)
  Library of Congress
  Name Authority Co-op
  1979– 83
Janet Lyons (GODORT)
  Illinois State Library
  1978– 83
Milton McGee (FLC)
  Federal Library Committee
  1978– 81
Sarah Whalen Mikel (FLC)
  Army Corps of Engineers Library
  1978– 83
Gail Nichols (GODORT)
  University of California
  at Berkeley Library
  1978– 80
Vi Moorhouse (GODORT)
  Government Printing Office Library
  1978– 83

Judy Myers (GODORT)
  University of Houston Library
  1982– 83
Sue Ellen Sloca (FLC)
  Department of Interior Library
  1978– 82
Virginia Snider (GPO—Sales)
  Government Printing Office
  Sales Service
  1979– 83
Charles Stewart (GODORT)
  Princeton University Library
  1978– 79
Johanna Thompson (GODORT)
  Washington & Lee University Library
  1978– 79
Alice Wickizer (GODORT)
  Indiana University Library
  1978– 83
Chong Yoon (GODORT)
  State University of New York
  at Albany Library
  1978– 83

(Dates included above indicate years served on the committee.)

Contents

Contents

Contents

Preface

For many years the government documents community has avoided using traditional cataloging rules for government documents. When the American Library Association (ALA) announced in 1975 a revision of the Anglo-American Cataloging Rules, the Government Documents Round Table (GODORT) seized the opportunity to participate in the revision, hoping to influence the rule-writing committee to produce rules that would make it easier for the searcher to find government information in traditional catalogs and would encourage libraries to include government documents in traditional catalogs.

GODORT submitted the following statement to the ALA Resources and Technical Services Division (RTSD) and the Joint Steering Committee of AACR2 in January of 1975.

RECOMMENDATIONS

1. The name or jurisdiction of the governmental unit should always appear first in the main entry and added entry.
2. Give complete hierarchy of government author in main entry. Give other variations of government author as added entries or see references.
   a. Unless the AACR Committee or IFLA can give a workable, understandable definition of the lowest identifiable agency.
   b. The *Monthly Catalog of U.S. Government Publications,* the *Monthly Checklist of State Publications,* and state checklists are all based on hierarchy. We cannot get along without these tools and would like to see AACR entries follow the same uniform entry.
   c. The user cannot function with the lowest identifiable agency.
3. Main entry under government author is preferred. If not, then we want a government author to be a required added entry.
4. We request a definition of a governmental agency—this should be an international standard. The government author is in essence the only world wide identifying factor.
5. In the glossary we request additional definitions and a clarification and change of some definitions. Also, a change in the footnote on page 11.

The Anglo-American Cataloguing Rules, second edition, are the product of six authors called the Joint Steering Committee (JSC). The American Library Association and the Library of Congress are the American participants. The Catalog Code Revision Committee (CCRC) was established as a committee of RTSD to formulate the ALA recommendations to the Joint Steering Committee. RTSD invited representatives from other units of ALA, as well as other library organizations, to participate in the revision as consultants. These consultants did not have a vote in CCRC.

The Government Documents Round Table sent Bernadine Abbott Hoduski as its representative. In order to advise her, GODORT established a Documents Cataloging Committee.

The GODORT Documents Cataloging Committee formulated a number of additional recommendations, and Ms. Hoduski presented them to CCRC along with those presented in 1975. A number of those proposals, such as the inclusion of a variety of numbers in the cataloging record (e.g., the Superintendent of Documents classification and stock numbers, the National Technical Information Service numbers and contract numbers), were included in the new rules. Other proposals, such as corporate body as the main entry for all government documents, were not accepted.

After the rules were adopted by the JSC in 1978, GODORT decided to establish a committee to write a government documents cataloging manual based on *AACR2*. GODORT believed that such a manual would promote standardized cataloging of government documents, would make it easier for libraries to accept each others records, and would encourage cooperative cataloging.

The Committee worked closely with the Library of Congress, the Superintendent of Documents, and the Federal Library Committee to develop rule interpretations that would provide for the best treatment of documents. Those rule interpretations include (1) how much hierarchy to include in the heading for a body after it has already been decided to enter the body subordinately and (2) the addition of geographic qualifiers to corporate headings.

The Committee worked with the Library of Congress (LC), the Superintendent of Documents, and the National Technical Information Service to determine such policies as how the bibliographic data sheet for scientific and technical documents would be used in the cataloging of such documents.

The Committee played an important role in encouraging the cooperative cataloging programs between LC and the Superintendent of Documents and between LC and libraries cataloging state documents, including the cooperative name authority program. Both the Superintendent of Documents and the LC staff were receptive to the Committee's suggestions. The LC staff was a gracious host on many occasions, providing not only meeting rooms but also coffee and encouragement.

GODORT would like to thank the Documents Cataloging Committee for its outstanding work and extend a special thanks to:

Bernadine Abbott Hoduski, who represented GODORT to the Catalog Code Revision Committee from 1975 to 1978 and its successor committee until 1983 and who, believing that GODORT could make a difference, encouraged the Documents Cataloging Committee to persevere in its work

Sue Ellen Sloca, U.S. Department of Interior, who did much of the editorial work on Part 1, including the creation of a number of the tables

Richard Fox, LC Geography and Map Division, who wrote most of chapters 3 and 23 and served on the editorial and proofing committee

Chong Yoon, State University of New York, Albany, who spent hours finding appropriate cataloging examples and checking the proofs for diacritical marks and cataloging errors

Nora Copeland, Colorado State University, who, even before she became a member of the Committee, gave good advice and contributed many cataloging examples

Ben Tucker, Chief of the Office of Descriptive Cataloging Policy at the Library of Congress, who reviewed the text several times and worked with the committee on rule interpretations

Suzanne Liggett and John Byrum, the Library of Congress, who patiently attended almost all the Committee meetings and were a constant source of excellent advice and assistance

Jim Coleman, who patiently keyed the text and countless changes to the manual into the computer

The Membership and Steering committees of GODORT who supported the principles of cooperative cataloging and the inclusion of documents in library catalogs.

Sandra K. Peterson, Chairperson, GODORT, 1983–84

Barbara Kyle, Chairperson, GODORT, 1982–83

Jeanne Isacco, Chairperson, GODORT, 1979–82

General Introduction

This manual has been designed to be used in conjunction with the second edition of the *Anglo-American Cataloguing Rules,* hereafter referred to as AACR2, for the cataloging of government documents. In this manual no new rules or additions to AACR2 are proposed. Rather, those rules especially pertinent to the cataloging of government documents are discussed. In so doing, this manual attempts

1) To clarify those rules in AACR2 that are unclear with regard to government document cataloging.
2) To address those special features of government documents pertinent to cataloging that remain unacknowledged by AACR2, and to interpret these features in a manner consistent with the spirit of AACR2.

The structure of this manual follows that of AACR2. Part 1 deals with description; Part 2 deals with headings, uniform titles, and references. The numbering of each chapter within these two parts corresponds to that of the chapter of AACR2 being discussed. (Consequently, there are no chapters 14– 19, for example.)

In this manual not all chapters of AACR2 are specifically addressed, or addressed in the same detail. Generally, government documents are more likely to be issued in certain types of formats rather than others (as printed monographs rather than as music, for example). In this manual an attempt has been made to deal with chapters of AACR2 in proportion to their relative likelihood of being of concern to government documents cataloging.

Not all rules of the chapters of AACR2 dealt with in this manual are individually discussed. Individual rules are addressed if, in the context of government document cataloging, they are unclear, require illustrative examples from government documents, or need further discussion before they can be applied to government documents. For ease of use of this manual, rule numbers of single rules or groups of rules not individually discussed are given in their appropriate order, followed by an extended dash.

0.1– 0.6 ———
2.3 ———

Often, it is not necessary to discuss individual subsets of rules separately; it is more useful to discuss several subrules with a single (joint) comment. In these instances, rule numbers for the subrules will not be given. Comments will be linked to the most specific rule or rule area to which the rules discussed are subordinate. Rules at the level of the first alphabetical subdivision and above, however, will always be given in their appropriate order, whether commented on or not. An example of the joint discussion of subrules is

2.0   GENERAL RULES
   2.0A Scope [text . . .]
   2.0B Sources of information [text   . . .]
   2.0C ———

The single (joint) comment for both subrules 2.0B1 and 2.0B2 is linked to 2.0B. Also, unless otherwise indicated, the references in the text to other rules refer to AACR2. References to Library of Congress rule interpretations are indicated by *RI*.

The provisions of this manual are intended to be applicable to documents issued by governments at all jurisdictional levels: local, midlevel (county, state, province, etc.), national, international, and combinations thereof. The definition of government document used in this manual includes all those types of materials for which chapters on descriptive cataloging have been provided in Part I of AACR2, whether the documents have been issued directly by, or in cooperation with, a government body, in any way.

Bibligraphically speaking, government documents are not simple materials. Typically, government documents are the joint product of a complex relationship of persons and corporate bodies. Any government document, like a more traditional item to be cataloged, may have one or more persons, acknowledged in its chief source of information, who bear a direct responsibility for its content. However, unlike such a traditional item, a government document is always, to a certain degree, also the product of at least one corporate body, and may often be the product of a number of corporate bodies. It is not uncommon for a government document, for example, to be written by the staff of a corporate contractor for a particular corporate body (government agency), with the funding or monitoring of the contract being provided for or performed by another corporate body, with the document itself being distributed by still another corporate body. Each of the involved corporate bodies may have incorporated the document into one of its own series. Complex materials call for complex cataloging. The manual for the interpretation of AACR2 for the cataloging of government documents that follows is intended to provide a bibliographic record that can be of maximum value to the wide variety of interests that must make use of it.

Description

Introduction

0.21 The rules in the chapters of Part I instruct the cataloger how to describe an item of library material, including documents, and how to set down statements of description, resulting in a whole called bibliographic description. Where the bibliographic description is filed in a library's catalog depends on the headings added to it to make it accessible to users of the catalog. These headings constitute points of access, which are chosen and constructed according to Part II.

0.22 AACR2 is the first cataloging code in the Anglo-American context that bases all bibliographic description on ISBD provisions for the formulation, arrangement, and punctuation of data elements. There are two noticeable effects of the pervasive influence of ISBD. Henceforth the bibliographic descriptions for book documents, serial documents, motion picture documents, etc., will all reflect ISBD arrangement and punctuation of data elements. A specific example of this point is the complete abandonment of the older idea of copying an element merely because it appears on the title page (or other chief source).

Structure of Part I. Methods of procedure

0.23 Unlike the chapters of Part II, which deal with sharply different matters, the chapters of Part I are extremely interrelated, because such factors as level of specificity of rule, bibliographic condition, and physical format of item, commonly cause the cataloger to select more than one chapter as a guide to bibliographic description of the item. The following illustrates the scope of these chapters in Part I:

> Chapter 1. Basic rules for description, applicable to all categories of library material
> Chapters 2–10. Rules for the description of specific categories of materials based on chapter 1. These rules cover only monographs.
> Chapters 11–13. Rules of partial generality, based on chapter 1, to be used with rules of chapters 2–10, as appropriate. Chapter 12 covers the bibliographic condition of serials, without regard to category of material.

0.24 As chapters of partial generality, however, chapters 11, 12, and 13 are themselves not otherwise comparable. They differ in the way in which they relate to chapters 2–10. Part I of AACR2 is based on the principle "that the description of a physical item should be based in the first instance on the chapter dealing with the class of materials to which that item belongs" (0.24). This means that items issued serially, cataloged according to chapter 12, are described primarily in terms of their individual physical formats as specified in chapters 2–10 and 11. This also means, however, that previously existing items issued in microform are to be cataloged according to chapter 11, with only a secondary consideration for the terms of their original individual physical formats as covered by chapters 2–10. Items in microform that are originally produced in microform are cataloged according to only chapter 11.[1] Microforms are described primarily in terms of their particular type of microformat. Chapters 2–10 are relied upon for the construction of notes, as appropriate. Chapter 13, dealing with analysis of individual parts of a larger item, provides guidelines for analyzing parts of all the categories of specific materials addressed in chapters 2-10. Consequently, the interrelationship of the chapters of Part I might be summarized in this way:

> Chapter 1 provides rules for bibliographic description which serve as the basic framework for all chapters of Part I.
>
> Within the basic framework, chapters 2–10 provide rules for the description of specific types of materials. These rules deal with the description of discrete units monographs).
>
> Within the basic frame work, chapter 11 provides rules for the description of microreproductions of any of the specific types of materials treated in chapters 2–10 (as well as of micro-original discrete units [monographs].
>
> Within the basic framework, chapter 12 provides rules for the description of series of units (serials) represented by any of the specific types of materials treated in chapters 2–10 (+11).
>
> Within the basic framework, chapter 13 provides rules for the description of parts of units represented by any of the specific types of materials treated in chapters 2–10 (+11) as either monographs or serials.

0.25 While the new area 3 is limited to serials and to cartographic material, it has recently been adopted by the Library of Congress for music, and it may eventually be considered for other materials.

Options and omissions

0.26 The publication, distribution, etc., area normally consists of three elements: place, publisher, and date. In the case of publications, some representation of the three elements must always be present, but this area for materials treated under chapter 4

---

1. Library of Congress has a special policy for cataloging of microforms of previously existing works.

needs only the date, with no sort of representation for elements of place and publisher. It is important to understand, consequently, that chapter 4 covers not only conventional manuscripts and typescripts, but also copies of the same, when copying is not accompanied by publication.

0.27 Not only are notes per se optional, but the formulation of them is also optional; how they are worded, how much standardization, how full or how brief the contents, etc., are all questions that are not legislated by the rules, to the extent that they are for data transcribed in the body of the entry. In fact, the note area becomes the place for assuaging all disappointments with transcription in the body of the entry.

0.28 ———

0.29 The three levels of description specified in 1.0D should *not* be confused with levels of description instituted by any specific bibliographic utility, etc., unless these levels are specifically keyed to AACR2. As noted in AACR2 0.29, "each of these levels is to be considered as a minimum in that, when appropriate, further information may be added to the required set of data." This means, in effect, that, according to local cataloging policy, items may be cataloged according to any intermediate combination of level specifications (level "1½, 1¾," etc.), but that bibliographic records created for these items must be coded, in any system (machine or otherwise) that includes such information, at the lowest level for which all mandatory specifications are met. For further discussion, see 1.0D in this manual.

1/ General Rules for Description

Chapter 1 of AACR2 contains the general rules for the descriptive cataloging of all types of materials, regardless of format. Specifically, chapter 1 presents the basic rules for the descriptive cataloging of books, pamphlets, and printed sheets; cartographic materials; manuscripts (including manuscript collections); music; sound recordings; motion pictures and videorecordings; graphic materials; machine-readable data files; three-dimensional artefacts and realia; serials; analytics . . . and even those materials whose formats are yet to be discussed in AACR2. (The chapter numbers 14–19 are not used, so chapters covering other categories of material can be added at a later date). Chapters 12–13 each deal with a particular category of material, while chapter 1 is applicable to all.

No single item can be described from chapter 1 alone; "it is a cardinal principle in the use of Part I that the description of a physical item should be based in the first instance on the chapter dealing with the class of materials to which that item belongs" (0.24). No single item can, however, be described without chapter 1. The rules for bibliographic description presented in chapter 1 are *not* systematically repeated in each succeeding chapter of Part I. In fact the rules in chapter 2 are frequently mere references back to chapter 1.

Government documents come in a variety of categories of material, making it necessary for the documents cataloger to move back and forth among the chapters of Part I, same as with materials other than documents.

1.0 GENERAL RULES

1.0A Sources of information
For each different category of material dealt with in Part I of AACR2 there is an appropriate "chief source of information" for bibliographic description. For a discussion of the details of each of these, refer to the chapter of this manual corresponding to the chapter of AACR2 applicable to the category of material.

United States federal government documents may include, in addition to or in place of the title page specified as the chief source of information in AACR2, a "bibliographic data sheet," which is a semi-standardized scientific and technical report title page. See the discussion of 2.0B in this manual for an in-depth treatment of bibliographic data sheets in the descriptive cataloging of government documents.

Occasionally government documents are issued without adequate self-identification. If the data for the description are available through research from a source other than the chief source of information, "give in a note the reason for and/or source of the supplied data" (1.0A2). If, however, exhaustive research into the source of any particular document is not possible, the item itself may have to serve as the only basis for the description.

1.0B–1.0C ———

1.0D Levels of detail in the description

As already indicated in 0.29, AACR2 provides for three different levels of bibliographic description. (See 0.29 and the discussion of it in this manual.) Each succeeding level includes more bibliographic elements than the preceding level. The highest—or, rather, fullest—level of bibliographic description, the third level, includes all bibliographic elements applicable to the item being described. Formally designated optional additions, however, are optional at all levels of bibliographic description. Such additions are indicated in AACR2 by the italicized terms *optional addition, optionally,* etc. Notes also are not suggested as optional additions. "All notes described in the chapters of Part I may be considered to be optional in that their inclusion in the entry depends on the nature of the item described and the purpose of the entry concerned" (0.27). The fact that all three levels of bibliographic description include notes among prescribed elements does not mean that all notes potentially applicable to any item must be included at all three levels. Because notes are optional in the sense that their inclusion depends partly on the purpose of the entry concerned, a cataloging agency has the authority at levels one and two to include only those notes deemed to be both necessary and appropriate at those respective levels. At level three, however, the bibliographic description of an item should include all applicable notes.

The following examples illustrate the application of the first, second, and third levels of bibliographic description as applied to books, pamphlets, and printed sheets (materials cataloged under chapter 2):

LEVEL 1
> List of treaty collections. — United Nations, 1956. — xv, 174 p. — Includes index.

LEVEL 2
> List of treaty collections (text) = Liste de recueils de traités. — New York : United Nations, 1956. — xv, 174 p.; 23 cm. — (ST/LEG/ ; 5) — Introduction in English, French and Spanish. — "Compiled by the Codification Division of the Office of Legal Affairs." — Includes index.

LEVEL 3
> List of treaty collections (text) = Liste de recueils de traités = Liste de colecciones de tratados. — New York : United Nations, 1956. — xv, 174 p.; 23 cm. — (ST/LEG/ ; 5) —Introduction in English, French and Spanish.

"Compiled by the Codification Division of the Office of Legal Affairs." — Includes index. — Contents: pt.1. General collections — pt.2. Collections by subject matter — pt.3. Collections by states.

Choice of appropriate level of description should be based not only on "the purpose of the catalogue or catalogues for which the entry is constructed" (1.0D), as instructed in AACR2, but also on the type of item being described. As discussed in the introduction to this manual, government documents are generally bibliographically complex items, often requiring complex cataloging. Whenever possible, government documents should be described at the fullest level of description, the third level of bibliographic description. Examples of complete bibliographic records presented in this manual will, therefore, reflect the third level of description. Aside from the unconditional exercise of option 1.1C, the display of the general material designation in eye-readable records (see the discussion of 1.1C below), these examples will faithfully reflect both the choice of formally designated options to be followed by LC/GPO, and the degree of detail deemed appropriate to bibliographic description of government documents by this manual.

It is recognized that it may not always be feasible for cataloging agencies to describe all items at the third level of description. Cataloging agencies choosing to describe government documents at either the first or second level should be aware of the varying scope of inclusion of bibliographic elements for each level. The single most serious deficiency of level one for the description of government documents— even for a simplified catalog—is the lack of a series statement. Agencies choosing to describe government documents at the first level ought to consider adding this element to their standard for description. Another point is that depending on the amount of bibliographic data pertinent to any particular item, it is likely that the description of a government document at level two will closely resemble its description at level three. (The gap between levels one and two is far greater than that between levels two and three.) The following examples illustrate the difference between the first and second levels of bibliographic description as applied to items of formats common to government documents:

LEVEL 1: serials
    Defense systems management review. — Vol.1, no. 1 (Winter 1976) — v. 3, no. 3 (Summer 1980) Defense Systems Management College, 1976– 1980. — v. Continued by: Concepts (Ft. Belvoir, Va.) — ISSN 0363-7727.

LEVEL 2: serials
    Defense systems management review (text). — Vol.1, no. 1 (Winter 1976) — v.3, no. 3 (Summer 1980). — Ft. Belvoir, Va. : Defense Systems Management College, 1976– 1980. — v. : ill. ; 27 cm. Continued by: Concepts (Ft. Belvoir, Va.) — ISSN 0363-7727 = Defense systems management review.

LEVEL 1: cartographic materials
    Official city map of Charlotte, Mecklenburg County, North Carolina / compiled

by the Engineering Division, Department of Public Works, city of Charlotte. — Scale 1:24,000. 1″ = 2,000′. — ₁Charlotte₁ : The Division, c1974. — 1 map. — Alternative title: Charlotte. — .''Grid based on North Carolina rectangular coordinate system.'' — Photocopy, blue line print. — ''A.A.S.C. 12730'' — Includes map of Mecklenburg County, North Carolina.

LEVEL 2: cartographic materials

Official city map of Charlotte, Mecklenburg County, North Carolina ₁map₁ / compiled by the Engineering Division, Department of Public Works, city of Charlotte ; photography & mapping by Abrams Aerial Survey Corporation. — Scale 1:24,000. 1″ = 2,000′. — ₁Charlotte₁ : The Division, c1974. — 1 map : photocopy ; 102 × 116 cm. — Alternate title: Charlotte. ''Grid based on North Carolina rectangular coordinate system.'' — Blue line print. — ''A.A.S.C. 12730.'' — Includes map of Mecklenburg County, North Carolina.

LEVEL 1: books, pamphlets, and printed sheets

January 1979 water levels, and data related to water-level changes, western and south-central Kansas / by M.E. Pabst. — United States, Department of Interior, Geological Survey, 1979. — 213 p.

LEVEL 2: books, pamphlets, and printed sheets

January 1979 water levels, and data related to water-level changes, western and south-central Kansas ₁text₁ / by M.E. Pabst; prepared in cooperation with the Kansas Geological Survey and the Division of Water Resources, Kansas State Board of Agriculture. — Lawrence, Kansas : United States, Department of Interior, Geological Survey, 1979. — 213 p ; 28 cm. + 3 maps. — (Open-file report / U.S. Geological Survey ; 79-925). — Chiefly tables.

1.0E–1.0G ———

1.0H Items with several chief sources of information

Single part items. When ''the chief sources of information present the item in different aspects (e.g., as an individual item and as part of a multipart item), prefer the one that corresponds to the aspect in which the item is to be treated'' (1.0H). This means when creating a bibliographic record for the individual item to use the title of it as the title proper, with the larger title (series or multipart monograph) transcribed in the series area (see 1.6)—as opposed to treating the title of the individual item, for example, as a subtitle to the title of the series or multipart monograph.

The range resource . . . (The use of high altitude, color and spectrozonal imagery for the inventory of wildland resources ; v.2)

not The use of high altitude, color and spectrozonal imagery for the inventory of wildland resources : Vol.2. The range resource . . .

Distinguish these cases from those in which the title of an item that is supplementary to or a section of another item appears in two or more parts not grammatically linked. (See 1.1B9.)

> Journal of biosocial science. Supplement.
> *not*   Supplement . . . (Journal of biosocial science)

Do not assume, however, that if the chief sources of information present the item being cataloged in different aspects (e.g., as an individual item and as part of a multipart item), that if, for example, only one part of a multipart item is available for cataloging, that the item necessarily ought to be described as an individual item. The decision of the cataloging agency to treat any such item as either an individual item or (part of a) multipart item ought to be based in part upon the nature of the item being described. Items with short, nondistinctive titles are generally better described, first of all, as (parts of) multipart items. Then, as is deemed necessary by the cataloging agency on a case-by-case basis, individual parts of the multipart items can be analyzed. (See chapter 13.)

> Movement of hazardous substances in soil : a bibliography . . . 2 v.
> . . . Contents: v.1. Selected metals.—v.2. Pesticides.

Multipart items. If items are issued as part of a multipart item that is not linked together bibliographically, as evidenced by any or all of the following characteristics:

> A single title (rather than a corporate name, such as a project name) for the work as a whole, as found on each part of the multipart set
> Individual part numbering/lettering, etc., placing the individual parts in a particular relationship to the item as a whole

but are, instead, merely linked together in the text (or preliminaries, etc., of the item) or in accompanying documentation, do *not* describe the collection of items as a "formal" (i.e., bibliographic) multipart item. Describe each item as an individual item. Include in the description of each, as is deemed necessary by the cataloging agency on a case-by-case basis, a note indicating the relationship of the item to the "informal" multipart item.

> Sourcebook for western coal/energy development ₍text₎ / prepared by Mountain West Research, Inc. for the Missouri River Basin Commission, (and) Resource and Land Investigations (RALI) Program. — Billings, Montana : Mountain West Research, 1979. — vi, 223, 8p. : ill. ; 28 cm. — At head of title: Western Coal Planning Assistance Project. — Identified in Foreword as vol. 4 of the Project's "Planning reference system."

1.1 TITLE AND STATEMENT OF RESPONSIBILITY AREA

1.1A ———

1.1B Title proper

It is essential for the accurate identification of government documents that the title proper be recorded in the exact form in which it is found on the chief source of information, aside from the modifications in punctuation, capitalization, accentuation, and diacritical marks prescribed in 1.1B1. In case of doubt as to which phrases constitute the title proper, provide added title entries for alternative phrases not chosen as the title proper which are likely to be regarded as such. (See 21.30J; also see the discussion of 2.1B in this manual.)

1.1C *Optional addition.* **General material designation**

LC/GPO are exercising this option for some but not all of the general material designations. LC's policy regarding the display of GMDs in its records is summarized in the following tables:

Category A: The material is cataloged by LC.
The GMD will be displayed.
1) filmstrip
2) kit
3) microform
4) motion picture
5) slide
6) sound recording
7) transparency
8) videorecording

Category B: The material is not cataloged by LC.
The GMD would be displayed if such material were to be cataloged by LC in the future.
1) chart
2) diorama
3) flash card
4) game
5) microscope slide
6) model
7) realia

Category C: The material is not cataloged by LC.
The decision as to the display of the GMD has not been made.
1) art original
2) picture
3) machine-readable data file
4) technical drawing

Category D: The material is cataloged by LC.
The GMD will not be displayed.
1) globe
2) map
3) manuscript
4) music
5) text (1)

1.1D Parallel titles

The titles of works in translation are sometimes to be recorded as parallel titles. 1.1D3 prescribes that if "an original title in a language different from that of the title proper" appears in the chief source of information, it is to be treated as a parallel title if

1) the item itself "contains all or some of the text in the original language"

or 2) "the original title appears before the title proper in the chief source of information."

If the original title appears after the title proper in the chief source of information for a work in translation, record it in a note. (See 1.7B4.)

1.1E Other title information

Often, with government documents, it may be difficult to determine which phrases constitute "other title information," as distinguished from both the title proper and statements of responsibility. For guidance, see the discussion of 2.1E below.

1.1E5 *Optionally.* Addition of other title information in other languages. LC/GPO are exercising this option.

1.1F Statements of responsibility

Statements of responsibility appearing "prominently" on items are to be recorded in the form in which they appear on the item. The term *prominently* as used here is a technical term. It "means that a statement to which it applies must be a formal statement found in one of the prescribed sources of information (see 1.0A) for areas 1 and 2 for the class of material to which the item being cataloged belongs" (0.8). For each different format dealt with in Part I of AACR2, there are appropriately defined "prescribed sources of information" for areas 1 and 2 of the bibliographic record. For this purpose note that area 1 is the title and statement of responsibility area and that area 2 is the edition area.

Statements of responsibility relating to persons or bodies appearing prominently on an item are to be recorded "in the form in which they appear there" (1.1F1). This means, especially for government documents, that in statements of responsibility involving corporate bodies, the names of these bodies are to be transcribed in the precise form and order (of hierarchical elements) that is presented on the item itself. Corporate names, therefore, in the title and statement of responsibility area, are *not*

1) to be rearranged so that the elements of corporate hierarchy as given are arranged in any order other than that which is given on the item
2) to be abbreviated, or shortened, in any fashion
3) to be extended, or lengthened, in any fashion.

When transcribing statements of responsibility as they appear on the item, the cataloger will notice that corporate affiliations of the people are also found in the source. With documents, the involvement of bodies named in this way amounts to a degree of responsibility that needs to be recorded, with added access points usually made under their headings. Consequently, when the names of those bodies would not otherwise be recorded, and information about them or access through them is considered essential, either record them with the personal name in the statement of responsibility, or give them in the note area. In recording the name of such corporate bodies, omit geographic addresses unless they are needed for adequate identification of the corporate bodies. Follow 1.1F7 in omitting, normally, a person's position or title in relation to the corporate body. When a group of people all belong to the same body, but the body's name is repeated after each individual, give the body's name once, after the person named last in the group, and enclose it within parentheses. Also enclose the body's name within parentheses when it appears once after the entire group. Otherwise, use a comma to separate the person's name from that of the body. Alternatively, record the names of these bodies in the note area, as when the necessary statement would be long, complex, or otherwise not easily handled in the title and statement of responsibility area.

Onset of condensation effects . . . / Robert M. Hall, Langley Research Center

Instream flow strategies for Arizona / by Wayne Nelson, Gerry Horak and Joe Solomon (Enviro Control, Inc.)

. . . / prepared by Morton J. Schussheim, senior specialist in housing, Joshua M. Kay, economic analyst, Richard L. Wellons, research assistant in housing, Congressional Research Service, Library of Congress

example of note
"Center for Systems Development, SRI International"

1.1F4 AACR2 indicates that a single statement of responsibility is to be recorded as such, whether the two or more parties named in it perform the same function or different functions. "Single statements of responsibility," as distinguished from "multiple statements of responsibility," are normally statements that are linked together by appropriate grammatical connectives (prepositions and conjunctions). Multiple statements of responsibility are normally not so grammatically linked, and, therefore, must be linked in the bibliographic record by the appropriate punctuation and spacing. (See 1.1A1.) Multiple statements of responsibility to which a word or short phrase is added, when the relationship between the title of the work and the parties named in the statements is unclear, may, with the addition of the work or phrase, be transformed into single statements of responsibility.

> Proposed zoning ordinance for the U.S. Virgin Islands / Walter H. Blucher ₍for the₎ Virgin Islands Planning Board

Grammar, therefore, can be quite helpful in distinguishing single statements of responsibility from multiple statements of responsibility. Remember, however, that in deciding whether any particular statement of responsibility represents a single statement of responsibility or a multiple statement of responsibility, the ultimate criterion lies in how the statement in question reads. The preposition "with," for example, may sometimes link multiple statements of responsibility.

> . . . / researched and drafted by James Q. Mason ; with a table of soil samples by Phyllis Marton

1.1F5 AACR2 prescribes that "when a single statement of responsibility names more than three persons or corporate bodies performing the same function, or with the same degree of responsibility" (1.1F5), all but the first of each group or such persons or bodies should be omitted in the transcription of the statement of responsibility. Strict adherence to practice of this omission—classically referred to as the practice of following "the rule of three,"—will result, for some government documents, in bibliographic records that have insufficient access points, particularly in regards to access via corporate body. AACR2 allows for the addition to the bibliographic record of as many other access points, not directly mandated by specific rules, as are needed "in the context of a given catalogue" (21.29D). For government documents, added entries may be created for each person or corporate body to whom/which responsibility for the items is attributed in the chief source of information. (See the discussion below of 21.29D.) Local cataloging policy will dictate when, and to what extent, the practice of providing these additional added entries for government documents is followed. When following this license as provided for in 21.29D, so that added entries beyond the limit of three are provided, record the names of persons or corporate bodies excluded from the statement of responsibility by 1.1F5 in an appropriate note.

1.1F7 Corporate names in conjunction with personal names. LC's rule interpretation will often be used by catalogers of government documents.

> If an added entry is required for a corporate body and the only prominently named source for the body's name being recorded is in a statement of responsibility, apply one of the following methods:

> a) enclose within parentheses the corporate name following the personal name(s) (e.g., "prepared by Morton J. Schussheim, Joshua M. Kay, Richard L. Wellons (Congressional Research Service, Library of Congress)";

> /by Miles Storfer and Edward Jove (Office of Policy and Economic Research).—

14

b) give the corporate name in a quoted note (e.g., "Building Economics and Regulatory Technology Division, Center for Building Technology, National Engineering Laboratory, National Bureau of Standards.").

GPO will follow option B.

1.1G ———

1.2 EDITION AREA

1.2A ———

1.2B Edition statement
Edition statements are found less typically in government documents than in publications issued by commercial publishers.

1.2B4 *Optional addition.* **Cataloger-supplied edition statement.** LC/GPO are exercising this option only in rather unusual circumstances. According to their policy, the option should never be applied to any case of *supposed* differences in issues that might make them different editions. If differences are manifest, however, but the catalog records needed would show exactly the same information in the areas beginning with the title and statement of responsibility area and ending with the series area. Otherwise, information about the differences between editions should be in the note area.

1.2C–1.2E ———

1.3 MATERIAL (OR TYPE OF PUBLICATION) SPECIFIC DETAILS AREA

According to printed text of AACR2, this area is used *only* for the bibliographic description of cartographic materials and serials. For cartographic materials, this area records "mathematical data," such as the item's scale, projection, coordinates and equinox, etc. (See 3.3 in this manual for a fuller discussion of this area as used for cartographic materials.) For serial items, this area records "numeric and/or alphabetic, chronological data," such as issue numbering, volume designation, etc. (See 12.3 in this manual for a fuller discussion of this area as used for serial items.)

1.4 PUBLICATION, DISTRIBUTION, ETC., AREA

1.4A ———

1.4B General rules
AACR2 specifies that the names of places, persons, or bodies are to be transcribed into the publication, distribution, etc., area "as they appear, omitting accompanying

prepositions unless case endings would be affected" (1.4B4). Publishers, distributors, etc., may be recognized in two ways: they may be found named in explicit statements of publication, distribution, etc., or these functions may be implied for the names by virtue of their position. (See 2.4 in this manual for a fuller discussion of this point in relation to title pages.) In any case, the names determined as publishers, distributors, etc., are to be transcribed in the precise form and order (of hierarchical elements) that is presented on the item itself. Corporate names, therefore, recorded in the publication, distribution, etc., area are *not*

1) to be rearranged so that the elements of corporate hierarchy given are arranged in any order other than that which is given on the item itself, whether this order be ascending, descending, or a combination of both
2) to be abbreviated or shortened in any fashion other than as prescribed in 1.4D2 and 1.4D4
3) to be extended or lengthened in any fashion other than as prescribed in 1.4C7 and 1.4E.

1.4B8 Multiple publishers, etc. LC rule interpretation says:

For items from the United States Government Printing Office (GPO), retain the statement that an item is for sale by the Superintendant of Documents since only a portion of GPO's items is distributed in that manner.

When a government printer or government printing office is named on the item, and there is no evidence that its functions are not that of a publisher or distributor, record it as the publisher. If, however, another body also appears on the item and the government printing office is named only in a less prominent position unaccompanied by a statement of printing or distribution, the likelihood is greater that it functions only as printer and that the body is the publisher.

For an item that does not name a publisher in imprint position but a corporate body is named at head of title, regard the corporate body named at head of title as the publisher. Transpose its name to publisher position in the publication, etc., area unless the item contains information indicating that the corporate body is not the publisher or casting doubt on this assumption. (If the body has been recorded in the title and statement of responsibility area, apply 1.4D2.)

[Freetown] : Sierra Leóne Govt., [1971] ([Freetown?] : Govt. Print. Dept.)

1.4C Place of publication, distribution, etc.

AACR2 specifies that the place of publication, distribution, etc., is to be recorded in "the form and the grammatical case in which it appears" (1.4C1). If additions to the form of the name of the place are deemed necessary to aid in identifying the place, such additions are to be placed in square brackets, as specified in 1.4C2, 1.4C3, and 1.4C4.

1.4C7 *Optionally.* **Addition of full address of publisher, distributor, etc.** LC/GPO are restricting their exercise of this option. The Library of Congress will add the full address of publishers, distributors, etc., to the publication, distribution, etc., area in the cases of U.S. imprints issued in the current three years provided there is no ISBN or ISSN recorded in the standard number and terms of availability area. The GPO does not apply the option at all in view of the policy of giving addresses of agencies in the *Monthly Catalog of U.S. Government Publications.* Other libraries wishing to apply the terms of the option as stated should note that at least the addresses of the Government Printing Office and the National Technical Information Service are unnecessary since these are major distributors of documents.

— ₁New York, N.Y. (71 Worth St. (4th Floor), New York, NY. 10013)₁

1.4D Name of publisher, distributor, etc.
AACR2 specifies that the names of publishers, distributors, etc., be transcribed "in the shortest form in which ₁they₁ can be understood and identified internationally" (1.4D2). Abbreviation of the names of corporate publishers, distributors, etc., in the publication, distribution, etc., area is, therefore, permitted only when of a particular corporate body, as, for example, in the cases listed below:

    1) The name of the corporate body had appeared previously in the bibliographic record in the title and statement of responsibility area in a recognizable form.

        Functional aspects of driver impairment : a guide for state medical advisory boards / U.S. Department of Transportation, National Highway Traffic Safety Administration ; in cooperation with American Association of Motor Vehicle Administrators. — Washington, D.C. : The Administration : For sale by the Supt. of Docs., U.S. G.P.O., 1980.
not   . . . Washington, D.C. : National Highway Traffic Safety Administration . . .

    2) There is an authorized abbreviation for the corporate body in question in the list of general abbreviations in AACR2 (B.9).

        G.P.O. or U.S. G.P.O.
not   Government Printing Office of United States Government Printing Office.

        H.M.S.O.
not   Her Majesty's Stationery Office

For government documents, abbreviation of the names of corporate publishers, distributors, etc., should be undertaken cautiously. With regard to case 1 above, the terms *incorporated, limited,* etc., and their respective abbreviations may be omitted, following the principle outlined in 24.5C1, unless they are an integral part of the names of corporate publishers, distributors, etc., or they are needed to make it clear that the names in question are those of a corporate body.

With regard to case 2 above, the names of corporate publishers, distributors, etc., may be abbreviated only if their names, as presented in the publisher, distributors, etc., statement on the chief source of information, are presented in the same form, or a form less full than that which is already transcribed into the title and statement of responsibility area of the bibliographic record. (If full transcription of the names of corporate publishers, distributors, etc., as presented on the chief source of information would add information to the bibliographic record, do not abbreviate these names. If, however, full transcription of the names of corporate publishers, distributors, etc., as presented on the chief source of information would merely repeat what has already been given earlier in the bibliographic record, these names may be abbreviated.) When abbreviating the names of corporate publishers, distributors, etc., in this manner:

> Avoid using initials in place of the name. Use a term from the name of the body itself to stand for the name. (Note: the example given in 1.4D4 for the Office de la langue française is *not* a good one, and should *not* be followed.)
> Do not further abbreviate the chosen term. (Do not, for example, use "The Dept." for "The Department.")
> Do not choose a term not found within the name of the body itself. (Do not, for example, use "The Firm" for "Anderson, Notter, Finegold, Inc.")

Notice in particular that the following abbreviations for the names of corporate bodies are authorized in B.9– B.15 for the publication, distribution, etc., area:

> U.S.
> *for*   United States

> Dept.
> *for*   Department

Add to these authorized abbreviations the following:

> N.T.I.S.
> *for*   National Technical Information Service
> *or*   Department of Commerce, National Technical Information Service

In using abbreviations authorized for the names of corporate bodies in the publication, distribution, etc., area, do not assume that an abbreviation stands for more of a corporate hierarchy than is specified in the abbreviation table. For example, the abbreviation for the Government Printing Office, as given in B.9, does not encompass the remainder of the hierarchy of the United States Government Printing Office, if this complete hierarchy is given on the chief source of information.

use G.P.O.
for Government Printing Office

use U.S. G.P.O.
for United States Government Printing Office
or U.S. Government Printing Office

If the only appearance of the name of a publisher, etc., is in a seal, insignia, or logo, treat the seal, etc., as a publisher statement. Record the name without brackets if the seal, etc., is in a prescribed source.

1.4E *Optional addition.* **Statement of function of publisher, distributor, etc.**
LC/GPO are exercising this option. Terms such as *distributor* and *publisher* will be added to entities named in the publisher, distributor, etc., area whenever necessary to clarify the function of the particular person or body. It is expected that the need for such clarification will vary from case to case, as will the cataloger's perception of this need. Consequently, no major effort at uniformity will be attempted.

1.4F Date of publication, distribution, etc.

1.4F5 *Optional addition.* **Addition of latest copyright date.** LC/GPO are exercising this option because of the importance of copyright dates.

1.4F7 Inferred publication dates. If no publication date, copyright date, or printing date is given on the item, a publication date can often be inferred from other dates or information appearing on the item. Inferred dates are enclosed in square brackets and may be questioned if there is doubt as to whether it is the actual date.

1.4F8 *Optionally.* **Addition of latest date to complete multipart item.** LC/GPO are exercising this option with respect to printed monographs.

1.4G Place of manufacture, name of manufacturer, date of manufacture

1.4G4 *Optional addition.* **Addition of place, name of manufacturer, date of manu-facture when different from publication data when considered important.** LC/GPO are exercising this option selectively so that valuable information about a manufacturer, such as a printer, will not be lost. No attempt to achieve a high degree of uniformity in regard to this practice will be made, however.

1.5   PHYSICAL DESCRIPTION AREA

1.5A Preliminary rule

Rules for the physical description of materials differ from category to category of material. Each item being described must be described in terms of the specific chapter dealing with the class of material to which it belongs.

1.5A3 *Optionally.* **Addition of notes as to other formats in which an item is available.** LC/GPO are exercising this option since it is often helpful for libraries using the cataloging data of these national agencies to find information about other formats of the same item. Often these national agencies have access to information about other formats that is not available to libraries generally. Moreover, many libraries prefer to describe only the format of the item they actually hold. Thus it may be that this option is one that is primarily for the national agencies, so that other libraries, when creating their own catalog records, may prefer to ignore the option, unless their own community of users requires the information. (When libraries are using Library of Congress cataloging data, they may have a concern about the note's suggesting that the other format(s) are available in the particular library. To allay this concern, the Library of Congress introduces the note with "Issued also . . . ," instead of "Also available . . ." as shown in AACR2 under rule 1.7B16.)

1.5B Extent of item (including specific material designation)

1.5B5 *Optionally.* **Addition of number of physical units when item is complete.** LC/GPO are exercising this option; continuing a long-standing tradition against which there seems to be no argument at all, apart from the obvious work involved in revising a bibliographic record to incorporate the information.

1.5C – 1.5D ———

1.5E Accompanying material

Material recorded in area 5 at the end of the physical description normally has the following characteristics:

1) It was issued at the same time as the main work.
2) Primarily it is useful only in conjunction with the main work it accompanies.
3) The same person(s) or body responsible for the main work is also responsible for the accompanying material (or if different, no additional access point is needed).
4) The title of the accompanying material either is a general term or is otherwise dependent on the title of the main work.

Separate bibliographic records (cf. 1.9A) or a note (cf. 1.7B11) should be considered for other types of material the contents of which are subordinate to a main work.

Note the following points about Library of Congress practice:

1) The Library does not employ multilevel description as a means of describing accompanying material.
2) The Library catalogs on separate records all supplements, etc., to serials, except for indexes or supplements that may be noted on the records for the main works (cf. 12.7B7 and 12.7B17).

1.5E1 *Optional addition.* **Addition of descriptions to method D.** LC/GPO are exercising this option on a case-by-case basis. The physical description of accompanying material dealt with by method D will be recorded when this accompanying material is substantial in extent or is particularly significant for some other reason, such as its nonbook nature.

> 82 p. : ill. ; 21 cm. + 7 maps (col. ; 77 × 58 cm. folded to 40 × 30 cm. in portfolio)

1.6 SERIES AREA

The rules that govern the recording of the series statement in the series area are, in general, the same as those that govern the transcription of bibliographic information in the title and statement of responsibility area. (See the discussion of 1.1 above.) The recording of the series statement differs from the recording of the title and statement of responsibility in that in transcribing the series information, not all elements of the information as given on the item are automatically transcribed. The conditions under which the following elements are transcribed differ:

> title proper
> parallel title
> other title information
> statements of responsibility

Each of these is discussed below.

Follow the provisions of 1.11 in describing facsimiles, photocopies, and other reproductions containing series statements. According to these rules, information relating to the original is to be transcribed in the note area, rather than in the series area. (See 1.7B12.)

When recording series statements, keep in mind the necessary distinction between bibliographic description (the form of the series statement recorded in the series area) and access points (the form of the series used as an added entry heading): the rules in chapters 21 and 25, which govern the situation from the point of view of access points, will often cause the tracing for the series added entry to depart from, or add to, the form transcribed in the series area. (See particularly 21.30L and the discussion of this rule in this manual for the treatment of series added entry headings selected and formulated according to AACR2.)

LC rule interpretation says:

> NUMBERS OR LETTERS NOT ASSOCIATED WITH A SERIES TITLE
> Do not treat as a series statement a number that cannot be associated with a series title. Give it as a quoted note instead. (Ignore the number altogether on a bibliographic record for a serial.)
> Do not treat as a series statement a combination of numbers and letters (or letters alone) that cannot be associated with a series title if there is evidence that the combination is assigned either to every item the entity issues for internal control purposes or to certain groups of items for identification. Give such a combination as a quoted note. (Ignore the combination altogether on a bibliographic record for a serial.) In any case of doubt, reject the combination as a series statement.
>
> "DOE/EIA–0031/2."
> "UC–13."
> "CRN 780206–00050."
> "SP–MN."

1.6A ———

1.6B Title proper of series
The title proper of a series is the most important element of the series statement. Unless an item is being cataloged at the first level of description (in which case the series statement is not recorded at all), the title proper is always transcribed. In presenting the rules for the transcription of the title proper of the series statement, 1.6B1 refers to 12.1B2. Familiarity with the entire section of 12.1B, which gives the rules for the recording of the title proper of serials, is helpful in recording the title proper in the series statement.

1.6C Parallel titles of series
The extent to which parallel titles are transcribed into the series statement depends on the level of description at which the item is being cataloged.

1.6D Other title information of series
Other title information is the least important element of the series statement. Other title information is to be transcribed in the series statement "only if it provides valuable information identifying the series" (1.6D1). In other words, do not include other title information in the series statement unless a series statement lacking it would not adequately identify the series. (Note: Do not include other title information in series statements containing statements of responsibility (either those integrated or those transcribed according to 1.6E), which normally assure adequate identification of series. See the discussion of these below.) For information pertaining to a subseries of the main series or to another series, rather than other title information for the series, see 1.6H and 1.6J for appropriate transcription.

1.6E Statements of responsibility relating to series

The conditions under which statements of responsibility are to be transcribed as part of the series statement, as specified in AACR2 1.6E1, are also stated in general terms: "Statements of responsibility appearing in conjunction with the series title [are to be transcribed as part of series statements] if they are considered to be necessary for identification of the series" Compare this with the statement above about other title information. To provide for greater consistency in the transcription of statements of responsibility in series statements for government documents, consider only those series with titles that are "generic" in nature to need improved identification via statements of responsibility. Identifying titles of such a weak nature that they need the support of the statement of responsibility is completely a matter of judgment. Some obvious examples of such titles are "Bulletin," "Official report," "Record," etc. When "support" is already present in the title, however, do not add the statement of responsibility. Two good examples of titles not needing "support" are (1) those consisting of a clearly generic term with an initialism added to this term, e.g., "B.E.A. staff paper" or "Research report ADM," and (2) those that are long, e.g., "Annual descriptive report of program activities for vocational education" or "Appropriation statements of departments and agencies, all funds." If in doubt as to the character of a title and its ability to stand alone, retain the statement of responsibility.

1.6F ISSN of series

In recording series statements, include the International Standard Serial Number (ISSN) of the series, if this number appears anywhere on the item being described, according to 1.6F. The ISSN is set off from what precedes it (title proper, parallel titles, other title information, statements of responsibility) by a comma, space, and from what follows it (numbering within the series) by a space, semicolon, space.

ISSNs are appearing on some series that are government documents. Because ISSNs provide unique identification for serials, ISSNs not appearing on the item being described (but appearing, instead, in a reference source, for example) may be included in the series statement if placed within square brackets.[1]

1.6G Numbering within series

The numbering pattern of many series that are government documents is complex and potentially confusing. Often this pattern consists of a combination of alphabetical and numerical characters. Research may be required to determine which characters constitute a series "number" and which, a part of the title proper. For example, in the United States Department of Agriculture, Forest Service's

---

1. Care should be taken in transcribing ISSNs from sources other than the item itself. A cataloger transcribing ISSNs from other sources should be familiar with both the nature of the ISSN and the authority of the particular reference sources from which such numbers are transcribed. ISSNs are associated with titles of particular serials—not with the serials themselves. If the title of a continuing serial changes, its ISSN must also change. Occasionally, this fact is not adequately reflected in references sources, where ISSNs of former titles are linked to later titles (continuations of the serials), and vice versa. It is better, bibliographically speaking, to transcribe no ISSN for any particular title than to transcribe the wrong ISSN.

it is difficult to determine from the item itself where the series title stops and where the series number begins. In general, if alphabetical characters appearing in conjunctionwith numerical characters are included as part of a series title, they will not be also included in the numbering of particular parts of the series. Care should be taken in the transcription of these numbers not to omit parts of numbers that may be significant simply to simplify a series number on bibliographic records. What may appear to be extraneous characters may turn out, upon research, to be significant elements of a numbering pattern. Omission of any of these characters can lead, if the numbering pattern transcribed into the series statement is also used for the series check-in record, to the discarding of unique numbers of series—as duplicate numbers—that are *not* duplicate numbers. In the following number, for example, taken from the United States Environmental Protection Agency's Ecological research series, there are four different significant numerical elements:

$$\underset{1}{\text{EPA-600}}\,/\,\underset{2}{3}-\underset{3}{80}-\underset{4}{032}$$

1.6G2 If a single bibliographic record for a noncontinuously numbered (within a particular series) multipart item is constructed, and all numbers are recorded as instructed in 1.6G2, make certain that it is clear from the bibliographic record which parts of the multipart item are linked to which particular numbers of the series. If necessary, include such information in a note, as instructed in 1.7B12.

Pt. 1 issued in 2 volumes as nos. 45 and 78. Pt. 2 issued as no. 108.

Note: 1.6G2 is *not* applicable to serials, for which a single bibliographic record is constructed, when the serials are issued as numbered parts of another series. See 12.6B for the treatment of these.

1.6H Subseries

In general, the same provisions as apply to the transcribing of bibliographic information into the series statement for the

> title proper
> parallel title
> other title information
> statement of responsibility

of the main series apply in regard to the transcription of a subseries. Notice, however, that if the ISSN of the subseries appears on the item being described, then the ISSN of the main series is *not* transcribed in the series statement, even if it appears also on the item. Be sure, if transcribing an ISSN from an item that has both a main series and a subseries, that the ISSN is linked to the appropriate series. (If the item is numbered both within the main series and the subseries, both series numbers (unlike ISSNs) are to be recorded in the series statement.)

1.6J ———

1.7 NOTE AREA

As indicated in 0.27, all notes "may be considered to be optional in that their inclusion in the entry depends on the nature of the item described and the purpose of the entry concerned. In addition, the wording of notes in the examples is not prescriptive . . . ." In general, significant information not included elsewhere in the bibliographic record is to be recorded in the note area. In this connection, note that the few restrictions on transcription, arrangement, and punctuation of data in the note area mean that the cataloger disappointed with the results of applying the restrictions pertaining to preceding areas may turn to the note area and take advantage of it as a place for clarifying, amplifying, etc., the earlier areas.

1.7A Preliminary rule
The Joint Steering Committee for Revision of AACR has approved the following as the final paragraph under rule 1.7A4 in the printed text of AACR2:

> Notes relating to items reproduced. In describing an item which is a reproduction of another (e.g., a text reproduced in microform; a manuscript reproduced in book form; a set of maps reproduced as slides), give the notes relating to the reproduction and then the notes relating to the original. Combine the notes relating to the original in one note, giving the details in the order of the areas to which they relate.

1.7B Notes
In general, the fuller the bibliographic record, in terms of level of description, the more numerous and lengthy the appropriate notes. The need for various types of notes differs from format to format, and from item to item within any particular format. Regardless of format, or level of description, however, numbers borne by the item (other than those covered in 1.8) ought to be recorded in the bibliographic record. It is very important for the adequate identification of government documents that such numbers, especially those assigned by the issuing government agency, and, for federal publications, by the Superintendent of Documents (of the Government Printing Office) be included in the bibliographic description of an item.

1.7B4 Variations in title. LC rule interpretation says:

> A note may be essential to show a variation from the chief source title appearing elsewhere in the item. Although the source may contain more than

one title, record in a note only the needed variant title, not titles already given in the description. [Always include in the note the source of the variant.]

1.8 STANDARD NUMBER AND TERMS OF AVAILABILITY AREA

1.8A ———

1.8B Standard number

1.8B2 *Optionally.* **Record multiple ISBNs, adding qualifications as needed.** LC/ GPO are exercising this option since ISBNs are being assigned to some government publications.

1.8C Key-title

The "key-title" of a serial is that form of its title that is recognized internationally as its unique identification. Generally a serial is assigned a key-title at the same time as an ISSN. (Once assigned to a particular key-title, an ISSN remains attached to that title. Should the title of a serial change, the serial will be assigned a new key-title and corresponding ISSN by the appropriate national center responsible for the operation of the International Serials Data System. The Library of Congress acts as the national center for the United States.) Record an ISSN in the standard number and terms of availability area even if the key-title is not available. Do not provisionally assign a key-title in such cases. The ISSN has become an extremely important means of access and therefore when known should always be recorded, regardless of the absence of the key-title.

ISSN 0160-1741 = Journal of Research of the National Bureau of Standards

1.8D *Optional addition.* Terms of availability
LC/GPO are exercising this option in the following ways:

1) The Library of Congress gives the price of monographs when the publication is cataloged according to chapters 2, 5, 6, 7, or 8 and was issued in one of the three current years. For serials, it records price in field 350 of the MARC serials format, which information does not appear on printed bibliographic records for serials.[2]
2) The Library of the Government Printing Office records only GPO sales information; prices for other distribution (e.g., NTIS) are not given.

Users have indicated that it is important to include terms of availability for government documents since many of them are available only from the issuing agency and not from the usual commercial sources. A number of federal, state, and local government agencies have their own sales or free distribution programs.

---

2. For an explanation of the role of national cataloging agencies in providing data such as price, see *Cataloging Service Bulletin,* no. 16 (Spring 1982), p. 22–31.

1.8E Qualification

1.8E1 *Optionally.* **Additional of qualification to terms of availability.** LC/GPO are exercising this option. It is felt that even single ISBNs are more useful in some cases when qualified as to the special nature of an item or edition of an item.

1.9 SUPPLEMENTARY ITEMS

AACR2 treats "supplementary items" in precisely the same way as it does "accompanying material." (See 1.5E.) In recording information about a supplementary item, as instructed in 1.9, be guided, in choice of the most appropriate method, by the nature of the supplementary item itself. If, for example, supplementary items have unique titles, and it is likely that they might be accessed by these titles, choose a method of recording information about them that would allow for added entries to be made for these titles as part of the bibliographic record. If, for example, supplementry items are both distributed and used separately from the material which it is intended to supplement, record the details of the items in separate entries.

1.10 ITEMS MADE UP OF SEVERAL TYPES OF MATERIAL

1.10A It is in chapter 1 of AACR2 that the rules for handling items made up of more than one category of material are provided; 1.10 deals primarily with two aspects of the bibliographic description of such items: general material designations and physical description.

1.10B AACR2 specifies that if an item to be described has one "predominant" component, all other components are to be regarded as "accompanying material." In such an instance, the bibliographic record for the item is based on the chapter of Part I that deals with the category of material to which the "predominant" component belongs. Details relating to all other components are relegated either to notes or to the accompanying material position of the physical description area. Because identifying predominance depends entirely on judgment, AACR2 makes no attempt to define the concept of "predominant" component. Depending upon the nature and interests of the particular cataloging agency, one agency's "predominant" component may well be another's "accompanying material." And of course one could debate this question even over the examples provided in 1.10B showing items containing a "predominant" component plus accompanying material. Rule 1.10C attempts to offer some help by saying, in effect, that if the cataloger has trouble in selecting a "predominant" component, the cataloger should assume that there is no such component, thereby treating these cases and the cases of "true" kits/multimedia items alike.

1.10C If an item to be described has no "predominant" component, or at least no clearly "predominant one," it is assigned as a general material designation, either *kit* or *multimedia* depending on whether the cataloging agency opted for GMDs and which list of GMDs, the American *kit* or the British *multimedia*, as given in 1.1C.

1.10C2 Physical description. The rule offers three different methods for recording the physical description, this being the area that needs the most attention when describing kits/multimedia items: method (a) is confined primarily to the statement of extent; method (b) gives a full physical description for each component (equal, really, to the quantity of data recorded if the component had been covered by a bibliographic record of its own); and method (c) provides only a brief statement in general terms that cover no more than extent. The Library of Congress cannot apply method *b* because this entails separate, complete physical description areas, this being one area that is not repeatable in the LC automation system at this time. Libraries that have the capability may wish to apply all three methods on a case-by-case basis: method *b* for the most important items, method *c* for the least important items, and method *a* for items of intermediate value. The choice depends upon what the library can afford.

1.10D Multilevel description

Multilevel description is similar to a greatly expanded contents note and is primarily feasible only in an automated environment. At the present time, LC has no plans for implementing this technique of analysis (cf. chapter 13).

1.11   FACSIMILES, PHOTOCOPIES, AND OTHER REPRODUCTIONS

AACR2's provisions for dealing with facsimiles, photocopies, and other reproductions are based upon the principle that "the description of a physical item should be based in the first instance on the chapter dealing with the class of materials to which that item belongs. For example, a printed monograph in microform should be described as a microform (using the rules in chapter 11). . . . In short, the starting point for description is the physical form of the item in hand, not the original or any previous form in which the work has been published" (0.24).

With the few exceptions, as detailed in 1.11A–F, details relating to the originals of facsimiles, photocopies, and other reproductions are to be given in the note area. In this regard, there are few significant differences between describing reproductions in printed form and reproductions in microform (as discussed in chapter 11 of Part I). In connection with microreproductions of books and analogous library materials, however, there is a special Library of Congress policy continuing traditional cataloging treatment, which will be discussed in relation to chapter 11.

When cataloging government documents, it is not always possible to determine, either from the items themselves, or from research, whether or not the items represent originals or reproductions. In the absence of evidence to the contrary, assume that an item is an original publication, and not a reproduction.

1.11A–1.11F ⸺

2/   Books, Pamphlets, and Printed Sheets

Chapter 2 of AACR2 applies the principles of bibliographic description outlined in chapter 1 to the traditional format of the printed book and its close relatives. (Most government documents that require cataloging are books.)

For cataloging purposes, some books that are government documents differ from other types of books. The typical government document book often does not look very much like the traditional one. These documents may be the size of typing paper, rather than that of the standard book. A document may have a soft or paper cover, or no real cover at all, and it may be held together only by staples or by a type of binding only slightly more permanent. In short, unlike normal books it may appear to be a draft that has not yet been formally transformed into a book by the processes of printing and publication. The structure and terminology of AACR2 lump together all monographic texts that appear in print or any degree of near-print, however, and consequently all such documents are described according to chapter 2.

Books that pass through the standardization process entailed in formal publication have typical characteristics. In contrast with such published books, government documents are often atypical. For example, they may contain either too few or too many sources of information significant for cataloging purposes. Government documents may, on the one hand, have no formal title page at all. The necessary title-page data may be found only on the cover or in an accompanying letter of transmittal. At the other extreme, government documents may have not only a formal title page, but also both a cover closely resembling a formal title page and a "bibliographic data sheet," which, for the purposes of the issuing agency, serves the many purposes of the formal title page. (The bibliographic data sheet is discussed in the treatment of 2.0B below.) Each of these sources may contain different or even conflicting information significant for bibliographic description.

Another characteristic of documents that sets them somewhat apart from conventional books is their relationship to agencies. Documents normally have a government agency associated with their genesis. These government agencies have some degree of responsibility for the "emanation" of the document. The document itself may bear both a designation for the agency as well as for other bodies responsible for preparation of the text, or for production and dissemination. These designations may appear at the head of title, in the imprint position, on the verso of the title page, or in the colophon (just to name a few of the more common locations). The cataloger then must decide how to interpret the evidence so as to transcribe a statement of responsibility, a statement of publisher, distributor, etc.

The discussion of chapter 2 of AACR2 that follows takes these special characteristics of documents into account and provides guidelines for dealing with them.

2.0   GENERAL RULES

2.0A   Scope
A large proportion of all government documents fall within the category of books, pamphlets, and printed sheets—in other words, within the category of printed monographs as covered by chapter 2 of AACR2. Note that the technical reports issued by government bodies also fall within this category.

Many documents issued by government bodies are issued in series for purposes of distribution and bibliographic control. Often the titles of such series are very general in nature, or consist only of acronyms, with the subject scope of such series often quite broad. Local cataloging and collection development policy will determine whether a single bibliographic record for such a series will suffice, or whether individual monographic parts of such a series should receive separate individual records in addition to the single bibliographic record for the series or in place of it. Generally,

1) A single bibliographic record should be created for a particular series if a significant proportion of the series is retained in the collection. In such a case, follow chapter 12 of AACR2.
2) Individual monographic parts of such a series should receive individual analysis if bibliographic access to these individual parts is needed. If a single bibliographic record for a series is not created, each individual monographic part of such a series should be analyzed. Chapter 13 of AACR2, which deals with the analysis of all types, provides a number of methods for achieving analysis without specifically mandating which method is to be followed for which particular situation. It does, however, note that "if the item is a part of a monographic series or a multipart monograph and has a title not dependent on that of the comprehensive item, prepare an analytical entry in terms of a complete bibliographic description of the part. Give details of the comprehensive item in the series area" (13.2).

This means, in effect, that separate bibliographic records should be created for such items. For such records, the provisions of chapter 2 of AACR2 should be followed.

2.0B   Sources of information
Rule 2.0B1 lists other sources of information to be used for monographs published without a title page, or without a title page applying to the whole work, but is *not* to be taken as an order of preference. Instead the rule states that the source to be used as the title page substitute is that part of the book which supplies the most complete information.

For United States federal government documents, the "bibliographic data sheet" should be considered as being on this list of other sources of information to be used as the title page substitute. Bibliographic data sheets are most commonly entitled:

> Report documentation page
> Technical report data
> Technical report standard title page, etc.

The bibliographic data sheet contains all of the information considered to be necessary by the federal government for accurately identifying and indexing a scientific or technical report. This information includes the following, as applicable:

> report number
> recipient's catalog/accession number
> title and subtitle
> report date
> author(s)
> performing organization report number
> performing organization name and address
> project/task/work unit number
> contract or grant number
> sponsoring agency name and address
> type of report/period covered
> supplementary notes
> abstract
> key words
> availability/distribution statement
> security classification of report
> security classification of sheet itself
> number of pages
> price

(The bibliographic data sheet was designed to include some information for a universal government coding scheme, which has never been developed, and so includes space for government accession number, performing code, and sponsoring organization code, although this information does not exist.)

The standardized format for the bibliographic data sheet was developed by the Committee on Science and Technology "to aid the interchange of scientific and technical information and to reduce the costs of preparing, storing, retrieving, reproducing, and distributing such [information]."[1] Bibliographic data sheets are included in scientific and technical reports prepared by or for certain federal government agencies as a

---

1. Guidelines to Format Standard for Scientific and Technical Reports Prepared by or for the Federal Government.—Washington, D.C. : Committee on Scientific and Technical Information, Federal Council for Science and Technology, 1968. p.3.

matter of regulation. (Indeed, the bibliographic data sheet, as the report documentation page, is an integral part of the American National Standards Institute's format for scientific and technical reports (ANSI Z39.18–1974).[2] The words designating each information field may vary from agency to agency, as may the numbering and arrangement of the fields, or the position of the sheet itself in relation to the other parts of the book. (Generally, if the bibliographic data sheet does not replace the title page altogether, it immediately precedes or follows it, or immediately precedes the back cover.) The bibliographic data sheet format (fig. 1) is used by the National Technical Information Service. Instructions for filling out the sheet (fig. 2) are used by the performing organization or sponsoring agency, as applicable.

If an item lacking a title page has both a cover closely resembling a formal title page (in terms of type and completeness of information presented) and a bibliographic data sheet, prefer the cover as the item's chief source of information. If an item lacking a title page does not have such a cover, prefer the bibliographic data sheet as the item's chief source of information. Specify in a note that the bibliographic data sheet has been used as the title page substitute for that item. (See 2.7B3.)

Title from bibliographic data sheet.

2.0C–2.0H ———

2.1 TITLE AND STATEMENT OF RESPONSIBILITY AREA

2.1A ———

2.1B Title proper

Title information found on the title page must be broken down into the two ISBD components called "title proper" and "other title information." The significance of these terms is comparable to that of the traditional terms *title* and *subtitle* as used by both librarians and nonlibrarians. The ISBD equivalent terms *title proper* and *other title information* are defined in the glossary of AACR2, albeit in a rather open-ended way. Notice particularly the wording in the definition of "other title information": "Any phrase . . . or other titles, indicative of the character, contents, etc., of the item, or the motives for, or occasion of, its production or publication." The wording, particularly the inclusion of "etc.," shows that the matter is left primarily up to catalogers' judgment. When one considers the division of title statements between "title proper" and "other title information," the cataloger then has considerable freedom in handling each case on its own merits, using his or her judgment, experience, etc.

With government documents, as with any other type of publication, many cases of deciding between "title proper" and "other title information" are relatively simple. For the more difficult cases, the following guidelines are offered:

---

2. American National Standard Guidelines for Format and Production of Scientific and Technical Reports. — New York : American National Standards Institute, 1974. — ANSI Z39.18–1974.

50272 - 101

REPORT DOCUMENTATION PAGE	1. REPORT NO.	2.	3. Recipient's Accession No.
4. Title and Subtitle			5. Report Date
			6.
7. Author(s)			8. Performing Organization Rept. No.
9. Performing Organization Name and Address			10. Project/Task/Work Unit No.
			11. Contract(C) or Grant(G) No. (C) (G)
12. Sponsoring Organization Name and Address			13. Type of Report & Period Covered
			14.
15. Supplementary Notes			
16. Abstract (Limit: 200 words)			
17. Document Analysis a. Descriptors			
b. Identifiers/Open-Ended Terms			
c. COSATI Field/Group			

18. Availability Statement		19. Security Class (This Report)	21. No. of Pages
		20. Security Class (This Page)	22. Price

(See ANSI–Z39.18)   **See Instructions on Reverse**   **OPTIONAL FORM 272** (4–77)
(Formerly NTIS–35)
Department of Commerce

Figure 1. Format of bibliographic data sheet used by National Technical Information Service

33

DO NOT PRINT THESE INSTRUCTIONS AS A PAGE IN A REPORT

INSTRUCTIONS

Optional Form 272, Report Documentation Page is based on Guidelines for Format and Production of Scientific and Technical Reports, ANSI Z39.18–1974 available from American National Standards Institute, 1430 Broadway, New York, New York 10018. Each separately bound report—for example, each volume in a multivolume set—shall have its unique Report Documentation Page.

1. Report Number. Each individually bound report shall carry a unique alphanumeric designation assigned by the performing organization or provided by the sponsoring organization in accordance with American National Standard ANSI Z39.23–1974, Technical Report Number (STRN). For registration of report code, contact NTIS Report Number Clearinghouse, Springfield, VA 22161. Use uppercase letters, Arabic numerals, slashes, and hyphens only, as in the following examples: FASEB/NS–75/87 and FAA/RD–75/09.

2. Leave blank.

3. Recipient's Accession Number. Reserved for use by each report recipient.

4. Title and Subtitle. Title should indicate clearly and briefly the subject coverage of the report, subordinate subtitle to the main title. When a report is prepared in more than one volume, repeat the primary title, add volume number and include subtitle for the specific volume.

5. Report Date. Each report shall carry a date indicating at least month and year. Indicate the basis on which it was selected (e.g., date of issue, date of approval, date of preparation, date published).

6. Sponsoring Agency Code. Leave blank.

7. Author(s). Give name(s) in conventional order (e.g., John R. Doe, or J. Robert Doe). List author's affiliation if it differs from the performing organization.

8. Performing Organization Report Number. Insert if performing organization wishes to assign this number.

9. Performing Organization Name and Mailing Address. Give name, street, city, state, and ZIP code. List no more than two levels of an organizational hierarchy. Display the name of the organization exactly as it should appear in Government indexes such as Government Reports Announcements & Index (GRA & I).

10. Project/Task/Work Unit Number. Use the project, task and work unit numbers under which the report was prepared.

11. Contract/Grant Number. Insert contract or grant number under which report was prepared.

12. Sponsoring Agency Name and Mailing Address. Include ZIP code. Cite main sponsors.

13. Type of Report and Period Covered. State interim, final, etc., and, if applicable, inclusive dates.

14. Performing Organization Code. Leave blank.

15. Supplementary Notes. Enter information not included elsewhere but useful, such as: Prepared in cooperation with . . . Translation of . . . Presented at conference of . . . To be published in . . . When a report is revised, include a statement whether the new report supersedes or supplements the older report.

16. Abstract. Include a brief (200 words or less) factual summary of the most significant information contained in the report. If the report contains a significant bibliography or literature survey, mention it here.

17. Document Analysis. (a). Descriptors. Select from the Thesaurus of Engineering and Scientific Terms the proper authorized terms that identify the major concept of the research and are sufficiently specific and precise to be used as index entries for cataloging.

(b). Identifiers and Open-Ended Terms. Use identifiers for project names, code names, equipment designators, etc. Use open-ended terms written in descriptor form for those subjects for which no descriptor exists.

(c). COSATI Field/Group. Field and Group assignments are to be taken from the 1964 COSATI Subject Category List. Since the majority of documents are multidisciplinary in nature, the primary Field/Group assignment(s) will be the specific discipline, area of human endeavor, or type of physical object. The application(s) will be cross-referenced with secondary Field/Group assignments that will follow the primary posting(s).

18. Distribution Statement. Denote public releasability, for example "Release unlimited", or limitation for reasons other than security. Cite any availability to the public, with address, order number and price, if known.

19. & 20. Security Classification. Enter U.S. Security Classification in accordance with U.S. Security Regulations (i.e., UNCLASSIFIED).

21. Number of pages. Insert the total number of pages, including introductory pages, but excluding distribution list, if any.

22. Price. Enter price in paper copy (PC) and/or microfiche (MF) if known.

☆U.S. Government Printing Office: 1978—261-647/3308   OPTIONAL FORM 272 BACK (4–77)

Figure 2. Instructions for filling out data sheet (fig. 1)

1) Typography and layout: Often the title proper is in larger type than other title information. Often it is set off, by some measurable distance, from other title information. Typography and layout should not be taken as the only factor, however. The title proper may not be distinguishable from other information presented in the chief source of information by either size of type or layout of the title page. The title proper can, occasionally, be found integrated into the artistic arrangement of the chief source of information.

2) Phraseology: Phrases such as

Final report
Environmental impact statement
Executive summary

if not linked grammatically to the rest of the title proper should be considered to be other title information rather than part of the title proper. Notice that in the layout of title pages the title proper does not always precede other title information. Other title information, especially if expressed in phrases such as the above, may be found above the title proper.

3) Consistency: The wording of the title proper should be consistent wherever the title appears on the item in a nonabbreviated form. (Compare the title as presented on the title page, the cover, the spine, the bibliographic data sheet, etc.)

AACR2 prescribes that the title proper is to be transcribed "exactly as to wording, order, and spelling" (1.1B1). This provision does *not* mean that all title information found on the chief source of information must be transcribed precisely in the order in which it is presented on the title page. AACR2 allows for other title information that precedes the title proper given on the chief source of information to be transcribed following the title proper in the cataloging record. In case of doubt as to which phrases constitute the title proper, provide added title entries for alternative phrases not chosen as the title proper when they are likely to be regarded as such. (See 21.30J.)

2.1C *Optional addition.* **General material designation**
LC/GPO are not exercising this option in relation to books, i.e., the general material designation (GMD) "text" will not be added after the title proper of documents.

2.1D Parallel titles
(See the discussion of 1.1D above.)

2.1E Other title information
Note that information may consist of:

1) a formal, easily recognizable subtitle immediately following the title proper.
2) words or phrases preceding or following the title proper, providing additional information about the nature of the item rather than about its origin, generally appearing in opposition to the title proper.

2.1E   *Other title information*

(For guidance in distinguishing the title proper from other title information, see the discussion of 2.1B above.)

Often other title information can be distinguished from statements of responsibility on the basis of the grammar of the statement as presented in the chief source of information. As a general rule:

> Other title information is expressed by noun phrases.
> Statements of responsibility are introduced by verb phrases (or their abbreviated equivalents, e.g., ''by'' phrases.)

> Mearns' quail capture method : a final report / prepared by Richard L. Brown

> Rehabilitation : an alternative for historic industrial buildings / edited by Selma Taylor

> The nation's water resources 1975– 2000 : second National Water Assessment / by the U.S. Water Resources Council

Notice that in this regard, statements of responsibility introduced by prepositions rather than verbs are sometimes to be considered part of other title information. AACR2 specifies that ''if the other title information includes a statement of responsibility or the name of a publisher, distributor, etc., and the statement or name is an integral part of the other title information'' (1.1E4), this statement of responsibility is to be transcribed as part of the other title information and *not* as a formal statement of responsibility. The examples presented in 1.1E4 and elsewhere in AACR2 (1.1F5, etc.) show that statements of responsibility, or the names of publishers, distributors, etc., linked with other phrases by certain prepositions as, for example, *of, to, for,* etc., are to be considered as ''integral parts of the other title information.''

> Federal management weaknesses cry out for alternatives to deliver programs and services to Indians to improve their quality of life : report to the Congress of the United States / by the Comptroller General

Additionally, in this regard notice that even if the first verbal statement of responsibility transcribed as such in the bibliographic record includes words or phrases that logically might be regarded as other title information (including the prepositions discussed above, as, for example, *of, to, for,* etc.), these words or phrases should still be included within the statement of responsibility if they follow the first word of the first verbal statement of responsibility.

> Open-pit mine demonstration of REAM : final report on contract no. H025011 / prepared for United States Department of the Interior, Bureau of Mines by Physics International Company.

Grammar alone, however, will not totally suffice to distinguish other title information from statements of responsibility. Rule 1.1F12 specifies that a noun phrase that is

36

indicative of the role of the involved party named in the statement of responsibility, rather than the nature of the work, is to be treated as part of the statement of responsibility, rather than as other title information.

International relations dictionary / ₍researching and writing by Carol Becker₎

In case of doubt, the noun phrase is to be treated as part of the statement of responsibility.

2.1F Statements of responsibility

(For guidance in distinguishing statements of responsibility from other title information, see the discussion of 2.1E above.)

According to AACR2, statements of responsibility relating to persons or bodies appearing "prominently" on an item are, once they have been properly identified, to be transcribed in the form in which they appear on the item. (See 1.1F1.) The term *prominently* as used here "means that a statement to which it applies must be a formal statement found in one of the prescribed sources of information (see 1.0A) for areas 1 and 2 for the class of material to which the item being catalogued belongs" (0.8). For the title and statement of responsibility area for books, pamphlets, and printed sheets, the prescribed sources of information are the title page, other preliminaries, the colophon, and the cover. Because the bibliographic data sheet (discussed in the treatment of 2.0B above) is so important that it should be considered as being on this list of potential title page substitutes, statements of responsibility appearing on it are also to be regarded as prominent in all cases. According to this provision, statements of responsibility, therefore, appearing in the following parts of the book are to be transcribed in the title and statement of responsibility area of the bibliographic record:

> title page, recto, and verso
> cover (all parts)
> bibliographic data sheet
> any page preceding the title page
> colophon

If an item has more than one statement of responsibility appearing prominently on it, and all such statements of responsibility appear on the chief source of information, such statements are to be recorded "in the order indicated by their sequence on, or by the layout of, the chief source of information" (1.1F6). If the sequence or layout of the chief source of information is ambiguous, or if an item has more than one statement of responsibility appearing prominently on it, and some statements of responsibility appear in prominent parts of the book other than the chief source of information, such statements are to be recorded "in the order that makes the most sense" (1.1F6).

Statements of responsibility appearing prominently on all prominent parts of the book (cf. list above except the title page recto) are to be placed in square brackets in the title and statement of responsibility area, unless the item lacks a title page proper. In this case, the source of the title page substitute should be acknowledged in a note (2.0B1) and statements of responsibility appearing in all other prominent parts other than this title page substitute placed in square brackets. (Statements of responsibility appearing in parts of the book that are not regarded as prominent or are taken from outside the publication are not normally transcribed. If transcribed, they must be placed in a note, not in the title and statement of responsibility area.) (See 1.1F2 and 2.1F2.)

In transcribing statements of responsibility appearing in the item (on prominent parts of the item other than the chief source of information) in square brackets, as discussed above, it is not necessary to record them as they would appear if quoted if the resulting statements of responsibility would be grammatically awkward. In particular, when transcribing statements of responsibility from the bibliographic data sheet, if these statements are to be placed in square brackets, it is not necessary to record, in addition to the names of persons and/or corporate bodies, as needed, the terms with which the bibliographic data sheet's respective information blocks are labeled.

on bibliographic data sheet:

Author(s)
  M. Beller
  C. Waide
  M. Steinberg

transcribe as: Treatment of acid mine drainage by ozone oxidation / [M. Beller, C. Waide, M. Steinberg]

not as: Treatment of acid mine drainage by ozone oxidation / [Author(s) M. Beller, C. Waide, M. Steinberg]

Statements of responsibility relating to persons or bodies appearing prominently on an item are to be recorded "in the form in which they appear there" (1.1F1). (For a detailed treatment of the implications of this statement for the transcribing of corporate names, see the discussion of 1.1F above.)

2.1G ———

2.2 EDITION AREA

2.2A ———

2.2B Edition statement

Government documents, like other types of printed books, do contain formally stated, classically recognizable edition statements of the type discussed in 2.2B1. However, unlike other types of printed books, government documents are often issued in different editions without these editions being clearly indicated as such on the actual items themselves. For example, different editions of government documents may be identified in the chief source of information only by differences in statements giving an issue date. In such a case, where there is definite evidence that a statement of this type indicates a new edition of a title issued earlier, transcribe it in the edition area rather than in a quoted note.

> Issued Mar. 1979.
>
> (Rev.) July 1979
>
> Jan. 6, 1979 (ed.)

Items that simply represent new printings of earlier titles (without any other changes) are not regarded as new editions. Statements relating to such printings should not be recorded as edition statements.

2.2B3 *Optional addition.* **Cataloger-supplied edition statement.** LC/GPO generally are not exercising this option. They recommend that information of this type be placed in the note area. (See 2.7B7.)

The LC interpretation says:

> Do not apply to any case of merely *supposed* differences in issues that might make them different editions. If differences are *manifest,* however, but the catalog records needed would show exactly the same information in the areas beginning with the title and statement of responsibility area and ending with the series area, apply the option.

A case in which it would be useful to apply the option is a Congressional document that is reprinted in order to correct some detail(s) of the text that do not alter the pagination. These are commonly called "star prints" because of the way the GPO printer designates them: an asterisk in the lower-left corner of the title page or cover. (At times, the words *star print* also appear adjacent to the asterisk.) Since it is known that these are corrected printings, supply an edition statement, for example:

> ₁Corr. print.₁
> (See 2.7B7 for a corresponding note.)

2.2C – 2.2E ———

2.3 ———

2.4 PUBLICATION, DISTRIBUTION, ETC., AREA

2.4A ———

2.4B General rule

AACR2 specifies that "if an item has two or more places of publication, distribution, etc., and/or names of publishers, distributors, etc., named in it, describe it in terms of the first named place of publication, distribution, etc., and the corresponding publisher, distributor, etc." (1.4B8).

Many government documents issued in the form of books, pamphlets, and printed sheets are published, distributed, etc., jointly by several corporate bodies. Generally, when such is the case, the responsibility of these involved corporate bodies extends beyond that of merely publishing, distributing, etc., the works in question. AACR2 recognizes the importance of such bodies in 21.30E, which prescribes added entries for them.

LC rule interpretation says:

> When two entities performing the same or different functions are named, record both. If three or more are involved, record the first and a subsequently named entity that is the only one located in the U.S. or is the one that is given prominence by typography as the principal publisher, etc. Record also a subsequently named entity whenever an added entry for it needs to be justified.
>
> When recording the names of two or more publishers, distributors, etc., and the names appear together in the item in a single statement that connects them linguistically, generally give them in a single statement rather than separating them with a space-colon-space. However, if the names need to be transcribed after different places, give each entity in a separate publisher statement in the publication, etc., area.

> Washington, D.C. : American Association of Colleges for Teacher Education in collaboration with the Teacher Corps, U.S. Office of Education
> (*source:* Published by American Association of Colleges for Teacher Education in collaboration with the Teacher Corps United States Office of Education)

2.4C ———

2.4D Name of publisher, distributor, etc.
Refer to the discussion in this manual of 1.4B and 1.4D in regard to the transcribing of the form and order of hierarchical elements, and to the abbreviation of elements of the names of publishers, distributors, etc.

2.4E *Optional addition.* **Statement of function of distributor**
LC/GPO are exercising this option. Terms such as *distributor* and *publisher* are added to entities named in the publication, distribution, etc., area whenever necessary to clarify the function of the particular person or body. It is expected that the need for such clarification will vary from case to case, as will the cataloger's perception of this need. Consequently, no major effort at uniformity will be attempted.

2.4F ———

2.4G Place of printing, name of printer, date of printing

2.4G2 *Optional addition.* **Addition of place, name of printer, date of printing when different from publication date when considered important.** LC/GPO are exercising this option. Significant information relevant to the place of printing, name of the printer, and date of printing, if different from the place of publication, name of publisher, and date of publication, if found on the item itself, will be included in the item's bibliographic record. The application of this option is specifically linked to the cataloging agency's perception of the significance of this information.

2.5 PHYSICAL DESCRIPTION AREA

2.5A ———

2.5B Number of volumes and/or pagination. *Single volumes*

2.5B1 ''Record the number of pages or leaves in a publication in accordance with the terminology suggested by the volume'' (AACR2 2.5B1). Describe a volume containing both leaves and pages not ordered in organized sequences in terms of whichever is predominant.

The list of terms given in 2.5B1 for describing single volumes—

> page(s)
> leave(s)
> column(s)
> broadside(s)
> sheet(s)
> case(s)
> portfolio(s)

—with the addition of any terms needed to indicate complicated or irregular paging, as discussed in 2.5B8 and 2.5B9, and any terms needed to indicate Braille or other raised types, as discussed in 2.5B23, is intended to be exhaustive. Of these terms, only the following is (and can be) abbreviated, according to Appendix B:

> page(s) to p.

(Note: *Case* is not defined in the Glossary, Appendix D. AACR2 distinguishes it from *portfolio* in 2.5B18.)

2.5B10 Plates are described in terms of either leaves or pages, according to whether there is only printing on the recto or on both recto and verso.

2.5B11 Folded leaves are described as such. Apparently, no mention is to be made of folded pages in the bibliographic record. However, if a ''sheet is designed to be used only in the folded form, describe it as *1 folded sheet and give the number of imposed pages . . .''* (2.5D4). The term *folded* is *not* abbreviated.

Publications in more than one volume

2.5B18 The list of terms given in 2.5B18 for describing publications in more than one volume, when the term *volume* is not appropriate, is:

> part(s)
> pamphlet(s)
> piece(s)
> case(s)
> portfolio(s)

and any terms needed to indicate complicated or irregular paging, as discussed in 2.5B8 and 2.5B9, and any terms needed to indicate Braille or other raised types, as discussed in 2.5B23. The list, plus the additional terms indicated, is intended to be exhaustive. Of these terms, only the following is (and can be) abbreviated, according to Appendix B:

> part(s) *to* pt(s).

(Note: AACR2 does authorize the abbreviation of *volume(s)* to *v.*)

2.5B19– 2.5B20 ———

2.5B21 *Optional addition.* **Addition of pagination of individual volumes of multi-volume sets.** LC/GPO are not exercising this option except in the case of rare books.

2.5C Illustrative matter

2.5C2 Illustrations. The list of terms given in 2.5C2 for designating types of illustrations—

> chart(s)
> coat(s) of arms
> facsimile(s)
> form(s)
> genealogical table(s)
> map(s)
> music
> plan(s)
> portrait(s)
> sample(s)

—in addition to the term *ill.* is intended to be exhaustive. Of these terms, only the following are (and can be) abbreviated, according to Appendix B:

facsimile(s) *to* facim(s).
genealogical table(s) *to* geneal. table(s)
portrait(s) *to* portr(s).

2.5C3 Colored illustrations. To be considered "colored," an illustration must be in two or more colors. Black is considered to be a color in the determination of whether or not illustrations are colored. (White, however, is not.) The term *colored* is abbreviated to *col*.

2.5C4– 2.5C5 ———

2.5C7 Illustrative matter in the physical description area is *not* described as folded. The term *folded* is used in describing the number of folded leaves in the volumes and/or pagination statement (2.5B11), in describing the size of folded sheets designed only to be used in the folded form in the volumes and/or pagination statement (2.5D4), and in a note indicating that folded illustrative matter is issued in a pocket inside the cover of items (2.5C7).

2.5D ———

2.5E Accompanying material
In recording information about accompanying material, as instructed in 2.5E (referencing 1.5E), be guided, in choice of the most appropriate method, by the nature of the accompanying material. If, for example, accompanying material has a unique title, and it is likely that it might be sought by this title, choose a method of recording information about it that would allow for an added entry to be made for this title as part of the bibliographic record. If accompanying material is both distributed and used separately from the material which it is intended to accompany, record its details in a separate entry.

2.5E1 *Optionally.* **Addition of physical description to accompanying material recorded at the end of the physical description.** LC/GPO are exercising this option on a case-by-case basis. The physical description of accompanying material dealt with by recording its details at the end of the physical description will be recorded when this accompanying material is substantial in extent or particularly significant for some other reason, such as its nonbook nature.

2.6 SERIES AREA

Refer to the discussion of 1.6 above, in regard to the series area.

2.6A– 2.6B ———

2.7 NOTE AREA

As indicated in 0.27, all notes "may be considered to be optional in that their inclusion in the entry depends on the nature of the item described and the purpose of the entry concerned. In addition, the wording of notes in the examples is not prescriptive . . . ." In general, significant information not included elsewhere in the bibliographic record is to be recorded in the note area.

2.7A Preliminary rule

Be aware that, as prescribed in 1.7A3: "If data in a note correspond to data found in the title and statement of responsibility, edition, material ₁or type of publication₁ specific details, publication, etc., physical description, and series areas, . . . the elements of the data (are to be given) in the order in which they appear in those areas."

In such cases, punctuation prescribed for these areas should be used, except that a full stop should be substituted for a full stop, space, dash, space.

2.7B Notes

2.7B3 Source of title proper. In suggesting that "notes on the source of the title proper ₁be made₁ if it is other than the chief source of information" (2.7B3), AACR2 is specifying that notes on the source of the title proper be made if the item being described lacks a title page altogether, or lacks a title page applying to the whole work. AACR2 is not suggesting here that if an item has a title page applicable to the whole work, that the title proper be taken from another source. (See 2.0B1.) The most common such notes, for government documents, are the following:

> Cover title
> Title from bibliographic data sheet
> Caption title
> *(See the discussion of 2.0B in this manual regarding the biblio-*
> *graphic data sheet.)*

2.7B9 Publication, distribution, etc. The LC rule interpretation says:

> When a publication has a date of release or transmittal in a prominent position, include it in the bibliographic description. Typically these special dates consist of month or month and day as well as year and appear on the title page or cover. If the date is in a phrase that is being recorded as an edition statement, so record it. If an edition statement is not appropriate, quote the date in a note, including with it any associated words:

> "May 1979."
> "May 1, 1979."
> "Issued May 1979."

Note that a date of release or transmittal is not a publication date. If the publication lacks a copyright date or a date of manufacture (cf. RI 1.4F6), the publication date *may* be inferred from the date of release or transmittal. Then give the inference in brackets in the publication, etc., area and follow the above instructions for the date of release or transmittal.

In case of doubt as to the character of the date in question, treat it as a date of release or transmittal.

2.7B17 Summary. Generally, a summary of the content of an item issued in the form of a book, pamphlet, or printed sheet is not provided. The subject content of such an item is generally indicated by the subject added entries provided for it in its bibliographic record and/or its classification number. (Additionally, it is possible to ascertain the subject content of a book, pamphlet, or printed sheet by physical examination of the item itself, i.e., by "browsing." For works intended for a juvenile audience and for many nonbook items, the summary note has considerable utility. It may guide teachers and librarians in assisting patrons of juvenile literature. In the case of many nonbook items, consulting the summary note may be much more practicable than an examination of the actual items to determine subject content.

2.7B19 Numbers borne by the item. In making notes of important numbers borne by the item other than ISBNs, precede such numbers with an indication of their source, if this information is given on the item or if otherwise known to be the case.

Each type of number is structured in a standardized way and is divided into elements which have meaning.

> Supt. of Docs. class no.: HE 19.120:39
> HE (parent body)
> 19. (subordinate body)
> 120: (series)
> 39 (unique book number)

> Supt. of Docs. S/N: 017-092-00025-1
> 017 - (department)
> 092 - (agency)
> 00025 - (unique publication number)
> 1 - (check digit)

> N.T.I.S.: PB-270 483/1GA

This number was used by NTIS prior to the American Standards Institute (ANSI) Z39 decision that there would be a unique American National Standard Technical Report Number (STRN) assigned to every technical report. In 1974, NTIS was asked to establish the Clearinghouse for Report Numbers.

> N.T.I.S. : FDA/ACA - 81/101
> FDA (parent body)
> /ACA (subordinate body)

-81 (year)
/101 (number of report)

ERIC: ED 131 424
ED (education)
131 424 (sequential number)

(Note: The coding requirements of some bibliographic utilities may result in some of these numbers being included elsewhere in the bibliographic record.)

2.8   STANDARD NUMBER AND TERMS OF AVAILABILITY

2.8A ———

2.8B International Standard Book Number (ISBN)

The coding requirements of some bibliographic utilities may result in the ISBN being included elsewhere in the bibliographic record.

2.8C   *Optional addition.* Terms of availability

LC/GPO are exercising this option with few exceptions, such as the description of noncurrent items. Their experience has proven that price and other data about the availability of an item are useful features of the item's bibliographic record.

2.8D Qualification

2.8D2   *Optional addition.* **Recording of the type of binding.** LC/GPO are exercising this option. ISBNs are more useful in some cases when qualified as to the special nature of an item or edition of an item, e.g., ''(library binding).''

2.9– 2.10———

2.11   FACSIMILES, PHOTOCOPIES, AND OTHER REPRODUCTIONS

Refer to the discussion in this manual of 1.11 in regard to facsimiles, photocopies, and other reproductions of books, pamphlets, or printed sheets or in the form of books, pamphlets, or printed sheets. If it is not possible to determine, either from the items themselves or from research, whether or not the items represent originals or reproductions, assume, in the absence of evidence to the contrary, that items are original publications, and not reproductions.

Early printed monographs

2.12– 2.18———

Early printed monographs (books, pamphlets, and broadsides published before 1821 in countries following European conventions in bookmaking) are not discussed in this manual.

3/ Cartographic Materials

Most cartographic materials produced today are government documents. They represent many specialized formats, such as aeronautical charts, remote sensing images, and relief models, as well as the more familiar forms: maps, atlases, and globes. The government agencies preparing and publishing these cartographic items are equally varied, ranging from local planning commissions to large international organizations. Because of this diversity in both format and producing agency, the rules for cataloging cartographic government documents must be comprehensive and well-documented with examples.

Chapter 3 of AACR2 provides sufficient instructions and guidance for applying many of the rules to government documents. Since many cartographic items are government documents, numerous examples in AACR2 have been taken from a variety of government sources.

There are several significant parts of chapter 3, however, which do not adequately treat government documents, or for that matter, cartographic materials in general. In these cases, the rules have been clarified, expanded, or rewritten in this manual when necessary, and appropriate examples have been added. These amendments include providing additional guidelines for selecting and transcribing the title proper, furnishing specific instructions for determining scales, and supplying a detailed description of a "map series." Also, a large number of examples of full bibliographic records for government cartographic materials has been included at the end of the chapter.

In addition, the GODORT manual has incorporated the major rule revisions and interpretations that have been adopted by the Anglo-American Cataloguing Committee for Cartographic Materials (AACCCM). This committee, which consists of representatives from the United States, Canada, Great Britain, Australia, and New Zealand, has recently prepared a comprehensive cataloging manual based on AACR2.[1] The rule interpretations and revisions adopted by AACCCM will be applied by the Library of Congress and the U.S. Government Printing Office and many will be issued as official Library of Congress rule interpretations.

---

1. Cartographic Materials, a Manual of Interpretation for AACR2. Chicago : American Library Association, 1982.

3.0   GENERAL RULES

3.0A Scope

Chapter 3 provides the rules for cataloging all types of cartographic materials. For some cartographic formats, however, other chapters in AACR2 in addition to chapter 3 may have to be consulted. For atlases, see also chapter 2; for manuscript cartographic materials, see also chapter 4; for microform reproductions of cartographic items, see also chapter 11; and for maps that are treated as serials, see also chapter 12.

3.0B Sources of information

3.0B1 Atlases. For sources of information for an atlas, see AACR2, 2.0B. Add, as an additional area of the description for atlases, "the mathematical data area" following the edition area. The prescribed source of information for the mathematical data area is "the whole publication."

An atlas is a systematically arranged collection of maps or charts intended to be shelved like a volume, either flat or vertically. Atlases share the characteristics of maps and books, having the content of maps and the format of books. An atlas is distinguished from other books by its emphasis on maps; any textual material is secondary and serves mainly to support and explain the cartographic content. An atlas is distinguished from other collections of maps by the publisher's apparent intent that the work be used like a book and shelved in the form as issued. Atlases may be bound or loose-leaf, flat or folded, in cases, portfolios, or folders.

3.0B2 Chief source of information. The chief source of information for cartographic materials (other than atlases) as instructed in AACR2 is:

> a) the cartographic item itself, including the entire recto (front) and verso (back) of the item; when an item consists of a number of physical parts (e.g., 4 maps), treat all the parts (including a title sheet) as the cartographic item itself.
>
> b) container (portfolio, cover, envelope, etc.) or case, the cradle and stand of a globe, etc.

If information is not available from the chief source of information, take it from any accompanying printed material (texts, indexes, etc.) that is issued with the cartographic item and is intended to be used in conjunction with it.

3.0B3 Prescribed sources of information. Follow the prescribed sources of information for cartographic materials as given in AACR2.

3.0C ———

3.0D Levels of detail in the description

Follow the instructions in AACR2, 3.0D and 1.0D. In addition, in a first-level description, include any series statements.

3.0E–3.0H ———

3.0J Description of whole or part

AACR2 says:

> In describing a collection of maps [which is often referred to as a "map set" or "map series," see 3.5B2 in this manual], describe the collection as a whole *or* describe each map (giving the name of the collection as the series), according to the needs of the cataloguing agency. If the collection is catalogued as a whole, but descriptions of the individual parts are considered desirable, see [AACR2] chapter 13. If in doubt whether to describe the collection as a whole or to describe each part separately, describe the collection as a whole.

When determining whether to describe a map collection as a whole or to describe each map of the collection separately, the following factors should be considered:

1) the number of maps in a collection. The number of maps in a collection can be as few as two or as many as 10,000 or more. If the collection consists of only a few maps, most libraries would find it economically feasible to catalog each map separately if so desired. If the collection, however, consists of a large number of maps, or if the maps are frequently revised, many libraries would find it impractical if not impossible to catalog each map separately.
2) the accessibility of the maps in a collection. Many map collections provide an index map (either printed on each map or on a special sheet) which indicates the numbering scheme and shows the layout and coverage of the maps in the collection. Libraries may find that describing these collections as a whole is bibliographically sufficient since the index map would permit adequate accessibility to the individual maps. If the collection, however, consists of maps covering various geographic areas or different subjects where an index map would not be useful or appropriate, libraries may find it desirable to provide a separate bibliographic description for each map of the collection.

Examples of the various descriptions follow. Although LC/GPO are currently not applying multilevel description to items in a collection, an example of a multilevel description is given.

Description of the collection as a whole
Geological Survey (U.S.)
    County map series (topographic), Connecticut / mapped, edited, and published by the Geological Survey. — Scale 1:50,000 ; Lambert conformal conic proj. (W 73°44′ — W 71°47′/N 42°03′ — N 40°57′). — Reston, Va. : The Survey, 1977– 1980.
    9 maps : col. ; 131 × 134 cm. or smaller.

Relief shown by contours and spot heights.
"Control by USGS and NOS/NOAA."
In upper margin on some maps: State of Connecticut, Department of Environmental Protection, Natural Resources Center.
In upper margin on some maps: State of Connecticut, Highway Department.
"Compiled from 1:24,000-scale maps."
Includes location map and "Index of 1:24,000 scale maps."
Contents: Litchfield County — Hartford County — Tolland County — Windham County — New London County — Middlesex County — New Haven County — Fairfield County (north half) — Fairfield County (south half)

I. Connecticut. Natural Resources Center. II. Connecticut. State Highway Dept. III. Title.

Description of one map—separate description
Geological Survey (U.S.)
New Haven County, Connecticut / mapped, edited, and published by the Geological Survey. — Scale 1:50,000 ; Lambert conformal conic proj. (W 73°20′—W 72°32′/N 41°39′—N 41°10′). — Reston, Va. : The Survey, 1980.
1 map : col. ; 108 × 134 cm. — (County map series (topographic))

Relief shown by contours and spot heights.
Title in lower right corner: New Haven Co., Conn.
"Control by USGS and NOS/NOAA."
In upper margin: State of Connecticut, Department of Environmental Protection, Natural Resources Center.
"Compiled from 1:24,000-scale maps."
Includes location map and "Index to 1:24,000 scale maps."

I. Connecticut. Natural Resources Center. II. Title. III. Series.

Description of one map—multilevel description.
Geological Survey (U.S.)
County map series (topographic), Connecticut / mapped, edited, and published by the Geological Survey. — Scale 1:50,000 ; Lambert conformal conic proj. (W 73°44′—W 71°47′/N 42°03′—N 40°57′). — Reston, Va. : The Survey, 1977–1980.
9 maps : col. ; 131 × 134 cm. or smaller

Relief shown by contours and spot heights.
"Control by USGS and NOS/NOAA."
In upper margin on some maps: State of Connecticut, Department of Environmental Protection, Natural Resources Center.
In upper margin on some maps: State of Connecticut, Highway Department.
"Compiled from 1:24,000-scale maps."
Includes location map and "Index of 1:24,000 scale maps."

New Haven, Connecticut. — (W 73°20′—W 72°32′/N 41°39′—N 41°10′).
—1980.
1 map : col. ; 108 × 134 cm.

Title in lower right corner: New Haven Co., Conn.
In upper margin: State of Connecticut, Department of Environmental Protection, Natural Resources Center.

  I. Connecticut. Natural Resources Center. II. Title.

3.1 TITLE AND STATEMENT OF RESPONSIBILITY AREA

3.1A–3.1A1 ———

3.1B Title proper

3.1B1 Record the title proper as instructed in AACR2, 1.1B. Transcribe the title exactly as to wording, order, and spelling, but not necessarily as to punctuation and capitalization.

USAF lunar wall mosaic

A comprehensive urban plan for Jacksonville, Texas

Bahamas air navigation chart

The national atlas of the United States of America

16-inch sculptural relief globe

Military map of the peninsula of Florida south of Tampa Bay

Wreck chart of the Great Lakes

1978 stream evaluation map, state of North Dakota

Reconnaissance of the western coast of the United States

Landsat image of western West Virginia

Tectonic map of the Carpathian-Balkan mountain system and adjacent areas

New York State transportation/planning map

Since the prescribed source of information for the title area is the entire cartographic item including any container (see AACR2, 3.0B3), the title proper can be taken from anywhere on the item. If the words or parts of the title are scattered over the face of the map so that the order is not obvious, formulate a title proper in a natural reading order, giving precedence to the name of the main geographic area covered. Add punctuation (preferably commas) when needed.

> Gordon County, Georgia, soil interpretative map of possibility for flooding
> (*"Gordon County, Georgia" appears in the lower right corner of the map;*
> *"soil interpretative map of possibility for flooding" appears in the upper*
> *right corner of the map*)

> Commonwealth of Virginia, county of Fairfax, voting precincts
> (*"Commonwealth of Virginia, county of Fairfax" appears in the upper right*
> *corner of the map; "voting precincts" appears in the lower left corner of*
> *the map*)

> Fort Hood Military Reservation, Texas 1:50,000, special map
> (*"Fort Hood Military Reservation" appears in the center of the upper*
> *margin; "Texas 1:50,000" appears on the left side of the upper margin;*
> *"special map" appears on the right side of the upper margin*)

3.1B2 If the title proper includes a statement of the scale, include it in the transcription, regardless of where it appears in the title. Transcribe the scale exactly as to punctuation and spacing.

> A topographic map of Willshire, on a scale of 2 inches to a mile

> Australia 1:5 000 000 relief map
> *not*   Australia 1:5,000,000 relief map

> 1:100,000-scale metric topographic map of Bartow, Florida
> *not*   1:100,000-scale metric topographic map of Bartow, Florida

3.1B3 If the chief source of information bears more than one title, choose the title proper according to the language as instructed in AACR2, 1.1B8. If both or all of the titles are in the same language, select the title proper on the basis of the locations of the titles on the cartographic item. Use the following list of locations (given in order of preference) as a guide for choosing the title proper.

a) title located within the neat line or border of the main map, etc.
b) title located on the recto (front) of the item outside the neat line or border of the main map, etc.
c) panel title (folded title) located on either the recto or verso of the item
d) title located on the verso (back) of the item
e) title located on a container (e.g., cover, portfolio, etc.)

In addition to selecting the title proper on the basis of location, the title chosen should be comprehensive. The intent is to provide a title proper that expresses the main geographic area covered and, when relevant, the primary subject content of the item. Select the title proper according to location but give precedence to a title that includes both area and subject. For example, if the title within the neat line of a thematic (subject-oriented) map includes only the name of the geographic area, and the panel title includes both the area and the subject, select the panel title as the title proper and record the title within the neat line as a variant title in a note (see 3.7B4 in this manual). If both titles on the map, however, indicate the geographic area and subject content, choose the title proper strictly on the basis of location. The following examples further illustrate this application of the rule.

> *title within neat line:* State of Texas
> *panel title:* Oil and gas map of Texas
> *Select the panel title as the title proper.*

> *title within neat line:* General highway map, Arenac County, Michigan
> *panel title:* Official road map of Arenac County, Michigan
> *Select the title within the neat line as the title proper.*

3.1B4 If the item lacks a title, supply one in the language of the item as instructed in AACR2, 1.1B7. For cartographic materials, the supplied title should include the name of the main geographic area covered and, when relevant, the primary subject content of the item. The scale of the item may be included in the form of a representative fraction (e.g., 1:100,000) if considered important.

> [Nautical chart of the coast of Maine from Cape Elizabeth to Monhegan Island]
>
> [Relief model of California showing vegetation, 1:335,000]
>
> [Carte départementale de la France]

3.1C *Optional addition.* **General material designation**

3.1C1 For cartographic materials, LC/GPO are not exercising the option of adding the general material designation following the title proper.

3.1C2 ———

3.1D Parallel titles

3.1D1 Record parallel titles as instructed in AACR2, 1.1D.

> Population distribution by census divisions, Canada, 1976 = Repartition de la population par division de recensement, Canada, 1976
>
> Soil map of the world = Carte mondiale des sols = Mapa mundial de suelos

3.1E Other title information

3.1E1 Record other title information as instructed in AACR2, 1.1E.

Use judgment in deciding whether a word or phrase is part of the title proper or is other title information. Make the title proper as concise as possible without the loss of essential information. For cartographic materials, normally consider the name of the main geographic area covered and, when relevant, the primary subject content of the item as part of the title proper and not as other title information.

The layout, typography, grammar, and punctuation of the title information on the cartographic item are other factors to consider. For example, information that is separated from the main elements of the title by punctuation (e.g., colon or semicolon) may indicate other title information. A word or phrase in smaller typeface may indicate other title information. Conjunctions, prepositions, and prepositional phrases may indicate the beginning of other title information. Fanciful appellations are often treated as other title information. In case of doubt, transcribe the word or phrase as part of the title proper.

> Map of Ft. Myers, Florida : including detailed insets of Cape Coral, Lehigh Acres, and North Ft. Myers
>
> Earthquake map of Oklahoma : earthquakes shown through 1978
>
> Michigan official transportation map : Great Lake State
>
> Map of Nairobi National Park : with a list of birds and animal species
>
> Topographic map of Lake Placid, New York : showing contours and elevations in meters
>
> Upper Chesapeake Bay, satellite image map : NASA LANDSAT imagery 1:500,000
>
> Map of Oregon and Upper California : from the surveys of John Charles Fremont and other authorities
>
> Ghost towns of New Mexico : showing historic and old centers of habitation, trading posts, ghost towns, stage and rail stops
>
> New York State map : four sheets, 1:250,000
>
> Alabama state parks : from mountain splendor and sparkling lakes to sun-kissed Gulf beaches
>
> Alaska's mineral potential : oil and gas, geothermal, uranium, metals, coal

but

> Map of Tuscaloosa County, Alabama, showing distribution of geologic formations and ground water supplies
>
> State of Tennessee, base map with highways and contours
>
> Massachusetts, a guide to the cultural and historic places to visit

54

3.1E2 If neither the title proper nor the other title information indicates the main geographic area covered or the primary subject content of the cartographic item, add as other title information a word or brief phrase indicating the geographic area and, when relevant, the subject content.

> Arizona : ₁land use map₁
>
> General development plan, land use, and transportation system : ₁Rochester, Minnesota₁
>
> Color image map : ₁ports of entry, United States-Canadian border₁

3.1F Statements of responsibility

3.1F1 For cartographic items, statements of responsibility relate to persons and corporate bodies who have contributed significantly to the intellectual or artistic content of the item. They can include cartographers, surveyors, engineers, draftsmen, engravers, artists, scientists, research institutions, and government mapping agencies. Persons or corporate bodies who have made only minor contributions to the item may be given in a note (see 3.7B6 in this manual).

Record statements of responsibility appearing prominently on the cartographic item as instructed in AACR2, 1.1F. Since the prescribed source of information for the statement of responsibility area is the entire cartographic item including any container (see AACR2, 3.0B3), a statement of responsibility may be taken from anywhere on the item.

Although a statement of responsibility may appear directly following the title proper, for cartographic materials such a statement will often be found elsewhere on the item separate from the main title. A statement of responsibility may be given in the upper or lower margin of the map, near the legend, following a variant title (e.g., panel title), or on a cover or other container.

Statements of responsibility will often include a term or phrase that indicates the function or responsibility of the person or corporate body named. Terms commonly used on cartographic materials include the following:

> artist, artwork by
> by
> cartographer, cartography by
> compiler, compiled by, compilation by
> designer, designed by
> draftsman, drafted by
> drawn by
> engraver, engraved by
> mapped by, mapping by
> preparer, prepared by
> producer, produced by
> surveyor, surveyed by

Copyright statements (e.g., copyrighted by . . .) and publication information (e.g., distributed by . . . , printed by . . . , etc.) are not to be considered formal statements of responsibility and should not be transcribed in the statement of responsibility area. Information relating to the publication and distribution of the item may either be recorded in the publication, distribution, etc., area (see 3.4 in this manual) or in a note (see 3.7B9 in this manual). A copyright statement may be given in a note if considered important (see 3.7B6 in this manual).

Examples of statements of responsibility follow.

Ecoregions of the United States / by Robert G. Bailey ; prepared in cooperation with the U.S. Fish and Wildlife Service

Lancaster Township, official zoning map / prepared by the Lancaster County Commission for the Lancaster Township Planning Commission

Land use 1976, Albany-Dougherty County, Georgia / the Albany Metropolitan Planning Commission ; urban planner, David A. Skarosi ; cartographer, Richard A. Walker ; compilation and drafting, Kayoko Gaddis

Residual total intensity aeromagnetic map of Kentucky / R.W. Johnson, Jr., C. Haygood, and P.M. Kunselman ; cartography by Roger B. Potts ; prepared in cooperation with the Tennessee Valley Authority and the United States Geological Survey

Mt. Sterling and vicinity / Neil C. Babb, county engineer ; L. Beach, draftsman ; traced by S. Adams

Official city map of Charlotte, Mecklenburg County, North Carolina / compiled by the Engineering Division, Department of Public Works, city of Charlotte ; photography & mapping by Abrams Aerial Survey Corporation

Oil and natural gas map of Asia / prepared under the sponsorship of the United Nations Economic and Social Commission for Asia and the Pacific (ESCAP) ; co-ordinator, V.V. Sastri, with guidance from B.S. Negri ; compilers, L.L. Bhandari . . . ₍et al.₎

Geologic map of the Republic of Zambia / compiled by J.G. Thieme and R.L. Johnson, 1974-1975 ; P.K. Banda, senior cartographer ; drawn by W. Overton

Gray Army Airfield (Fort Lewis) Washington, air-crash search-and-rescue map / prepared and published by the Defense Mapping Agency, Topographic Center ; aero data furnished by the D/A, HQ 9th Infantry Div. & Fort Lewis, Fort Lewis, Washington

> Geothermal resources of Utah / geothermal data compiled by the Utah Geological and Mineral Survey ; map prepared by the National Geophysical and Solar-Terrestrial Data Center, National Oceanic and Atmospheric Administration for the Division of Geothermal Energy, United States Department of Energy ; geothermal data compiled under the direction of Peter J. Murphy ; map produced by Albert E. Theberge and Joy A. Ikelman in cooperation with Earth Science Laboratory, University of Utah Research Institute

Frequently cartographic materials will not have a statement of responsibility given. If no statement of responsibility is recognized on the item, do not construct one for the bibliographic record.

3.1F2 Add a word or short phrase to the statement of responsibility if the relationship between the title of the item and the person(s) or body (bodies) named in the statement is not clear.

> Master plan, city of Grandville, Michigan / prepared by Scott Bagby and Associates ; ₁prepared for₁ Grandville Planning Commission

> Official visitor's map and guide to Portland / ₁cartography by₁ Richard J. Williamson ; text by Arthur K. Johnson

In the example given in AACR2, the punctuation is incorrect. The example should read:

> Maps of the Mid-west ₁GMD₁ / ₁edited by₁ D.M. Bagley

3.1G Items without a collective title

3.1G1 If a cartographic item lacks a collective title and no one map, etc., is predominant, either describe the item as a unit (see 3.1G2 in this manual), or make a separate bibliographic description for each separately titled map, etc. (see 3.1G4 in this manual), or if the item consists of a large number of physically separate maps, etc., supply a collective title (see 3.1G5 in this manual).

If a cartographic item lacking a collective title has one map, etc., that is predominant, treat the title of that map as the title proper and regard the other maps as secondary maps and describe them in a note (see 3.7B18 in this manual).

Use judgment in deciding whether a map, etc., is predominant. Determine a predominant map, etc., on the basis of publisher's preference as indicated by the relative size and scale of the maps, their arrangement on the sheet, and the placement or prominence of title information.

3.1G2 When describing a cartographic item lacking a collective title as a unit, record the titles of the individual maps, etc., as instructed in AACR2, 1.1G.

> Political map of Nigeria ; Physical map of Nigeria / Federal Surveys, Nigeria
> *(Item consists of 2 maps on 1 sheet; both maps by the same author)*

3.1G3

>Plan of Perth Amboy, New Jersey : from an actual survey / by James Grant,
>deputy surveyor. Sketch of Bonham Town, New Jersey / by Alexander Suther-
>land, engineer
>
>>*(Item consists of 2 maps on 1 sheet; maps by different authors)*
>
>Map of North Island, New Zealand ; Map of South Island, New Zealand /
>cartography by Department of Lands & Survey
>
>>*(Item consists of 2 physically separate maps; both maps by the same author)*

3.1G3 ———

3.1G4 If desired, make a separate bibliographic description for each separately titled
map, etc., of an item lacking a collective title. For the description of the extent in each
of the descriptions, see 3.5B4 in this manual. Link the separate descriptions in a note
(see 3.7B21 in this manual).

LC/GPO are normally applying this provision only when the item consists of a
number of physically separate maps, etc. If the item consists of a number of maps, etc.,
which are not physically separate (e.g., 2 maps on 1 sheet), LC/GPO will either
describe the item as a unit (see 3.1G2 in this manual), or will consider one of the maps
to be predominant and will catalog that one as the main map.

3.1G5 If a cartographic item lacking a collective title consists of a large number of
physically separate maps, etc., supply a collective title in the language of the item that
includes the name of the main geographic area covered and, when relevant, the primary
subject content of the item. The scale of the item may be included in the form of a
representative fraction (e.g. 1:100,000) if considered important.

>[Pennsylvania state park maps]
>
>[Flood-prone area maps of Iowa]
>
>[Loran charts of the North Pacific Ocean, 1:1,094,400]

3.2 EDITION AREA

3.2A – 3.2A1 ———

3.2B Edition statement

3.2B1 Record the edition statement as instructed in AACR2, 1.2B.

>Ed. 5-SK
>
>1st ed.-D.O.S.

Minor corrections made 1974

Photorevised 1978

Partially rev. 1973

4th ed., 1978 ed.
   (*Two edition statements given on the item*)

3.2B2 In case of doubt as to whether a statement on a cartographic item is to be considered an edition statement, take the presence of such words as *edition, issue,* and *version* as evidence that such a statement is an edition statement as instructed in AACR2, 1.2B3.

Bicentennial ed.

Provisional issue

Statements that are not considered edition statements may be recorded in a note if considered important (see 3.7B7 in this manual).

"Experimental"

"Proof copy"

"Special printing"

3.2B3 *Optional addition.* LC/GPO are exercising the option of supplying an edition statement as instructed in AACR2.

[Rev. ed.]

3.2B4–3.2C1 ———

3.2D Subsequent edition statement

3.2D1 In the first example given in AACR2, abbreviate "Reprinted" to "Repr." in accordance with AACR2, Appendix B.9.

3.2E–3.2E1 ———

3.3 MATHEMATICAL DATA AREA

3.3A–3.3A2 ———

3.3B Statement of scale

3.3B1 Scales can be expressed in a variety of ways on cartographic items, the most common forms being a representative fraction, a verbal scale statement, and a bar or graphic scale. The scale is recorded in the statement of scale in the form of a representative fraction expressed as a ratio (e.g., Scale 1:10,000). If the scale on the item is given only as a verbal scale statement or bar scale, it must be converted into a representative fraction for it to be recorded in the statement of scale. All derived scales are given in square brackets in the scale statement.

Most verbal scale statements can be computed into a representative fraction mathematically. On most government maps published in the United States, the verbal scale statement is given in the customary system, often stated as 1 inch (on the map) representing so many miles (on the earth), e.g., 1 inch = 2 miles. If the scale on the map is given in miles to the inch, the representative fraction is calculated by multiplying the number of miles per inch by 63,360 (the number of inches in one mile).

Verbal scale statement on item: 1 inch = 2 miles

Multiply the number of miles per inch by 63,360: 2 × 63,360 = 126,720

Record the scale in the statement of scale as: Scale [1:126,720]. 1 in. = 2 miles

On most foreign government cartographic items and on some recently published U.S. government maps, the verbal scale statement is given in the metric system, often expressed as 1 centimeter (on the map) representing so many kilometers (on the earth), e.g., 1 cm. = 5 km. If the scale on the map is given in such terms, the representative fraction is determined by multiplying the number of kilometers per centimeter by 100,000 (the number of centimeters in one kilometer).

Verbal scale statement on item: 1 centimeter = 5 kilometers

Multiply the number of kilometers per centimeter by 100,000: 5 × 100,000 = 500,000

Record the scale in the statement of scale as: Scale [1:500,000]. 1 cm. = 5 km.

For additional guidelines for determining a representative fraction from a verbal scale statement, consult *Cartographic Materials*.

For some cartographic items, the scale may be given only in the form of a bar or graphic scale. A bar or graphic scale is a horizontal line or diagram, often found near the title or legend, which is subdivided to show distances at a given scale. To derive a representative fraction from a bar or graphic scale, the use of a natural scale indicator is recommended.[2] A natural scale indicator resembles a graduated ruler with various units of measure printed on it. The scale is determined by laying one edge of the natural scale indicator against the printed bar scale on the item. The representative fraction can then be usually read directly from the indicator. Since nearly all scale indicators give miles, feet, and kilometers, most graphic scales can be easily and accurately computed into a

---

2. Natural scale indicators were available in 1984 from: National Ocean Service, Physical Science Services Section, N/CG 3341, Riverdale, Md. 20737.

representative fraction by using this tool. The representative fraction is preceded by *ca.* when recorded in the statement of scale.

> Scale ₍ca. 1:48,000₎

If the cartographic item does not give a scale in the form of a representative fraction, and it cannot be computed either mathematically or with the use of a natural scale indicator, LC/GPO are not normally determining the scale by comparison with a map of a known scale. In the statement of scale, LC/GPO are giving the phrase *Scale not given* and not *Scale indeterminable* as indicated in AACR2. In the exceptional instance in which an effort is made to determine the scale of an item by comparing it with other maps and the scale still cannot be ascertained, then LC/GPO will use the phrase *Scale indeterminable*.

If the cartographic item is a facsimile, photocopy, or other type of reproduction, see 3.11 in this manual for instructions for recording the scale.

3.3B2 *Optional addition.* LC/GPO are exercising the option by recording additional scale information that is given on the cartographic item. The information is given in English in accordance with AACR2, 3.3A2.

> Scale 1:125,000. 1 cm. represents 1.25 km. 1 in. represents approx. 2 statute miles
>
> Scale 1:14,000,000. 1 in. equals 221 statute miles at the equator
>
> Scale ₍ca. 1:50,000₎ not "1 inch=1/2 mile"

3.3B3 If the scale within a single map varies (e.g., perspective map or view) and the outside values (largest and smallest scale) are given on the item or can be determined, record both scales connected by a hyphen.

> Scale 1:47,000,000– 1:57,000,000

If the values are not known, give the phrase *Scale varies* in the statement of scale.

3.3B4 If the cartographic item is multipart, consisting of a number of physically separate maps, etc., that have two different scales, record each scale as a separate scale statement instead of as one combined scale statement as indicated in AACR2. Give the larger scale first.

> Scale 1:63,360. — Scale 1:126,720
> *not* Scale 1:63,360 and 1:126,720

3.3B5 If the cartographic item is multipart consisting of a number of physically separate maps, etc., that have three or more different scales, LC/GPO are using the phrase *Scales differ* in the statement of scale and not *Scales vary* as indicated in AACR2.

3.3B6 If the cartographic item consists of two or more main maps on a single sheet (e.g., 3 maps on 1 sheet) and all the maps have the same scale, record the scale. If the maps have two different scales, record each scale as a separate scale statement (see 3.3B4 above). If the maps have three or more different scales, LC/GPO are using phrase *Scales differ* and not *Scales vary* as indicated in AACR2.

3.3B7 For celestial charts, maps of imaginary places, views (bird's-eye views or map views), and maps with nonlinear scales, record the scale only if it is given on the item.

> East-west street scale approx. double to north-south avenue scale

If the cartographic item is not drawn to scale, give the phrase *Not drawn to scale* in the statement of scale.

3.3B8 For relief models and other three-dimensional items, record the vertical scale (specified as such) following the horizontal scale if the vertical scale is given on the item or if it can be determined.

> Scale 1:250,000. Vertical scale 1:125,000. Vertical exaggeration 2:1

3.3C Statement of projection

3.3C1 Record the statement of projection if it is given on the cartographic item. The projection and any associated statements are given in English in accordance with AACR2, 3.3A2. Capitalize the first word of the projection statement as well as any proper name (e.g., Mercator, Lambert, Albers, etc.). *Projection* is abbreviated to *proj.* in accordance with AACR2, Appendix B.9.

Cartographic items are made with a variety of map projections. The most commonly used projections include the following:

> Albers equal-area
>
> Azimuthal equidistant
>
> Bonne
>
> Gauss-Kruger
>
> Lambert azimuthal
>
> Lambert conformal conic
>
> Lambert equidistant
>
> Mercator
>
> Miller cylindrical

Mollweide

Orthographic

Polyconic

Sinusoidal

Stereographic

Transverse Mercator

Universal transverse Mercator

Van Der Grinten

3.3C2 *Optional addition.* LC/GPO are exercising the option by adding any associated phrases connected with the projection statement if they are given on the cartographic item.

Lambert conformal conic proj. based on standard parallels 33° and 45°

Transverse Mercator proj., central meridian 35°13'33"E

3.3D *Optional addition.* **Statement of coordinates and equinox**
LC/GPO are exercising the option conditionally. LC/GPO are recording the coordinates or equinox of the cartographic item if the information is readily available (e.g., if the coordinates are printed on the item).

3.3D1 Statement of coordinates. Record the statement of coordinates as instructed in AACR2. Be consistent in transcribing the coordinates; record only degrees, only degrees and minutes, or only degrees, minutes, and seconds. Supply zeros when necessary to ensure consistency. Do not use square brackets in the statement of coordinates when supplying numbers.

(W 76°30'—W 74°00'/N 41°15'—N 39°00')
not   (W 76°30'—W 74°/N 41°15'—N 39°)

The statement of coordinates is to reflect only the main map(s) being described. The coordinates of insets and other secondary maps on the cartographic item are not to be included unless these maps are a continuation (uninterrupted extension) of the main map(s). For example, Alaska and Hawaii are usually shown on maps of the United States as insets. Since these insets do not generally show a continuous area of the main map, they are not included in the statement of coordinates as their inclusion would indicate coverage for extremely large geographic areas not covered by the map.

If the cartographic item is multipart, consisting of a number of physically separate maps, etc., or if one map is printed on two or more sheets, record the maximum extent of the coordinates as if the maps or sheets were joined together.

3.3D2

If the coordinates printed on the item do not extend to the neat line or border of the main map(s) or to the edge of the item, determine them as accurately as possible by extrapolation.

If the cartographic item has a prime meridian other than Greenwich, do not record the coordinates unless they can be determined by using Greenwich as the prime meridian. Cartographic items produced prior to the twentieth century may have used other prime meridians (e.g., Philadelphia, New York, Washington, Paris, Ferro, etc.).

LC/GPO are exercising the option of recording in a note other meridians given on the item (see 3.7B8 in this manual).

For world maps, disregard any overlap and the relative location of the continents. Record the coordinates for world maps and globes as:

(W 180°—E 180°/N 90°—S 90°)

If the latitudinal coordinates do not extend to the North and South Poles (N 90° and S 90° respectively) for a world map, record the maximum extent of the coordinates.

(W 180°—E 180°/N 80°—S 65°)

For atlases, LC/GPO are transcribing the coordinates only when their cartographic content is drawn at one or two dominant scales. Record the coordinates are transcribed for the maximum extent of the geographic area covered by the atlas.

For maps of the Moon, planets, and other celestial bodies, LC/GPO are not recording the coordinates (until a coding system is developed to differentiate the earth coordinates from those of other celestial bodies).

3.3D2 The instructions and examples for recording the declination, right ascension, and equinox for celestial charts in AACR2 are incorrect. For transcribing such data in the mathematical data area, consult *Cartographic Materials*.

3.4 PUBLICATION, DISTRIBUTION, ETC., AREA

3.4A–3.4B2 ———

3.4C Place of publication, distribution, etc.

3.4C1 Record the place of publication, distribution, etc., as instructed in AACR2, 1.4C.

3.4D Name of publisher, distributor, etc.

3.4D1 Record the name of the publisher as instructed in AACR2, 1.4D.

If the publisher is not explicitly stated on the cartographic item (e.g., published by . . . , produced by . . . , etc.), in the absence of information to the contrary, normally regard the name of a government mapping agency or other corporate body appearing prominently on the item (e.g., at head of title) as the publisher. Since corporate authorship can be applied to cartographic materials (see 21.1B2), the author and publisher will often be the same body for many cartographic items. Many government mapping agencies are responsible for both the preparation and the publication of their cartographic products.

Do not consider a personal author to be the publisher, however, unless there is clear evidence on the cartographic item that the person actually published the item.

LC/GPO are exercising the option by adding the name of the distributor as instructed in AACR2, 1.4D.

> Reston, Va. : U.S. Geological Survey ; Denver, Colo. : For sale by Branch of Distribution, U.S. Geological Survey

> Frankfort, Ky. : Dept. of Transportation : Distributed by Dept. of Public Information

3.4E *Optional addition.* **Statement of function of publisher, distributor, etc.**

3.4E1 LC/GPO are exercising the option by adding a statement of function to the name of the publisher, distributor, etc., as instructed in AACR2, 1.4E.

> Ottawa : Surveys and Mapping Branch : Information Canada ₍distributor₎

In the example given in AACR2, the punctuation is incorrect. The example should read:

> København : Geodætisk Institut ; ₍London₎ : Stanford ₍distributor₎

3.4F Date of publication, distribution, etc.

3.4F1 Record the date of publication, distribution, etc., as instructed in AACR2, 1.4F.

If no publication date, copyright date, or printing date is given on the item, a publication date can often be inferred from other dates or information appearing on the cartographic item. Inferred dates are enclosed in square brackets and may be questioned if there is doubt as to whether it is the actual publication date.

The date of publication may be inferred from the following sources on the cartographic item:

> a) date in the title proper, other title information, or variant title

> *title:* 1980 official highway map
> *record publication date:* ₍1980₎

b) date in the statement of responsibility

statement of responsibility: prepared by the Dept. of Lands and Surveys, 1978
record publication date: [1978]

c) date in the edition statement

edition statement: rev. 1975
record publication date: [1975]

edition statement: 1979– 80 ed.
record publication date: [1979]

d) printing or publisher's code

code on U.S. Central Intelligence Agency map: 503821 6-78
record publication date: [1978]

code on United Nations map: CART-M-74-3
record publication date: [1974]

e) other information appearing elsewhere on the item

statistical data in text: 1975 estimated population
record publication date: [1975?]

note on map: freeway to open in fall 1980
record publication date: [1980?]

Certain information found on the cartographic item, however, should not be considered when inferring a date of publication. This information includes:

a) date of geodetic control:

1927 North American datum

b) date of magnetic declination:

1975 magnetic north declination

c) dates of boundaries:

cease-fire lines as of 1967

international boundaries as of Sept. 1, 1939

d) dates in base map notes:

based on the 1972 Forest Service class A map

base map prepared by U.S. Geological Survey in 1969

3.4G Place of printing, etc., name of printer, etc., date of printing, etc.

3.4G1 Publisher unknown. If the name of the publisher is unknown, record the place and name of the printer, etc., if it is given on the item, as instructed in AACR2, 1.4G.

[S.1. : s.n., 1977?]₁ (Washington, D.C. : U.S. G.P.O.)

3.4G2 *Optional addition*. LC/GPO are exercising the option by adding the place, name of the printer, etc., and/or date of printing, etc., when it differs from the publisher, etc., and if it is considered important. For cartographic items published before 1900 and for relief models and globes regardless of the date of publication, information concerning the printer or manufacturer should normally be given. For contemporary maps, give the printer if it is a well-known map publisher or cartographic firm and the printing date when it differs from the date of publication.

Washington, D.C. : War Dept., 1870 (Washington, D.C. : J. Bien)

Richmond, Va. : Division of Mineral Resources, 1978 (Washington, D.C. : Williams & Heintz Map Corp.)
   (*Williams & Heintz Map Corp. is a well-known cartographic firm*).

Austin : Texas Dept. of Water Resources, 1977 (1978 printing)

3.5 PHYSICAL DESCRIPTION AREA

3.5A–3.5A1 ———

3.5B Extent of item (including specific material designation)

3.5B1 Record the number of physical units of a cartographic item (extent of item) by giving the number of units in arabic numerals.

1 map

1 atlas

2 views

4 maps

If the item is multipart, consisting of a large number of physically separate maps, etc., and the exact number cannot be readily determined, give an approximate number. Precede the number by *ca*.

ca. 500 maps

3.5B1

If the multipart item is not yet complete, do not record the extent of the item. Give the specific material designation (in the plural form) alone preceded by three spaces as instructed in AACR2, 1.5B5. LC/GPO are exercising the option by adding the number of maps, etc., when the item is complete. Record in a note the number of maps, etc., required to complete the item if it is known (see 3.7B10 in this manual).

[3 spaces] maps

Record the specific material designation immediately following the extent of the item. LC/GPO are not using the list of specific material designations given in AACR2, but instead are using the following list of terms which has been adopted by the Anglo-American Cataloguing Committee for Cartographic Materials. In addition, terms from other chapters in AACR2 will be used as required.

atlas

diagram
(includes block diagram)

globe
(includes celestial globe)

map
(includes aerial chart, anamorphic map, celestial chart, chart, hydrographic chart, imaginative map, photomap, plan, topographic drawing, and topographic print)

model
(includes relief model)

profile
(includes map profile)

remote-sensing image
(includes aerial remote-sensing image, orthophoto, photo mosaic, space remote-sensing image, and terrestrial remote-sensing image)

section
(includes map section)

view
(includes bird's-eye view and map view)

For the definition and further description of these cartographic terms, consult the following reference sources (in addition to AACR2 and the *Cartographic Materials*):

Department of Defense Glossary of Mapping, Charting, and Geodetic Terms. 4th ed.
Washington, D.C. : Defense Mapping Agency,
Hydrographic/Topographic Center, 1981

68

Multilingual Dictionary of Technical Terms in Cartography.
Wiesbaden, Germany : F. Steiner, 1973

If the cartographic item is a manuscript, LC/GPO are indicating this in other physical details of the physical description area (see 3.5C1 in this manual) instead of in the statement of extent as indicated in AACR2.

3.5B2 If there are two or more maps, etc., of comparable importance on a single sheet, give the number of maps, etc., followed by the phrase *on 1 sheet.*

4 maps on 1 sheet

2 remote-sensing images on 1 sheet

If the maps, etc., are printed on two or more sheets but so designed that they could be fitted together to form a single map, etc., or more than one map, etc., give the number of complete maps, etc., followed by the number of sheets. LC/GPO are using the phrase *on . . . sheets* instead of *in . . . sections* as indicated in AACR2.

1 map on 4 sheets
not   1 map in 4 sections

2 maps on 8 sheets
not   2 maps in 8 sections

A single map printed on two or more sheets is often referred to as a "multisheet single map." A multisheet single map can often be identified (and distinguished from a collection of maps or a map series) by the following characteristics:

a) The number of sheets normally does not exceed 12.
b) The individual sheets are usually published together by the same body and are sold as a unit.
c) Each sheet often has an incomplete border, existing only on one or two sides of the sheet (the map has a complete border when the sheets are joined together).
d) Only one of the sheets may have the main title or legend data (each sheet, however, may have its own sheet title or designation, e.g., northeast sheet, sheet no. 3, etc.) .

The most important feature of a multisheet single map is that the individual sheets are not complete maps in themselves, only when taken together do they constitute a complete map. The separate sheets cannot be used independently—they must be used together as a unit.

3.5B2

Map series

If the item consists of a number of sheets each having the characteristics of a complete map, etc., treat it as a collection and describe it as instructed in 3.5B1 in this manual.

250 maps

10 views

2 profiles

A collection of maps, etc., is often referred to as a "map set" or more recently as a "map series." A map series is not to be confused with a "monographic series" (see AACR2, Appendix D) although there are some similarities between them. The number of maps in a map series can be as few as two or as many as 10,000 or more. Regardless of the number, the maps in a map series have common unifying characteristics. Since most map series are produced by government agencies, a further description of a map series is appropriate.

The maps within a map series generally conform to a uniform size, format, scale, and projection. The maps of some series, however, may have varying dimensions or scales. The maps of a series will also use the same system of cartographic symbolization. For example, each map will apply the same method to depict relief features (e.g., contours and spot heights) or will use the same coloring scheme to show vegetation.

A map series resembles a multisheet single map in that the maps of a series can often be assembled together to form a large single map. Differing from the sheets of a multisheet single map, the maps of a series are complete maps in themselves and can be used independently. Each map in a series will normally have the collective or series title, authorship and publication information, and legend data. Some map series may have a separate title sheet or legend sheet.

A map series is identified by a collective or series title, consisting of a special title, series designation, scale, or a combination of these elements.

International map of the world 1:1,000,000

New York 7.5 minute series planimetric

Ordnance Survey of Great Britain, 1:50 000 second series

Carte géologique de la France a 1/50 000

Australia 1:100 000 topographic survey

1:250 000-scale map of Atlantic coast ecological inventory

City of Durban, 500 feet to 1 inch cadastral series

Topographic lunar maps 1:250,000

In addition to the series title, each map in a series will have its own sheet title or designation, consisting of the name of the geographic area covered, a map or sheet number, etc.

Monteagle quadrangle, Tennessee

Map no. J-18

Calvert County

Sheet 1459. San Rafael

West sheet

Figure 6. Metallogenic provinces in Alaska

Plate 20. Present use of reclaimed land

A map series is usually produced and published by one government body; however, for some series that are issued over a long period of time or are international in scope, several agencies may be involved. The International map of the world 1:1,000,000 series, for example, is an international cooperative mapping project which involves many foreign government mapping agencies.

The maps of a series may be issued simultaneously or over a period of time. Some large series are issued over many years. In addition, the maps within some series are frequently revised or updated. The maps may be completely revised or may only be overprinted with new or corrected information. For example, topographic maps produced by the U.S. Geological Survey are often "photorevised" with the revision information being printed on the maps in a distinctive color.

The primary intent of most map series is to cover a contiguous geographic area (e.g., city, state, country, the world, etc.) in a systematic arrangement. Each map of a series covers a specific area (e.g., quadrangle area, administrative unit, etc.). The maps of a series may be general-purpose by showing only general geographic features (e.g., planimetric and topographic maps) or may be thematic by emphasizing a particular theme or subject (e.g., highways, geology, soils, vegetation, land use, etc.). An example of each type of series is given below.

New York (State). Dept. of Transportation.
New York State map : four sheet, 1:250,000 / prepared and published by the New York State Department of Transportation, in cooperation with the Federal Highway Administration, U.S. Department of Transportation. — Rev. in 1979 from Dept. of Transportation 1:24,000 scale quadrangle maps, highway construction plans, municipal boundary maps, and various other sources. — Scale 1:250,000 ; Transverse Mercator proj. (W 79°52′30″ — W 71°45′00″/N 45°00′00″ — N 40°22′30″). — Albany : New York State Dept. of Transportation : For sale by the Map Information Unit, New York State Dept. of Transportation, 1980.
4 maps : col. ; 95 × 132 cm.

Shows minor civil divisions.
New York transverse Mercator (NYTM) grid.
Includes sheet index.
Contents: West sheet — North sheet — Central sheet — South sheet.

I. United States. Federal Highway Administration. II. Title.

U.S. Fish and Wildlife Service.
1:250 000-scale map of Atlantic coast inventory / produced by U.S. Fish and Wildlife Service. — Scale 1:250,000 ; Transverse Mercator proj. (W 82°00′ — W 66°00′/N 45°16′ — N 25°00′). — ₁Washington, D.C.₁ : The Service ; Reston, Va. : For sale by U.S. Geological Survey, 1980.
31 maps : col. ; 89 × 71 cm. or smaller, folded to 21 × 10 cm.

Relief shown by spot heights.
Panel title.
Title in lower right corner: Atlantic coast ecological inventory.
Base map prepared by U.S. Geological Survey.
Accompanied by: Atlantic coast ecological inventory, user's guide and information base / by Angelo D. Beccasio . . . ₁et al.₁
Includes indexes of land and water species and location map.

I. Geological Survey (U.S.). II. Title. III. Title: Atlantic coast ecological inventory.

A map series may also consist of maps covering a common geographic area with each map displaying a different or related theme or subject. In the first example given below, each map of the series covers the entire state of Alaska, but shows a different mineral resource. In the second example, each map of the series covers the entire state of Colorado, but shows a different topic relating to land use and regional planning.

Alaska Field Operation Center.
Alaska's mineral potential, 1978 : oil and gas, geothermal, uranium, metals, coal / prepared at the request of the Federal-State Land Use Planning Commission of Alaska by Alaska Field Operation Center, U.S. Bureau of Mines, and C.C. Hawley. — Scale ₁ca. 1:5,068,800₁. 1 in. = approx. 80 miles (W 172° — W 130°/N 72° — N 54°). — Juneau : The Center, 1977.
8 maps : col. ; 41 × 59 cm., folded in portfolio 33 × 26 cm.

Title from portfolio.
Base map: Alaska, 1977 / United States Department of the Interior, Bureau of Mines.
Accompanied by text.

Some sheets include indexes, notes, and inset of the Aleutian Islands.
Contents: Figure 1. Relative importance for oil and gas development in
Alaska — Figure 2. Relative importance for coal development in Alaska —
Figure 3. Relative importance for geothermal development in Alaska —
Figure 4. Mineral potential areas and historical mining regions in Alaska —
Figure 5. Sedimentary basins having uranium potential in Alaska — Figure
6. Metallogenic provinces in Alaska — Figure 7. Present and state proposed
transportation corridors in Alaska — Figure 8. Proposed ''Four systems''
withdrawals.

I. Hawley, C. C. (Charles Caldwell), 1929– . II. Joint Federal-State Land Use
Planning Commission for Alaska. III. Title.

Colorado Land Use Commission.
Colorado land use map folio. — Scale 1:500,000. 1 in. equals approx. 8
miles ; Lambert conformal conic proj., standard parallels 33° and 45° (W
109°—W 102°/N 41°—N 37°). — Denver : Colorado Land Use Commission, 1974.
12 maps : col. ; 93 × 126 cm., folded in portfolio 26 × 22 cm.

Relief shown by spot heights.
Title from portfolio.
Accompanied by: A land use program for Colorado : report.
Includes text.
Contents: Existing land use, Colorado, 1973 — Land ownership, Colorado,
1974 — Selected energy resources pipelines, Colorado, 1974 — Electrical
power plants and distribution systems, Colorado, 1974 — Selected mineral
lode resources, Colorado, 1974 — Potential available groundwater, Colo-
rado, 1974 — Snow depth, Colorado, 1974 — Water service areas, Colo-
rado, 1974 — Potential for irrigated agriculture, Colorado, 1974 — Potential for non-irrigated agriculture, Colorado, 1974 — Sediment yield, Colo-
rado, 1974 — Soil shrink-swell potential, Colorado, 1974.

I. Colorado Land Use Commission. A land use program for Colorado : report.
II. Title.

For some map series, it may be desirable to catalog each map separately instead of
describing the series as a whole. Consult the guidelines given in 3.0J in this manual
when determining which method to use.

3.5B3 For atlases, record the pagination or the number of volumes in the statement of
extent as instructed in AACR2, 2.5B.

1 atlas (xii, 132, 44 p.)

3.5B4 If the description is of a separately titled map, etc., of a cartographic item lacking a collective title (see 3.1G4 in this manual) and the map, etc., is physically separate from the rest of the item, record the statement of extent as instructed in 3.5B1–3.5B3 in this manual.

If the description is of a separately titled map, etc., of a cartographic item lacking a collective title (see 3.1G4 in this manual) and if the map, etc., is not physically separate from the rest of the item (e.g., 2 maps on 1 sheet), do not record the statement of extent as instructed in AACR2, 3.5B4. Record instead the statement of extent as instructed in 3.5B1–3.5B3 in this manual. Give further details of the physical description of the item in a note.

3.5C Other physical details

3.5C1 Record other physical details of the cartographic item, as appropriate, following the statement of extent. In addition to those physical details given in AACR2, LC/GPO are indicating in this area whether the item is printed on both sides of sheet, is a manuscript, or is a photoreproduction, according to the order set below.

a) Printed on both sides of sheet. If a map is printed so that it continues from one side of the sheet to the other at the same scale, use the phrase *both sides*.

    1 map : both sides ; 62 × 85 cm., on sheet 66 × 72 cm.

b) Manuscript. If the cartographic item is a manuscript, use the abbreviation *ms.* in accordance with AACR2, Appendix B.9. Record details describing the manuscript (e.g., pen-and-ink drawing, pencil tracing, etc.) in a note (see 3.7B10 in this manual).

    1 map : ms. ; 46 × 33 cm.

c) Photoreproduction. If the cartographic item is a photoreproduction, use the term *photocopy*. Record the method of reproduction (e.g., blue line print, blueprint, etc.) in a note (see 3.7B10 in this manual).

    1 map : photocopy ; 42 × 76 cm.

d) Number of maps in an atlas (see 3.5C2 in this manual)
e) Color (see 3.5C3 in this manual)
f) Material (see 3.5C4 in this manual)
g) Mounting (see 3.5C5 in this manual)

3.5C2 Number of maps in an atlas. Record the number of maps in an atlas as instructed in AACR2, 2.5C.

    1 atlas (viii, 132 p.) : 72 col. maps ; 24 cm.

3.5C3 Color. The determination of whether the item is colored is made on the basis of the cartographic data which appears within the neat line or border of the main map, etc., being described, and not on the basis of material outside the border or on the verso of the item (e.g., secondary maps, illustrations, etc.).

The cartographic item may be printed in color (requiring more than one printing plate for reproduction) or may be hand colored (a printed map, etc., which has been systematically colored by hand). Monochromatic items (having only a single color) are not to be considered colored regardless of the color of ink or paper used.

Colored is abbreviated to *col.* in accordance with AACR2, Appendix B.9. If the item consists of a number of maps, etc., some of which are colored, indicate the number that are colored if it can be easily determined, otherwise, use the phrase *some col.*

> 1 map : col. ; 36 × 47 cm.
>
> 6 maps : 3 col. ; 57 × 44 cm.
>
> 120 maps : some col. ; 84 × 59 cm.

If the cartographic item is colored by hand, use the phrase *hand col.* Additional information concerning the hand coloring of the item may be given in a note (see 3.7B10 in this manual).

> 1 map : hand col. ; 50 × 48 cm.

3.5C4 Material. Record the material of which the cartographic item is made if it is considered to be significant. These materials include silk, plastic, wood, plaster, vellum, parchment, and metal. Materials like cardboard and plastic-coated paper are usually not considered significant enough to mention.

> 1 model : col., plastic ; 46 × 65 × 4 cm.
>
> 1 map : ms., parchment ; 30 × 27 cm.

3.5C5 Mounting. Indicate if the cartographic item is mounted.

> 1 map : mounted on linen ; 37 × 29 cm.

3.5D Dimensions

3.5D1 Maps, plans, etc. Record the dimensions of maps and other two-dimensional cartographic items as instructed in AACR2. Give the height of the item followed by its width. Measure between the neat lines or inner borders of the main map(s) being described.

> 1 map ; 42 × 28 cm.

3.5D1　*Maps, plans, etc.*

For circular maps, give the diameter of the item specified as such. *Diameter* is abbreviated to *diam.* in accordance with AACR2, Appendix B.9.

> 1 map ; 37 cm. in diam.

If the map, etc., is irregularly shaped, or has no neat lines or borders, or has bleeding edges (cartographic content extends right to the edge of the sheet without any margin or border), give the greater or greatest dimensions of the map itself. If the map itself cannot be easily measured, give the size of the sheet specified as such.

> 1 map ; on sheet 62 × 50 cm.

All measurements will be given in centimeters. LC/GPO are not exercising the option of giving dimensions to the nearest millimeter for early and manuscript cartographic items.

> 1 map : ms. ; 124 × 153 cm.
> *not*　1 map : ms. ; 123.6 × 152.4 cm.

When recording more than one dimension in the physical description area, LC/GPO are separating each set with a comma.

> 1 map ; 35 × 45 cm., on sheet 40 × 50 cm., folded to 20 × 10 cm.

If a single map, etc., is printed on two or more sheets at the same scale (multisheet single map), if it can be easily measured, give the size of the entire map, etc., as if the sheets were joined together, as well as the size of the individual sheets. LC/GPO are using the phrases *sheets* and *on . . . sheets* instead of *sections* and *in . . . sections* as indicated in AACR2.

> 1 map on 2 sheets ; 110 × 84 cm., sheets 58 × 88 cm.
> *not*　1 map in 2 sections ; 110 × 84 cm., sections 58 × 88 cm.

If the size of either dimension (height or width) of the map, etc., is less than half the same dimension of the sheet on which the map, etc., is printed, or if there is substantial additional information on the sheet (e.g., text, illustrations, secondary maps, etc.), give the size of the sheet as well as the size of the map.

> 1 map ; 24 × 28 cm., on sheet 60 × 66 cm.

If the map, etc., is printed with an outer cover within which it is intended to be folded or if the sheet itself contains a panel or section designed to appear on the outside when the sheet is folded, give the size of the sheet in its folded form as well as the size of the map.

> 1 map ; 53 × 68 cm., folded to 23 × 9 cm.

76

If the map, etc., is printed so that it continues from one side of the sheet to the other at the same scale, if it can be easily measured, give the size of the map, etc., as a whole, as well as the size of the sheet. The phrase *both sides* is given as other physical details in the physical description area (see 3.5C1).

> 1 map : both sides ; 54 × 80 cm., on sheet 58 × 65 cm.

If the maps, etc., in a collection or a map series are of two sizes, give both sizes with the predominant size first.

> 6 maps ; 38 × 54 cm. and 32 × 48 cm.
> *(4 maps are 38 × 54 cm., 2 maps are 32 × 48 cm.)*

If the maps, etc., in a collection or a map series are of more than two sizes, give the greatest height of any of the maps, etc., followed by the greatest width of any of the maps, etc. Follow the dimensions by the phrase *or smaller*.

> 36 maps ; 80 × 60 cm. or smaller
> *(There may be no single map with these actual dimensions)*

3.5D2 Atlases. Record the dimensions for atlases as instructed in AACR2, 2.5D.

> 1 atlas (viii, 92, 24 p.) : 60 col. maps ; 26 cm.

3.5D3 Relief models. Record the dimensions for relief models by giving the height and width of the item as instructed in 3.5D1 in this manual. LC/GPO are exercising the option by adding the depth as well.

> 1 model : col., plastic ; 52 × 49 × 3 cm.

3.5D4 Globes. Record the dimensions for globes by giving the diameter of the item specified as such. *Diameter* is abbreviated to *diam.* in accordance with AACR2, Appendix B.9.

> 1 globe : col., plastic, mounted on a metal stand ; 41 cm. in diam.

3.5D5 *Optional addition.* **Containers.** LC/GPO are exercising the option by adding the dimensions of any container of the item. Types of containers for cartographic items include covers, cases, slipcases, envelopes, and portfolios.

> 4 maps : col. ; 88 × 60 cm., folded to 42 × 28 cm., in portfolio 45 × 31 cm.

3.5E Accompanying material.

3.5E1 Record the name of any material that is issued with the cartographic item and is intended to be used in conjunction with it, as instructed in AACR2, 1.5E. If the accompanying material, however, has a distinctive title or a complex description that cannot be easily or fully described in the physical description area, record the accompanying material in a note (see 3.7B11 in this manual).

Describe the accompanying material in the physical description area by recording its title if it consists of a general term (e.g., index book), otherwise, supply a generic term in English (e.g., index, index map, text, directory, bibliography, legend sheet, errata sheet, etc.).

LC/GPO are exercising the option conditionally by recording the physical description of the accompanying material if considered important.

1 map : col. ; 88 × 72 cm. + 1 index (16 p. ; 22 cm.)

44 maps ; 58 × 69 cm. + 1 index map
(Physical description of the index map is not given as it has the same dimensions as the main maps).

3.6 SERIES AREA

3.6A – 3.6A1 ——————

3.6B Series statements.

3.6B1 Record each series statement of a cartographic item as instructed in AACR2, 1.6. Do not consider stock numbers, order numbers, and other similar numbers as series statements. These numbers can be recorded in a note if considered important (see 3.7B19 in this manual).

(Map series / Colorado Geological Survey ; 12)

(Kentucky map facsimile series ; no. 3)

(National park series (topographic))

(Resource map / New Mexico Bureau of Mines & Mineral Recources ; 10)

(Open-file report ; 78-1034)

(Series V603 / Defense Mapping Agency, Topographic Center)

(Miscellaneous investigations series / United States Geological Survey ; map I-1115)

(Australia small scale thematic map series ; 19)

3.7 NOTE AREA

3.7A – 3.7A2 ———

3.7B Notes.

3.7B1 Nature and scope of the item. Record notes describing the nature or scope of the cartographic item if it is not apparent from the rest of the bibliographic description (e.g., title area, other notes, etc.). Include notes relating to the date of information of the item, particularly if that date differs from the date of publication. Also give notes on unusual or unexpected features of the item.

> Shows city wards
>
> Shows radial distances from City Hall
>
> Cadastral map showing land ownership
>
> ''Forest Service map class A''
>
> Points of interest shown pictorially
>
> ''Map information as of July 1, 1979''
> *(Item published in 1980)*
>
> Also shows geologic formations
> *(Item entitled:* Mineral resources map of Wyoming)
>
> Does not show land capability
> *(Item entitled:* Bennington County, Vermont, land capability plan)
>
> Covers area between Cape Cod and Assateaque Island
> *(Item entitled:* Bathymetric map, Atlantic coast, United States)
>
> ''Bathymetric information is not intended for navigational purposes''

Record notes describing relief when it is depicted on the item, regardless of whether the depiction occurs on the land or below sea level. Relief can be shown in a variety of ways on cartographic items. The terms most commonly used to describe relief are *contours, hachures, shading, gradient tints, spot heights, form lines, soundings,* and *pictorially.*

> Relief shown by contours, hachures, and spot heights
>
> Relief and depths shown by gradient tints
>
> Depths shown by contours and soundings
>
> ''Contour interval 200 feet with supplementary contours at 100 foot intervals''

The following examples given in AACR2 are notes describing the physical description of the item and should instead be given as physical description notes (see 3.7B10 in this manual).

> Maps dissected and pasted onto the sides of 42 wooden blocks to form an educational game

> Free ball globe in transparent plastic cradle with graduated horizon circle and ''geometer''

3.7B2 Language. Record the language or languages of the cartographic item and its contents (including titles, place names, legend data, text, and indexes) when it is not apparent from the rest of the bibliographic description.

> Title in English, French, German, and Russian
>   *(Only the English and French titles are given in the title area)*

> Title and legend in English, Afrikaans, and German. Place names in English and Afrikaans. Text in English

3.7B3 Source of title proper. Record the source of the title proper in a note when it is taken from outside the chief source of information, such as an accompanying text, a published reference source, or another edition of the item. LC/GPO are also recording the source when the title proper is taken from the verso of the cartographic item or from its container (e.g., cover), or when the title proper is a panel title (folded title).

> Title from publisher's catalog

> Title from: Monthly Checklist of State Publications, v. 73, no. 11

> Title from 1976 ed.

> Title from verso

> Cover title

> Panel title

3.7B4 Variations in title. Record other titles appearing on the cartographic item or its container that differ from the title proper. Include the source of the title.

> *Title in upper margin:* State of Oregon

> *Panel title:* Padre Island National Seashore, Texas
>   *(Title proper:* Padre Island National Seashore)

> *Title on envelope:* Land use and land cover in the greater Pittsburgh region, 1973

> *Spine title:* Atlas of the state of Minnesota

3.7B5 ———

3.7B6 Statements of responsibility. Record information relating to the authorship of the cartographic item if not given in the title and statement of responsibility area and if considered important.

> "Ground control was supplied by the U.S. Coast and Geodetic Survey"
>
> "Imagery from NASA Earth Resources Technology Satellite (ERTS-1)"
>
> Bathymetry compiled by the National Ocean Survey
>
> Source of data: Office of the Geographer, Dept. of State
>
> "This map approved by Charles T. Wilson, county surveyor"
>
> "Geology modified from F.S. MacNeil"
>
> "Base map prepared by the U.S. Geological Survey in cooperation with the U.S. Soil Conservation Service"
>
> "Road update furnished by Washington State Department of Natural Resources"
>
> "Based on research and exploration supported by the U.S. Navy Office of Naval Research and the National Science Foundation"
>
> "Copyright by City of New York"

3.7B7 Edition and history. Record information relating to the edition or history of the cartographic item if not given in the edition area and if considered important.

> "Reprinted in 1974 from the original copper plates in the possession of the Hydrographic Office"
>
> Reproduced from a manuscript in the National Archives
>
> "This is no. 16 of an edition limited to 100 copies"
>
> Differs from earlier edition in coloration
>
> "Experimental"
>
> "Proof copy"
>
> "Advance copy, subject to corrections"
>
> "Special printing"
>
> "Re-drawn from 1961 map"
>
> Originally published in U.S. House of Representatives report, 1827
>
> "This map was reproduced by electronic color scanning of an earlier printing (1965)"

"Reprinted from the Geological World Atlas published by UNESCO in association with the Commission for the Geological Map of the World."

3.7B8 Mathematical and other cartographic data. Record other mathematical and cartographic data additional to or elaborating on that given in the mathematical data area. Include notes on meridians, grids, and orientation. Record relief in a scope note (see 3.7B1 in this manual).

Record the prime meridian if stated on the cartographic item and if other than Greenwich. The prime meridian is the north-south reference line on the earth's surface (0° longitude) from which longitude is measured. The Greenwich meridian, the meridian which passes through Greenwich, England, near London, has been accepted almost universally since 1884 as the prime meridian. For cartographic items produced prior to that date, meridians other than Greenwich were often adopted. For example, maps published in the United States in the early 19th century often used Philadelphia, Washington, or New York as the prime meridian. On some maps, two different prime meridians were given.

> Prime meridian: Washington
>
> Prime meridians: Philadelphia and London

In addition to the prime meridian, record any local or principal meridian given on the cartographic item. A principal meridian, for example, is often stated on maps of the U.S. Forest Service.

> "Michigan meridian"
>
> "Sixth principal meridian"
>
> "Boise and Willamette meridian"

Record the type of grid if stated on the cartographic item and if considered important.

> Irish national grid
>
> "20,000-metre universal transverse Mercator grid, zones 16 and 17"
>
> Military grid
>
> Arbitrary grid
>
> "Grid based on North Carolina rectangular coordinate system"
>
> UTM grid

Most cartographic items are produced with north located at or near the top of the item. If the item indicates that north is located in a position 45° or more from the top of the item, record the orientation in a note.

Oriented with north toward the upper left

Oriented with north to the left

Oriented with north toward the lower right

Oriented with north to the bottom

3.7B9 Publication, distribution, etc. Record information on the publication, distribution, etc., of the cartographic item if not given in the publication, distribution, etc., area and if considered important. Record notes relating to the date of information of the item in a scope note (see 3.7B1 in this manual).

Published in cooperation with the U.S. Geological Survey under the auspices of the U.S. Agency for International Development

Some maps published by the U.S. Army Map Service
(Item is a map series, most maps are published by the U.S. Defense Mapping Agency which is given in the publication area).

Not distributed outside the U.S.

"Published by the U.S. Navy as a memorial to Dr. Bruce C. Heezen"

"Published and issued February 1976"

"Distribution limited—destroy when no longer needed"

3.7B10 Physical description. Record information relating to the physical description of the cartographic item if not given in the physical description area and if considered important.

Has watermark in shape of anchor

Has grommets in upper corners for hanging

"This map is red-light readable"

If the item is a photoreproduction (i.e., photocopy), LC/GPO are indicating this in the physical description area (see 3.5C1 in this manual) and not in a note as indicated in AACR2. The method of reproduction, however, is recorded in a note.

Blue line print

Blueprint

If the item is a manuscript, record details further describing the hand-drawn item.

Pen-and-ink drawing

Pencil tracing

If the item is multipart and is not yet complete (see 3.5B1 in this manual), record the number of maps, etc., required to complete the item if it is known. (This information can sometimes be determined by an index map on the item or by consulting the publisher's catalog.)

> Geographic coverage complete in 48 maps

If the item is hand colored or is printed on both sides of the sheet, LC/GPO are recording these physical details in the physical description area (see 3.5C1 and 3.5C3 in this manual) instead of in a note as indicated in AACR2.

3.7B11 Accompanying material. Record the accompanying material of the cartographic item in a note when it is not stated in the physical description area (see 3.5E in this manual) or given as a separate entry. (LC/GPO are currently not applying multi-level description to accompanying material).

> Accompanied by: Explanatory brochure, oil and natural gas map of Asia
>
> Accompanied by: Millersville borough ordinance no. 99
>
> Accompanied by: Description of disturbed and reclaimed surface-mined coal lands in eastern Oklahoma
>
> Accompanied by 7 regional texts: Alaska wildlife management plans : a public proposal for the management of Alaska's wildlife
>
> Some maps accompanied by texts
>> *(Item is a map series.)*
>
> Accompanied by introductory letter indicating maps are to be part of an economic atlas of Quebec

3.7B12 Series. Record notes on series data that cannot be given in the series area.

> Sheets 8, 10, and 12 have series: D.O.S. 30
>> *(Other sheets have a different D.O.S. series which is given in the series area)*.
>
> "First in a series which will eventually cover the whole country"

3.7B13 ———

3.7B14 Audience. Record notes indicating the intended audience of the cartographic item. In addition, include notes concerning any restricted use of the item.

> "For official use only"
>
> Restricted to U.S. Government officials
>
> Unclassified

3.7B18 Contents. Record notes describing the contents of the cartographic item as instructed in AACR2. Include secondary maps, insets (secondary maps located within the neat line or border of the main map), indexes, text, illustrations, distance charts, statistical tables, diagrams, and advertisements. If information is given on both the recto and verso of the item, describe each in a separate note. Information on a container (e.g., cover, envelope, etc.) may be described in a separate note if considered important. Use abbreviations in accordance with AACR2, Appendix B.

Includes indexes, text, distance chart, and 4 insets

Includes location map, boundary diagram, and elevation guide

Index to points of interest, col. ill., maps of Richmond and Norfolk, and advertisements on verso

Text, glossary, list of sources, and geologic profile on verso

Insets: Alaska — Hawaii — Puerto Rico and the Virgin Islands — Guam — American Samoa

Index on cover

LC/GPO are using the term *Contents:* and not *Parts:* as indicated in AACR2. A formal *Contents:* note is used:

a) to record the titles of individual maps, etc., in a collection or map series and a collective title is used as the title proper

Contents: Central and western Massachusetts — Cape Cod and islands — Northeast Massachusetts — Southern Massachusetts
(Item consists of 4 physically separate maps; collective title: Massachusetts sites & attractions)

Contents: Geologic map, Routt County, Colorado — Energy and resources map, Routt County, Colorado
(Item consists of 2 physically separate maps; collective title: Routt County, Colorado)

b) to record the titles of two or more main maps, etc., on a single sheet and a collective title is used as the title proper

Contents: Existing land use, Byhalia, Mississippi — Future land use, Byhalia, Mississippi
(Item consists of 2 maps on 1 sheet; collective title: Community development plan, Byhalia, Mississippi)

Contents: Topography — Land apportionment — Average annual rainfall — Land use
(Item consists of 4 maps on 1 sheet; collective title: Southern Rhodesia)

Titles recorded in a *Contents:* note are to be transcribed exactly as they appear on the cartographic item. LC/GPO are generally recording no more than 12 titles in such a note.

3.7B19 Numbers. Record important numbers given on the item and its container other than an ISBN or ISSN number (see AACR2, 3.8B). Important numbers for cartographic items include stock numbers, order numbers, plate numbers, classification numbers, and any other number or alpha-numeric code which would further identify the item or distinguish it from other similar items.

Supt. of Docs. S/N: 024-005-00704-1

"Plate no. 27"

Order no.: FPC M/63

"Chart no. 694"

"Drawing no. 72-A"

United Nations sales publication no.: E.74.1.3

3.7B20 Copy being described and library's holdings. Record notes describing any annotations made to the cartographic item by hand before being received by the library. Include the method and color of the annotation, and, if it can be determined, the nature of the annotation.

LC copy annotated in red ink to show boundaries, black ink to show place names, and blue ink to show routes

LC copy signed in pencil on verso: S.A. Douglas, 1846

LC copy stamped on: North Dakota state depository document

Record any imperfections of a cartographic item if they are significant enough to affect its use. For old or rare items (e.g., manuscript maps) even minor imperfections should be noted.

LC copy imperfect: Index lacking

LC copy imperfect: Deterioration along folds and edges of sheet
(Manuscript map)

For a multipart cartographic item, record the library's holdings, including any wanting maps or sheets.

> LC copy lacking northwest sheet

3.7B21 "With" notes. If the description is of a separately titled map, etc., of a cartographic item lacking a collective title (see 3.1G4 in this manual), make a note listing the other separately titled maps, etc., of the item in the order in which they appear.

> With: Surface-water availability, Jefferson County, Alabama, map 167, plate 2
> *(Item being described is plate 1)* .

> Issued in portfolio with 19 other facsim. maps of New Jersey
> *(Other 19 maps cataloged separately, with same note)*

3.8   STANDARD NUMBER AND TERMS OF AVAILABILITY AREA

3.8A–3.8C1 ———

3.8D   *Optional addition.* **Terms of availability.**

3.8D1 LC/GPO are exercising the option conditionally by adding the terms of availability only to cartographic items that have been issued within the current three years.

3.8E–3.8E1 ———

3.9–3.10 ———

3.11   FACSIMILES, PHOTOCOPIES, AND OTHER REPRODUCTIONS

Describe facsimiles, photocopies, and other reproductions of cartographic materials as instructed in AACR2, 1.11. If the reproduction has either been reduced or enlarged from that of the original, record the scale of the reproduction in the statement of scale area. Record the scale of the original item in a note if it is known or can be determined.

> Fremont, John Charles, 1813–1890.
> Map of Oregon and Upper California : from the surveys of John Charles
> Fremont and other authorities / drawn by Charles Preuss under the order of
> the Senate of the United States. — Scale ₍ca. 1:2,700,000₎ (W 125°—W
> 103°/N 49°—N 31°). — ₍Washington, D.C.₎ : U.S. Army Corps of Engi-
> neers, ₍1975₎
> 1 map ; 85 × 65 cm.

Shows area of U.S. west of the Continental Divide.
Relief shown by hachures and spot heights.
Facsim. of map originally published in 1848.
Scale of original: 1:3,000,000.
Includes notes and "Profile of the travelling route from the South Pass of the Rocky Mountains to the Bay of San Francisco."
"C-2a."

I. Preuss, Charles, 1803–1854. II. United States. Army. Corps of Engineers. III. Title. IV. Title: Oregon and Upper California. V. Title: Upper California.

Cartographic materials — examples

United States. National Park Service.
Valley Forge National Historical Park, Pennsylvania / National Park Service, U.S. Department of the Interior. — Scale ₁ca. 1:16,000₁. — Washington, D.C. : The Service : For sale by the Supt. of Docs., U.S. G.P.O., ₁1979₁ 1 map : col. ; 26 × 42 cm., folded to 10 × 21 cm.

Relief shown by shading.
Selected buildings shown pictorially.
Panel title.
Includes text, descriptive index to points of interest, and col. ill.
Text, map of "Campaign of 1777," and col. ill. on verso.
"Stock number 024-005-00760-1."

I. Title.

Lines, Gregory C.
Water availability of Randolph County, Alabama / by Gregory C. Lines and Robert V. Chandler ; prepared in cooperation with the United States Geological Survey. — Scale ₁ca. 1:126,720₁ (W 85°40'—W 85°15'/N 33°30'—N 33°05'). — University, Ala, : Geological Survey of Alabama, 1975.
1 map : col. ; 48 × 49 cm., folded in envelope 23 × 31 cm. — (Map / Geological Survey of Alabama ; 137)

Shows surface and underground water flow.
Relief shown by spot heights.
"Base map modified from Alabama Highway Department maps and field notes."

Accompanied by text: Water availability, Randolph County, Alabama.
Includes text and location map.

I. Chandler Robert V. II. Geological Survey (U.S.). III. Geological Survey of
Alabama. IV. Title. V. Series: Map (Geological Survey of Alabama) ; 137.

Geological Survey (U.S.).
Oregon, base map with highways and contours / compiled, edited, and
published by the Geological Survey. — Rev. in 1979, highways corr. to
1979. — Scale 1:500,000. 1 in. equals approx. 8 miles ; Lambert conformal
conic proj., standard parallels 33° and 45° (W 124°—W 117°/N 46°—N
42°). — Reston, Va. : The Survey, 1979.
1 map : col. ; 100 × 132 cm. Relief shown by contours and spot heights.
Title in upper margin: State of Oregon.
Title in upper right margin: Oregon.
"Advance copy, subject to corrections."
"Compiled in 1964– 1965."
"Source data: U.S. Dept. of the Interior, Geological Survey topographic
maps; U.S. Dept. of the Army, Corps of Engineers topographic maps."

I. Title. II. Title: State of Oregon.

Charlotte (N.C.). Engineering Division.
Official city map of Charlotte, Mecklenburg County, North Carolina /
compiled by the Engineering Division, Department of Public Works, city of
Charlotte ; photography & mapping by Abrams Aerial Survey Corporation.
—Scale ₍1:24,000₎. 1″ = 2,000′. — ₍Charlotte₎ : The Division, 1974.
1 map : photocopy ; 102 × 116 cm.

Alternate title: Charlotte.
"Grid based on North Carolina rectangular coordinate system."
Blue line print.
Includes map of "Mecklenburg County, North Carolina."
"A.A.S.C. 12730."

I. Abrams Aerial Survey Corporation. II. Title.

Louisiana. Dept. of Public Works.
Official map of Louisiana / prepared by the Department of Public Works,
under authority of Act no. 159 of 1928 of the Louisiana State Legislature
from the most authentic information available ;
cartographers, W. Douglas Agee, Barbara C. Hawkins. — 1776– 1976
bicentennial ed. — Scale ₍1:380,160₎. 1/6 of an in. equals 1 statute mile ;

Polyconic proj. (W 94°— W 89°/N 33°—N 29°). — ₁Baton Rouge₁ : The
Department, 1976.
1 map : col. ; 131 × 150 cm.

Depths shown by soundings.
"Published and issued February 1976."
Includes source data.

I. Agee, Wilmer D. II. Hawkins, Barbara C. III. Title.

United States. Central Intelligence Agency.
Angola / Central Intelligence Agency. — Scale 1:4,000,000 ; Lambert
conformal conic proj., standard parallels 6° N and 30° N (E 11°—E 25°/S
4°—S 20°). — ₁Washington, D.C.₁ : The Agency, ₁1981₁.
1 map : col. ; 51 × 44 cm.

Relief shown by shading and spot heights.
Includes location map, comparative area map, and maps of "Population,"
"Major tribal groups," "Vegetation," "Economic activity," and "Major
Angolan oilfields."
"504590 (545154) 4-81."

I. Title.

Wray, James R.
Land use and land cover in the greater Pittsburgh region, Pa., 1973 / by
James R. Wray ; prepared in cooperation with the Appalachian Regional
Commission. — Scale 1:125,000. 1 cm. represents 1.25 km. 1 in. repre-
sents approx. 2 statute miles (W 80°32′30″—W 78°55′00″/N 41°12′30″—N
39°55′00″). — Reston, Va. : U.S. Geological Survey ; Arlington, Va. : For
sale by Branch of Distribution, U.S. Geological Survey, 1980.
1 map : col. ; 115 × 110 cm., folded in envelope 30 × 24 cm. —
(Miscellaneous investigations series / United States Geological Survey ; map
I-1248)

Title in upper margin: Land use in the greater Pittsburgh region.
Title on envelope: Land use and land cover in the greater Pittsburgh region,
1973.
Universal transverse Mercator grid.
Includes index, text, list of references, 3 statistical tables, and 2 distance
measurement diagrams.

I. Appalachian Regional Commission. II. Geological Survey (U.S.). III. Title.
IV. Title: Land use in the greater Pittsburgh region. V. Series: Miscellaneous
investigations series (Geological Survey (U.S.)) ; map I-1248.

Geological Survey (U.S.).
    State of Georgia, NASA LANDSAT-1 satellite image mosaic / prepared and
    published by the U.S. Geological Survey in cooperation with the National
    Aeronautics and Space Administration and the Earth and Water Division of
    the Georgia Department of Natural Resources. — Scale 1:500,000. 1 cm.
    equals 5 km. ; Lambert conformal conic proj. based on standard parallels
    33° and 45° (W 85°—W 81°/N 35°—N 31°). — Reston, Va. : The Survey,
    1976.
    1 remote-sensing image : col. ; 109 × 95 cm.

    Title in lower margin: Georgia satellite mosaic, 1973–1974.
    "Imagery recorded in discrete spectral bands with multispectral scanner
    (MSS) on NASA LANDSAT-1 (formerly ERTS-1). Orbital altitude 920 km.
    (570 mi.)."
    "20,000-meter universal transverse Mercator grid, zones 16 and 17."
    Includes text and 4 diagrams.

    I. United States. National Aeronautics and Space Administration. II. Georgia.
    Earth and Water Division. III. Title. IV. Title: Georgia satellite mosaic, 1973–
    1974.

Brown County (Ill.). County Engineer.
    Mt. Sterling and vicinity / Neil C. Babb, county engineer ; L. Beach,
    draftsman ; traced by S. Adams. — Corr. to 5-26-73. — Scale ₍ca. 1:2,400₎.
    —₍Mt. Sterling, Ill.₎ : County Engineer, 1973.
    1 map : photocopy ; on sheet 81 × 105 cm.

    Cadastral map showing land ownership.
    "Re-drawn from 1961 map."
    Oriented with north toward the upper right.
    Blue line print.

    I. Babb, Neil C. II. Beach, L. III. Title.

United States. Bureau of Land Management.
    State of Utah, land ownership and public management / U.S. Department of
    the Interior, Bureau of Land Management. — Scale [ca. 1:126,720] ;
    Polyconic proj. (W 114°—W 109°/N 42°—N 37°). — ₍Washington, D.C.₎ :
    The Bureau, 1980– .
        maps : col. ; 93 × 78 cm. or smaller

    "Contour interval 200 feet with supplementary contours at 100 foot
    intervals."

91

"The base grid was compiled by the Bureau of Land Management from official records of cadastral surveys."

"The land status was compiled for printing by the Bureau of Land Management from the official federal records with additional data furnished by the Utah State Land Board, and U.S. Forest Service maps."

Geographic coverage complete in 23 maps.

Includes index map.

I. Title.

Brawley (Calif.). City Engineer.
City of Brawley, county of Imperial, California / A.J. Pion, city engineer. —Scale ₍ca. 1:7,400₎. — ₍Brawley₎ : City Engineer, 1976.
1 map : col. ; 48 × 68 cm.

Cadastral map.
Accompanied by letter from City Clerk's Office.
LC copy annotated in yellow and green ink to show the downtown redevelopment area.

I. Pion, A.J. II. Title.

United States. Forest Service. Southwestern Region.
Coronado National Forest, Arizona and New Mexico : Chiricahua, Peloncillo, Dragoon mountain ranges / U.S. Department of Agriculture, Forest Service, Southwestern Region ; compiled and drafted at Regional Office, Albuquerque, New Mexico, from U.S. Forest Service planimetric maps. — Rev. 1975, repr. 1980. — Scale ₍1:126,720₎. 1/2″ = 1 mile ; Polyconic proj. (W 110°15′—W 108°45′/N 32°10′—N 30°19′). — Albuquerque : The Office, ₍1980₎
2 maps on 1 sheet : both sides, col. ; 80 × 64 cm. and 51 × 63 cm., sheet 82 × 65 cm., folded to 11 × 22 cm.

"Forest Service map class A."
Relief shown by hachures and spot heights.
Panel title.
"Gila and Salt River meridian, New Mexico principal meridian."
Includes location map, recreation indexes, "Vicinity map and U.S.G.S. index," col. ill., and text.
Contents: Douglas Ranger District, Coronado National Forest (Chiricahua-Peloncillo Mts.) Arizona and New Mexico — Douglas Ranger District, Coronado National Forest (Dragoon Mts.) Arizona.

I. Title.

United States. Defense Mapping Agency.
   The world / prepared and published under the direction of the Department of
   Defense by the Defense Mapping Agency and the U.S. Naval Oceanographic Office. — Ed. 1-DMA. — Scale 1:14,000,000. 1 in. = 221 statute
   miles at the equator ; Mercator proj. (W 180°—E 180°/N 84° —S 70°). —
   ₍Washington, D.C.₎ : The Agency : The Office, ₍1981₎
   6 maps : col. ; 100 × 122 cm. or smaller. — (Series 1150)

   "Compiled from information to 1980."
   "Boundary information as of October 1980."
   Relief shown by gradient tints, shading, and spot heights.
   Depths shown by gradient tints and contours.
   Includes index map.
   Sheet 4 has "Standard time zone chart of the world."
   DMA stock nos.: 1150X1-1150X6.

I. United States. Dept. of Defense. II. United States. Naval Oceanographic
Office. III. Title. IV. Series: Series 1150 (United States. Defense Mapping
Agency)

World Bank. Agriculture and Rural Development Dept. Resource Planning
Unit.
   Nepal / prepared by the Resource Planning Unit, Agriculture and Rural
   Development Department, World Bank ; cartographic drafting by Williams
   and Heintz Map Corp. ; compilation, design, and supervision by W. Drewes
   and K. Willett, World Bank. — Scale 1:500,000. 1 in. equals approx. 8
   miles (E 80°—E 88°/N 31°—N 26°). — Washington, D.C. : World Bank,
   1980.
   1 remote-sensing image on 2 sheets : col. ; 72 × 169 cm., sheets 78 × 85
   cm. and 78 × 95 cm.

   Relief shown by spot heights.
   "The Universal transverse Mercator (UTM) grid overlay is based on the
   Everest geodetic system."
   Includes "Location map, LANDSAT coverage."
   Insets: Kathmandu Valley — Kathmandu streets in city center — Stereo-
   scopic pair of the Kathmandu Valley images.

I. Drewes, Wolfram U. II. Willett, K. III. Williams and Heintz Map Corporation. IV. Title.

Australia. Division of National Mapping.
   Australia statistical divisions and local government areas, 1976 census

/ produced as part of the Australia 1:5,000,000 map series by the Division
of National Mapping, in collaboration with the Australian Bureau of Statistics. — Scale 1:5,000,000 ; Simple conic proj. with 2 standard parallels 18°
S and 36° S (E 110°—E 155°/S 10°—S 45°). — Canberra : The Division,
c1978.
1 map : col. ; 79 × 88 cm.

At head of title: Natmap.
Includes notes, 6 insets, and lists of statistical divisions for each state.
"Index to local government areas" on verso.
"NMP 77/148."

I. Australian Bureau of Statistics. II. Title.

Blaskowitz, Charles.
Sketch of the White Plains / by Captain Blaskowitz. — Scale ₁1:6,000₁. 500
ft. to an in. — ₁1776?₁
1 map : ms., col. ; on sheet 47 × 57 cm. — (Peter Force map collection ;
150)

Shows the disposition of British, Hessian, and American troops during the
Battle of White Plains, 1776.
Relief shown by hachures and shading.
Pen-and-ink and watercolor.

I. Title. II. Series.

United States. Army Map Service.
Mare Nectaris and vicinity, lunar plastic relief map / produced by Army
Map Service, Corps of Engineers. — Scale 1:5,000,000. Vertical scale
1:1,000,000. Vertical exaggeration 5:1. — Washington, D.C. : The Service,
₁1965₁
1 model : col., plastic ; 31 × 22 × 2 cm.

"Prepared by the Army Map Service (AM), Corps of Engineers, U.S.
Army, Washington, D.C., from Lunar topographic map, 1:5,000,000, Army
Map Service, provisional edition, 1961."

I. Title. II. Title: Lunar plastic relief map.

National Foreign Assessment Center (U.S.)
Polar regions atlas / ₁produced by the National Foreign Assessment Center,

CIA₁. — Scales differ. — ₁Washington, D.C.₁ : Central Intelligence
Agency, 1978.
1 atlas (66 p., ₁2₁ folded leaves of plates) : ill. (some col.), col. maps ; 37
cm.

Includes index.
"GC 78-10040."

I. United States. Central Intelligence Agency. II. Title.

United States. Bureau of the Census. Geography Division.
Michigan / prepared by Geography Division in cooperation with Data
Preparation Division. — Scale 1:750,000. 1 in. represents approx. 12 miles
(W 90° – W 82°/N 48° – N 41°), – Washington, D.C. : U.S. Dept. of
Commerce, Bureau of the Census : For sale by the Supt. of Docs., U.S.
G.P.O., ₁1983₁
1 map ; 102 × 89 cm.

"Sources: Base map from U.S. Geological Survey, Michigan, 1970.
County, county subdivision, and place boundaries certified by local offi-
cials, January 1, 1980."
Includes indexes.

I. United States. Bureau of the Census. Data Preparation Division. II. Title.

9/ Machine-Readable Data Files

Chapter 9 of AACR2 applies the principles of descriptive cataloging outlined in chapter 1 to machine-readable data files, for example, magnetic tapes, punched cards, aperture cards, punched paper tapes, disk packs, cassettes, floppy disks, laser disks, video disks, mark-sensed cards, and optical character recognition font documents. Governments generate a great many such machine-readable data files.

For cataloging purposes, few government-issued machine-readable data files have, in the recent past, been regarded as government documents. Fewer still have been brought under the same degree of bibliographic control as have books, pamphlets, and printed sheets, or cartographic materials. And even fewer still have been brought under bibliographic control within a single integrated catalog including other forms of government documents. What bibliographic control has been exercised over such files has generally been by standards promulgated and practiced by an agency's automatic data processing unit, and not by its library.

Nonetheless, it is becoming increasingly the case that such machine-readable data files do stand in need, first of all, of being brought under adequate bibliographic control, and secondly, of being brought under bibliographic control in the context of other government documents. Inadequate bibliographic control of government-issued machine-readable data files has made it extremely difficult for either the employees or the constituents of a government agency to locate, let alone access, these files in a cost-effective manner. Unintegrated bibliographic control of government-issued machine-readable data files has made it necessary for both employees and constituents to turn to two different types of catalogs maintained by two different units within an agency to find both data and documents dealing with a particular topic.

The problems involved with the description of government-issued machine-readable data files are legion, to say the least. Traditionally, the approach to bibliographic description upon which the rules for such have been based has involved the cataloger in an examination of not only the physical object itself, but also its intellectual content. While this approach has proved to be more awkward and more expensive with nontraditional "nonbook" materials, it has at least proved to be surmountable. Most cataloging agencies have been able to afford access to microform readers so that they might describe microforms; record players and tape recorders so that they might describe sound recordings; etc. However, this approach is somewhat impractical in the case of the bibliographic description of machine-readable data bases. The intellectual content of machine-readable data bases, encoded in them, is not accessible to the cataloger without machines, typically computers. In view of this fact, the most significant problem involved with the description of government-issued machine-readable data files is the location of a source of information for describing them.

Currently, no requirement exists that government-issued machine-readable data files be accompanied by standardized descriptions. Many files have accompanying documentation, each varying in its degree of thoroughness. Chapter 9 of AACR2 provides for the describing of this documentation along with the files themselves; it is this documentation that will provide the cataloger with most of the needed information. In addition to the accompanying documentation, it is advisable that, insofar as possible, the cataloger rely on the creator of the file as the ultimate authority for its description. It is quite possible that the telephone or mails will have to be used in solving problems or obtaining essential information.

Catalogers who are unfamiliar with machine-readable data files as a medium to be described would be well advised to consult the Glossary, Appendix D, before beginning study of chapter 9, in order that they might gain an adequate understanding of the terms used in the chapter. They should remember, in their study of chapter 9, that its rules, as are the rules of every other chapter in Part I, are based on the general rules for description presented in chapter 1. A sound understanding of chapter 1 will enable catalogers to deal with machine-readable data files, once the terminology of the chapter has been digested, and a source of descriptive information has been located.

9.0   GENERAL RULES

9.0A ———

9.0B Sources of information

9.0B1 Chief source of information. AACR2 prescribes that the chief source of information for a machine-readable data file is its internal user label. This identifier is not always available. Furthermore, when it is available, it is not eye-readable; a cataloger cannot read it without the aid of a computer. Therefore, the documentation produced by the creator is almost invariably the most likely source of information for the bibliographic description of the file.

9.0B2 Prescribed sources of information. The list of prescribed sources of information for the description of machine-readable data files presents the cataloger with considerable scope for obtaining the necessary information. The use of brackets will frequently be necessary.

9.0C – 9.0H ———

9.1   TITLE AND STATEMENT OF RESPONSIBILITY AREA

9.1A ———

9.1B Title proper.

The rules for transcribing the title proper of a machine-readable data file refer to "a locally assigned data set name." A locally assigned data set name, or DSN, is an arbitrarily assigned set of characters unique to a file, e.g., CEN4CT. It is unlikely that a DSN would be the title proper of the file.

9.1C   *Optional addition.* **General material designation**

LC/GPO are exercising this option. The general material designation *machine-readable data file* will be stored in machine-readable form with every bibliographic record constructed according to the provisions of chapter 9, AACR2. LC will display the GMD *machine-readable data file* in the eye-readable form of its records.

9.D–9.1G ———

9.2   EDITION AREA

9.2A ———

9.2B Edition statement

When transcribing what might appear to be an edition statement from the chief source of information, or suitable substitute, make sure that the statement refers to an official edition in the sense of a formal reissue, and not merely minor changes or updates. Generally, machine-readable data files do not have official edition statements.

9.2B3   *Optional addition.* **Cataloger-supplied edition statement.**   LC/GPO are exercising the option conditionally. (See 1.2B4 and 2.2B3.)

9.2C–9.2E ———

9.3 ———

9.4   PUBLICATION, PRODUCTION, DISTRIBUTION, ETC., AREA

9.4A–9.4D ———

9.4E   *Optional addition.* **Statement of function of publisher, producer, distributor, etc.**

LC/GPO are exercising this option. Terms such as *publisher, producer,* and *distributor* —but primarily the latter two—will be added to entities named in the publication, production, distribution, etc., area whenever necessary to clarify the function of the particular party. It is likely that this application will occur frequently in the description of government-issued machine-readable data files.

9.4F ———

9.5 FILE DESCRIPTION AREA

9.5A – 9.5C ———

9.5D Accompanying material

9.5D1 *Optionally.* **Add to the designation the number of statements or logical records.** LC/GPO are exercising this option when the material is readily available.

9.5D2 *Optionally.* **Record the physical description of other accompanying material.** LC/GPO are exercising this option when the material is readily available.

9.6 ———

9.7 NOTE AREA

9.7A ———

9.7B Notes

9.7B4 Variations in title. *Optionally.* **Record a data set name differing from the title proper.** LC/GPO are exercising this option.

9.8 STANDARD NUMBER AND TERMS OF AVAILABILITY AREA

9.8A – 9.8C ———

9.8D *Optional addition.* Terms of availability
LC/GPO are exercising this option.

9.8E ———

9.9 – 9.10 ———

11/ Microforms

Chapter 11 of AACR2 applies the principles of descriptive cataloging outlined in chapter 1 to all kinds of material in microform, whether reproductions of existing textual or graphic materials, or original publications in their own right. Increasingly, more and more government documents are being issued in microformat.

For cataloging purposes it is necessary to differentiate between microform reproductions and microform originals. Both types of microforms are, to be sure, described primarily as microforms. Part I of AACR2 is based on the principle that "the description of a physical item should be based in the first instance on the chapter dealing with the class of materials to which that item belongs. For example, a printed monograph in microform should be described as a microform (using the rules in chapter 11). . . . In short, the starting point for description is the physical form of the item in hand, not the original or any previous form in which the work has been published" (0.24).

However, the complete description of a microform reproduction includes, in addition, a brief description of the original. For this description, it will generally be necessary to consult the chapter dealing with the form of the original item. All details of the description of the original are to be given in the note area.

When cataloging a government document in microform, it is not always possible to determine, either from the item itself or from research, whether or not the microform is an original. In the absence of evidence to the contrary, assume that a microform is an original publication, and not a reproduction.

Policy for cataloging of microreproductions

The *Library of Congress Information Bulletin* (Nov. 21, 1980) included an announcement of an interim Library of Congress policy for the cataloging of microreproductions, pending a final resolution of questions that arose from a consideration of the application of AACR2 to such materials. The ALA/RTSD/CCS Committee on Cataloging: Description and Access sponsored extensive discussions of the questions raised and finally in June 1981 at its meeting in San Francisco voted to favor the thrust of the Library's interim policy as an alternative to provision 0.24 in AACR2. When the Joint Steering Committee for Revision of AACR2 considered the same issue on July 2, 1981, at its meeting in San Francisco, the committee decided not to take action at this time in relation to rule revision that would incorporate an alternative for microreproductions—

particularly since the issues had not been as thoroughly discussed in the other countries represented as in the United States.

The statement, below is the final Library of Congress policy for the cataloging of microreproductions. The policy will be applied and recommended by the Library as "rule interpretation" rather than rule revision.

1) *Materials covered.* This policy applies to reproductions in micro- and macroform of previously existing materials. Specifically the policy applies to micro- and macroreproductions [1] of

> books, pamphlets, and printed sheets
> cartographic materials
> manuscripts
> music
> graphic materials in macroform
> serials

It applies to reproductions of dissertations issued by University Microfilms International and "on demand" reproductions of books by the same company.

It is the intent of this policy to apply AACR2 in determining the choice and form of access points but to emphasize in the bibliographic description data relating to the original item, giving data relating to the reproduction in a secondary position. As a result, rule 1.11 and chapter 11 of AACR2 will not be applied to these materials except to provide directions for the formulation of the note describing the micro- or macroform characteristics of the reproduction. (Items that are microreproductions of material prepared or assembled specifically for bringing out an original edition in microform will be cataloged as instructed in chapter 11 of AACR2.)

2) *Bibliographic description*

a) *General.* Apply chapter 2 to books (including dissertations cataloged as books), pamphlets, and sheets; chapter 3 to cartographic materials; chapter 4 to manuscripts (including dissertations not cataloged as books); chapter 5 to music; relevant portions of chapter 8 to graphic materials in macroform; and chapter 12 to serials. Transcribe the bibliographic data appropriate to the work being reproduced in the following areas:

> title and statement of responsibility
> edition
> material (or type of publication) specific details for cartographic
>   materials and serials
> publication, distribution, etc.
> physical description
> series

---

1. For the purpose of this statement the term *macroreproduction* refers only to macroreproductions produced "on demand."

Record in the note area all details relating to the reproduction and its publication/availability. Introduce the note with the word that is the specific material designation appropriate to the item.

b) *Microreproductions*. Add the general material designation "ₜmicroformₗ" in the title and statement of responsibility area according to 1.1C2. Record in the note area the bibliographic details relating to the reproduction required by 11.4, in the order and form provided by this rule, followed by the details required by 11.5–7. If a note of the 11.7B10 type is necessary, transcribe it before any series statement required by 11.6.

Microfilm. Ann Arbor, Mich. : University Microfilms, 1981. 1 microfilm reel ; 16mm. High reduction.

Microfilm, Washington : Library of Congress, 1981. 1 microfilm reel ; 5 in., 35 cm.

c) *Macroreproductions*. Do not use a general material designation in the title and statement of responsibility area. Use the word "Photocopy" to introduce the note giving the details of the macroreproduction.

Photocopy. Ann Arbor, Mich. : University Microfilms, 1965. 20 cm.

Photocopy. ₜS.1., s.n., 1981?ₗ. 23 cm.

Photocopy. Seattle, Wash. : University of Washington, 1979. 28 cm.

11.0 GENERAL RULES

11.0A Scope
Chapter 11 of AACR2 applies equally to microforms (including microfilms, microfiche, microopaques, and aperture cards) issued as monographs or as serials, as originals or as reproductions.

11.0B Sources of information
The chief source of information for microfilms, microfiche, and microopaques is the title frame ("i.e., a frame, usually at the beginning of the item, bearing the full title and, normally, publication details of the item" (11.0B1)) supplied by the producer of the microform. Do not confuse this title frame with the first frame of text reproduced from another format (for microform reproductions). If a microfiche or microopaque does not have such a title frame—or if the information on this frame is bibliographically insufficient—"treat the eye-readable data printed at the top of the fiche or opaque as the chief source of information" (11.0B1). (Note: If a microfiche or a microopaque has a title frame that is sufficient for bibliographic description, and the data presented on it differs in any bibliographically significant manner with the eye-readable data printed at the top of the fiche or opaque, indicate this in a note.) Additionally, provide added entries for access points indicated in the eye-readable data, according to the provisions of 21.29B.

The Joint Steering Committee for Revision of AACR has approved the addition of the following next to last sentence in rule 11.0B1 in the printed text of AACR2: "If, however, the title appears in a shortened form on the 'header' and appears in a fuller form on the accompanying eye-readable materials or the container, treat the accompanying eye-readable materials or the container as the chief source of information."

11.0C–11.0H ―――

11.1   TITLE AND STATEMENT OF RESPONSIBILITY AREA

11.1A–11.1B ―――

11.1C   *Optional addition.* **General material designation**
LC/GPO are exercising this option. The general material designation *microform* will be stored in machine-readable form with every bibliographic record constructed according to the provisons of chapter 11, AACR2. Local policy (together with choice of bibliographic utility, etc.) should govern the use of this GMD for display on catalog cards, book catalogs, CRT terminals, etc. LC will display the GMD *microform* in the eye-readable form of its records.

11.1D – 11.1G ―――

11.2   EDITION AREA

11.2A ―――

11.2B   Edition statement
AACR2 prescribes that "a statement relating to an edition of a microform that contains differences from other editions, or that is a named reissue of that microform" (11.2B1) be transcribed into the edition area as an edition statement, according to the provisions of 1.2B. AACR2 does not, however, indicate with sufficient clarity precisely what constitutes an "edition" of a microform, as distinguished from another "copy" of a microform. The definition of "edition" as applied to microforms in the Glossary (Appendix D) of AACR2 is only partially helpful: "In the case of nonbook materials, all the copies of an item produced from one master copy and issued by a particular publishing agency or a group of such agencies. Provided the foregoing conditions are fulfilled, a change of identity of the distributing body or bodies does not constitute a change of edition."

As was suggested earlier, it is not always possible to determine, either from an item itself or from research, whether or not a microform is an original, or a reproduction. Happily, this problem has no direct bearing on the problem of distinguishing between editions and copies as far as AACR2 is concerned. (Note: This problem may have a bearing on distinguishing between editions and copies in shared cataloging data bases, such as are maintained by bibliographic utilities, that have an economic interest in limiting the number of bibliographic records contained therein to one record per unique "work.")

It is, however, often the case with government documents issued in microform that the same "work" may be issued by a number of different distributors. In issuing the same "work," each of these distributors may identify the "work" differently on the microform itself in terms of information provided as eye-readable data, in terms of unique numbers assigned to it, etc. It is also the case with government documents issued in microform that the same issue of a particular microform, as distributed by any one of the different distributors discussed above, may be duplicated and further distributed by a number of different institutions. In duplicating the same issue, each of these institutions will (generally) *not* add any bibliographic information to the microform itself, or change any bibliographic information already existing on the microform. It may, however, distribute the duplicate of the microform in its own container, upon which may be printed bibliographic data unique to that particular institution or distribution point.

For purposes of distinguishing between editions and copies as far as AACR2 is concerned, regard the presence of unique bibliographic data on the microform itself, either in eye-readable form or not, as evidence that the microform represents a different edition of a "work" and not merely a different copy of an edition. Disregard for such purposes unique bibliographic data printed only on a microform's container, provided that the bibliographic details of the microform itself are identical to those of another such microform distributed by another institution. (If such unique bibliographic data is regarded as important to the cataloging agency, give such data in a note, according to the provisions of 11.7B9. In the context of a shared cataloging data base, such as would be maintained by a bibliographic utility, such a note should be regarded as a "local note.")

In any event, nonetheless, transcribe into the edition area only specific statements that may be regarded as "edition statements." "In case of doubt about whether a statement is an edition statement, follow the instructions in 1.2B3" (11.2B2) .

11.2B3 *Optional addition.* **Cataloger-supplied edition statement.** LC/GPO are exercising the option conditionally. (See 1.2B4 and 2.2B3.)

11.2C–11.2E ———

11.3 ———

11.4 PUBLICATION, DISTRIBUTION, ETC., AREA

In following the provisions of 11.4 for recording data in the publication, distribution, etc., area, it is necessary, when dealing with microform reproductions, to distinguish between "editions" and "copies" in order to determine the appropriate place of publication, name of publisher/distributor, etc. In so doing, following the guidelines given above in the discussion of 11.2B, do *not* transcribe bibliographic details relating only to a "copy" in the publication, distribution, etc., area. (If such details are regarded as important to the cataloging agency, give such details in a note, according to the provisions of 11.7B9. In the context of a shared cataloging data base, such as would be maintained by a bibliographic utility, such a note should be regarded as a "local note.")

11.4A–11.4D ———

11.4E *Optional addition.* **Statement of function of publisher, distributor, etc.**
LC/GPO are exercising this option. Terms such as *distributor* and *publisher* will be added to entities named in the publisher, distributor, etc., area whenever necessary to clarify the function of the particular person or body. It is expected that the need for such clarification will vary from case to case, as will the cataloger's perception of this need. Consequently, no major effort at uniformity will be attempted.

11.4F ———

11.5 PHYSICAL DESCRIPTION AREA

11.5A ———

11.5B Extent of item (including specific material designation)

11.5B1 Record the number of physical units of a microform item according to the provisions of 11.5B1. LC/GPO are not exercising the option of dropping the prefix *micro* from the designated terms.

11.5C–11.5D ———

11.5E Accompanying material

11.5E1 Record the name of any accompanying material as instructed in AACR2, 11.5E. LC/GPO are exercising the option conditionally by recording the physical description of the accompanying material, if it is considered important.

11.6 ———

11.7 NOTE AREA

11.7A ———

11.7B Notes

11.7B10 Physical description. Film. *Optionally.* **Details of the nature of the film.** LC/GPO are exercising this option on a case-by-case basis.

11.7B11–11.7B21 ———

11.7B22 Notes relating to original. The Joint Steering Committee for Revision of AACR has approved the following addition to the printed text of AACR2: "Give information on the original of a microform item."

> Sacred music for one, two, three, or four voices [GMD] : from the works of the most esteemed composers, Italian and English / selected, adapted, and arranged by R.J.J. Stevens. — New York : New York
> Public Library Photographic Service, 1980.
> 1 microfilm reel ; 35 cm.
> Reproduction of original : London : Printed for the editor, [1798– 1807].
> 1 score (3 v.) ; 32 cm.

11.8   STANDARD NUMBER AND TERMS OF AVAILABILITY AREA

11.8A–11.8C ———

11.8D   *Optional addition.* **Terms of availability**
LC/GPO are exercising the option by adding the terms of availability as instructed in AACR2, 1.8D. The price, however, will not normally be given for noncurrent items.

11.8E ———

11.9– 11.10 ———

12/ Serials

Chapter 12 of AACR2 applies the principles of descriptive cataloging outlined in chapter 1 to materials of any of the specific types treated in chapters 2–11 that are issued serially. A very significant proportion of all government documents are issued in series.

For cataloging purposes, serials that are government documents differ from serials issued by sources other than governments, in general, to the degree that monographs of these same formats differ from their nongovernmental counterparts. Serials are, after all, not a specific type or format of material; they are, ultimately, merely monographs issued in an indefinite number of parts over time. The description of a complete serial is no more complicated in principle than the description of a monograph of similar number of parts.

In practice, however, this is not the case, first of all, because the description of a serial cannot wait until the serial has, at last, "died." Serials must be described while they are still in a state of actual—or potential—change. A serial described from one particular issue may change its name, merge with another serial, split into parts, or even cease publication altogether with the very next issue. In short, serials are dynamic. Their description, like that of a living organism, is never complete or finished until they have ceased to be.

Additionally, the description of a serial is more complicated in practice than that of a monograph because, in contrast to monographs, it is the essence of any particular issue of a serial that it is related to all others. A monograph basically may be described in isolation. (Note: A monograph issued in a number of parts is a hybrid creature; its existence must not be allowed to confuse the essential contrast.) It is bibliographically interesting that a monograph may be related to another monograph, but it is not bibliographically essential; the item may be accepted at "face value," and described precisely as it presents itself to the world. This is generally not the case with a serial. Unless one has the first issue of a serial, one is never sure, with only a single issue, whether or not this is the issue that is the anomaly, that this is the very issue that represents the classic "variant title." Except for the first issue then, a single issue of a serial short of the first issue can never be trusted; some degree of research is invariably necessary.

The description of serials that are government documents, therefore, is more complicated than that of monographs that are government documents simply because they are serials. Adding to this complexity, however, is the fact that because they are government documents, they have not passed through that standardization process entailed in formal publication. As a result, all too often there is insufficient information available from the items themselves as to which government agency has issued the particular series, or even whether or not the items themselves are truly part of a series at all. Some degree of research is, therefore, once again mandatory.

The rules for describing serials presented in chapter 12, like those given in chapter 11 (when describing microform reproductions) or chapter 13, must be used in conjunction with the specific chapter of AACR2 that deals with the physical form of the items in question. Rules presented in these chapters are not repeated in chapter 12. It should be noted that chapter 12, dealing with description, does not contain rules for choice of entry of serials. For choice of entry, chapter 21 is to be consulted. Chapter 12 is, therefore, *not* a stand-alone prescription for serials cataloging.

12.0   GENERAL RULES

12.0A Scope
Chapter 12 of AACR2 applies equally to serial publications of all types, including the full range of what are commonly referred to as serials, series, and periodicals. Whether a serial is a newspaper, journal, yearbook, annual report, conference transaction, or monographic series, it shares with items of its type the characteristic of being indefinite in its term of publication. It is this quality of continuous publication that distinguishes the serial from the monograph, and creates the need for special treatment for the serial within the rules of bibliographic description.

This aspect of unconditional or indefinite publication serves both to include and exclude classes of documentation from serial treatment. For example, most "contractor's reports" are not described as serials. Although these reports are issued with regularity, usually monthly or quarterly, the term of the report expires with the completion of the specific contract. The describing of contractor's reports, therefore, should be done in accordance with the appropriate monographic rules, rather than with those for serials. Likewise, the rules for describing monographs should be used for the bibliographic treatment of manuals, handbooks, guides, etc., which are issued with basic manuals at irregular intervals, but with regular or frequent updates. In case of doubt as to whether or not an item should be described as a serial or monograph, if the item does not pass the criterion of continuous publication, treat it as a monograph. If its publication status is unclear—even after research—treat it as a monograph. Better an item be misdescribed as a monograph when it is a serial, than misdescribed as a serial when it is a monograph! (If the item is truly a serial, the mistake will be noted and can then be corrected with the receipt of the next issue of the serial. If, on the other hand, the item is truly a monograph, the mistake will rarely if ever be noted, and probably not be corrected. If there was some suspicion on the part of the cataloger that another issue of the serial might have been released, then the fact that the cataloging agency may not have that other issue, or be able to get that other issue, is not proof positive that it did not exist. From the point of view of the catalog user, however, the result is the same: no other issue of the item is available.)

In principle, additionally, chapter 12 of AACR2 applies equally to both "numbered" and "unnumbered" series, should the cataloging agency wish to create a separate bibliographic description for an "unnumbered" series. Note: A "serial" is defined in the Glossary (Appendix D) of AACR2 as being "a publication in any medium issued in successive parts bearing numerical or chronological designations and intended to be continued indefinitely." A "series," on the other hand, is defined, in one sense, as "a group of separate items related to one another by the fact that each item bears, in addition to its own title proper, a collective title applying to the group as a whole. The individual items may or may not be numbered." Despite this definition of a serial, chapter 12 of AACR2 is the *only* chapter that could possibly apply to an "unnumbered" series as a whole. If a cataloging agency wishes to so describe such an "unnumbered" series, adjustments in the bibliographic record, such as in the numeric and/or alphabetic designation (12.3B), etc., will have to be made.

12.0B Sources of information

In general, the chief source of information for a serial is the same source of information, in terms of being a part of the physical item itself, as for a monograph of the same medium. Because, by definition, a serial is issued in more than one part, the rules for bibliographic description of a serial must specify which issue's chief source of information, for any serial, takes precedence over all others. AACR2 indicates that for printed serials the "chief source of information" is the title page or title page substitute of the first issue of a serial, or failing this, the first issue that is available to the cataloging agency. Curiously, AACR2 does not explicitly extend this principle to nonprinted serials. It would be illogical to suppose, however, that such was not at least the implicit intent of the chapter.

In dealing with printed serials, it is important to remember that the bibliographic data sheet is to be considered as being on the list of other sources of information to be used as title page substitutes. For a fuller discussion of the bibliographic data sheet, see the discussion of 2.0A in this manual.

12.0C–12.0H ———

12.1 TITLE AND STATEMENT OF RESPONSIBILITY AREA

12.1A ———

12.1B Title proper

The title proper of a serial is its "cataloging title," as distinguished from its "key-title," as assigned according to the rules of the International Serials Data System (ISDS). AACR2 does not contain rules for the formulation of key-titles. See 12.8C1 for their inclusion in the bibliographic record of a serial. The titles proper of two different serials may be identical, in contrast to their respective key-titles, which, by definition, must be unique. Serials with identical titles proper may be distinguished by unique uniform titles. See chapter 25 of AACR2 for a treatment of this matter.

12.1C *Optional addition.* **General material designation**
LC/GPO are exercising this option. The appropriate general material designation will be stored in machine-readable form with every bibliographic record constructed according to the provisions of chapter 12, AACR2. Local policy (together with choice of bibliographic utility, etc.) should govern the use of this GMD for display on catalog cards, book catalogs, CRT terminals, etc. Notice that "serial" is *not* an approved GMD; GMDs refer to the physical, not bibliographic, format of items.

12.1D– 12.1F ⸺

12.2 EDITION AREA

12.2A ⸺

12.2B Edition statement

12.2B3 *Optionally.* **Add parallel edition statements.** LC/GPO are exercising this option.

12.2C– 12.2E ⸺

12.3 NUMERIC AND/OR ALPHABETIC, CHRONOLOGICAL, OR OTHER DESIGNATION AREA

12.3A– 12.3C ⸺

12.3D No designation on first issue
For purposes of clarification, this rule is not mandatory. A numeric, alphabetic, chronological, or other designation is not required to be on the bibliographic record in this instance. The decision to include such a statement rests with the individual cataloging agency. In those instances in which it is deemed necessary to include a numeric and/or alphabetic, chronological, or other designation where one is not provided for on the document, the examples cited in 12.3D should be followed.

12.3E– 12.3G ⸺

12.4 PUBLICATION, DISTRIBUTION, ETC., AREA

12.4A– 12.4D ⸺

12.4E *Optional addition.* **Statement of function of publisher, distributor, etc.**
LC/GPO are exercising this option. Terms such as *publisher* and *distributor* will be added to entities named in the publisher, distributor, etc., area whenever necessary to clarify the function of the particular person or body. It is expected that the need for such clarification will vary from case to case, as will the cataloger's perception of this need. Consequently, no major effort at uniformity will be attempted.

12.4F ———

12.4G Place of manufacture, name of manufacturer, date of manufacture

12.4G2 *Optional addition.* **Addition of place, name of manufacturer, date of manu-facture when different from publication date when considered important.** LC/GPO are exercising this option. Significant information relevant to the place of manufacture, name of the manufacturer, and date of manufacture, if different from the place of publica-tion, name of publisher, and date of publication, if found on the item itself, will be included in the item's bibliographic records. The application of this option is specifically linked to the cataloging agency's perception of the significance of this information.

12.5 PHYSICAL DESCRIPTION AREA

12.5A – 12.5D ———

12.5E Accompanying material

12.5E1 *Optionally.* **Record the physical description of regularly issued accompa-nying material.** LC/GPO will exercise this option.

12.6 ———

12.7 NOTE AREA

12.7A ———

12.7B Notes

12.7B7 Relationships with other serials

12.7B7c Continued by. *Optionally.* **Add the date of change.** LC/GPO are exercis-ing this option whenever the information is readily available.

12.7B7e Split. *Optionally.* **Add the names of other serials resulting from the split.** LC/GPO are not exercising this option.

12.7B7f Absorption. *Optionally.* **Add the date of absorption.** LC/GPO are exercis-ing this option when the information is readily available, and does not require additional research.

12.7B19 Numbers. Care must be exercised in the transcription of important numbers borne by serials other than ISSNs to ensure that the numbers recorded are, indeed, numbers assigned to a particular serial, and not to individual items included within it. A serial record is constructed to be used indefinitely and for many individual issues of a serial. For this reason, when transcribing numbers, from numbering schemes that allow for the addition of characters to represent the individual numbers of particular issues of a serial to the base number assigned to the serial, it is important that these additional characters be omitted from the numbers as found on the individual items. The following examples will illustrate this point as it relates to the Superintendent of Documents Classification Schedule:

AA   1.14: (nos.)

HE   20.3173/2:CB 08/(nos.)

TD   5.6:V 63/7/(date)

12.8 STANDARD NUMBER AND TERMS OF AVAILABILITY AREA

12.8A ———

12.8B International Standard Serial Number (ISSN)

A brief description of the ISSN and key-title assignment procedures can be found in the brochure "ISSN: A Brief Guide," available from the National Serials Data Program, Library of Congress, Washington, D.C. "Guidelines for Key-Title Assignment," issued by the same office, should be consulted for background information and instruction in the use of key-titles. In the United States, the National Serials Data Program is the authorized center for the assignment and authentication of ISSNs and key-titles. The "ISSN-Key Title Register" (1977) and "CONSER Microfiche" (1979) are the two most reliable sources for the determination and verification of ISSNs. The "ISSN-Key Title Register" covers all assignments by the National Serials Data Program through February 1975. The "CONSER Microfiche" lists all records authenticated by the National Library of Canada and the Library of Congress for the period 1975–78. Requests for both issuances should be sent to the Cataloging Distribution Service, Library of Congress, Washington, D.C. In addition, ISSNs appear in *Ulrich's International Periodical Directory, Irregular Serials and Annuals,* and *New Serial Titles.* All of these are commonly known reference works on serial publications. However, a number of the ISSNs appearing in these pubications were not compatible with the ISDS standards for key-titles at the time of their assignment. While the publications are generally reliable for verifying ISSNs, individual inaccuracies in information will be found.

12.8C ———

12.8D *Optional addition.* Terms of availability

LC/GPO are exercising the option of providing additional information. Information that can be included in the bibliographic record under this rule includes, but is not limited to, pricing information. Examples of other types of information that may be transcribed into this area are:

Publication not available for sale or distribution.

For official use only.

Available for free upon request.

Distribution limited to members of Congress.

12.8E Qualification

12.8E1 *Optional addition.* **Add qualifications to the terms of availability.** LC/GPO are exercising this option.

12.9– 12.10 ———

13/ Analysis

Chapter 13 of AACR2 applies the principles of descriptive cataloging outlined in chapter 1 to parts of items issued in all types of formats. Most government documents lend themselves to some degree of analysis, should a particular cataloging agency choose to describe them in this detail.

For cataloging purposes, the issue, with respect to the analysis of government documents, is twofold, involving both cataloging policy and procedures.

   1) To which parts of which documents should analysis be applied?
   2) Through which methods of analysis should analysis be achieved?

AACR2 makes no attempt to prescribe when analysis should be undertaken, leaving this matter of policy to the cataloging agencies involved. AACR2 does, however, attempt to suggest in certain cases which methods of analysis are more appropriate to describing which particular types of "parts."

In order for a particular part to be analyzed, it must have either a bibliographically or physically distinguishable identity. It must, in other words, have either its own individual title (or similar "name") or separate physical identity (within the whole), as, for example, with the individual pieces of a kit. Within these broad limits, any government document can be seen as composed of a multitude of potentially analyzable parts.

The decision on the part of the cataloging agency, as to whether or not any particular part that can be analyzed should be analyzed, ought to be based on two specific factors:

   1) the perceived utility for the catalog user of providing analysis of a particular part or types of parts
   2) the overall cost of providing such analysis

Analysis of a part means at the very least that the particular part will be specifically mentioned in the bibliographic description of the whole; analysis of a part usually means that direct access to that particular part will be provided to the catalog user by the part's own "name" used as an access point. There are a great many government documents whose various parts are insufficiently indexed from the point of view of the catalog user. Analysis should be considered for all of these.

Before deciding whether or not to provide analysis for these parts, however, the cataloging agency must balance the cost of analysis against its overall budget and cataloging workload. Generally, analysis should not be provided if it means that other items acquired for the agency's collection will, due to lack of funds or staff time, not then be cataloged, unless the parts in question have so little utility to the catalog user in an unanalyzed state that they are, for all practical purposes, themselves uncataloged. (The parts of some monographic series may fall into this category.)

As a practical matter, analysis should be provided to categories of parts according to the individual cataloging agency's policy. It should not be left to the individual cataloger to decide whether or not any particular item warrants analysis on its own, apart from any such policy. (Practically any document can be analyzed; no document must be analyzed, according to AACR2.) A cataloging agency's policy in this regard can be based on any appropriate factor, as, for example, one or more of the following:

1) type of part (i.e., part of a monographic series, etc.)
2) subject content of a part
3) party responsible for the part (i.e., personal author or corporate body)
4) "substantiality" of the part (i.e., length, ualue for research, as opposed to ephemeral nature, etc.)
5) nature of identification of a part (i.e., whether the part has a distinct title, etc.)
6) format of the part (i.e., cartographic item, etc.)
7) date of publication of the part (i.e., before 1821, etc.)

13.1 SCOPE

Analysis, as "the process of preparing a bibliographic record that describes a part or parts of a larger item" (13.1), can be achieved by a variety of different methods, as described in chapter 13. Each of these methods, when compared with one another, can be regarded as levels of increasing complexity (and independence) of bibliographic description and adequacy of access by means of entry headings. The diagram on page 116 illustrates this point.

In certain cases, AACR2 does attempt to suggest which methods of analysis are more appropriate to describing which particular types of "parts." (See, for example, 13.2.) Within its broad guidelines, however, cataloging agencies are free to choose the particular method of analysis to be used with the particular type of part to be analyzed, based on their perception of the need for access to, and description of, that type of part. It must be recognized, however, that the form of an agency's catalog, or the choice of bibliographic utility by which an agency's catalog is produced, may limit the agency's options, or even make such a choice unnecessary. For example, a bibliographic utility may not be able to accommodate "In" analytics or multilevel descriptions. An online catalog with sophisticated retrieval capabilities may allow for adequate access of parts buried within the description of the whole without further specific provision of access points.

ACCESS

complete bibliographical description	
multilevel description	multilevel description
analytical added entry	+
''in'' analytic	
D	
E	
S	
C	
R	
I	
P	contents note
T	
I	
O	analytical added entry
N	

13.2   ANALYTICS OF MONOGRAPHIC SERIES AND MULTIPART MONOGRAPHS

AACR2 here recommends that parts of monographic series and independently titled parts of multipart monographs be described as if, in effect, the respective series and multipart monograph were not themselves also described elsewhere in the catalog. Analytics prepared according to the provisions of 13.2 are identical with monographs prepared according to the provisions of chapter 2, in terms of their bibliographic descriptions. (They do differ in respect to their call numbers.)

Parts of monographic series that themselves constitute a subseries may be cataloged according to the provisions of chapter 12 and 13.2. If, however, the numbers of the subseries parts do not constitute consecutive parts of the main series, as, for example:

SUBSERIES	MAIN SERIES
no. 1	no. 12
	no. 13
	no. 14
no. 2	no. 15
	no. 16
no. 3	no. 17

it is not recommended that they be cataloged as a series, insofar as, short of creating an additional added entry for each newly issued part of the subseries, indicating its position in the numbering scheme of the main series, it is difficult to clearly show the relationships between the two numbering schemes in the main entry for the subseries should it have more than one or two distinct parts. The series note for the subseries illustrated above would read, for example:

(——— ——— ; no.12, 15, 17, etc.)

Without creating such additional added entries, it is impossible to file the one added entry for the main series and still acknowledge the presence in the collection of the other numbers of the series.

13.3   NOTE AREA

Even contents notes are a form of analytic!

13.4   ANALYTICAL ADDED ENTRIES

Analytical added entries can provide access points for parts analyzed by means of notes or multilevel descriptions.

13.5   "IN" ANALYTICS

"In" analytics provide an appropriate method for the analysis of journal articles and the like. The examples provided in AACR2 suggest that "In" analytics can be serial, as well as monographic. In giving the details of the whole item, a series statement found on the whole item is not included in the "In" analytic, unless, as is indicated in 13.5B, the larger item itself is also cataloged by means of an "In" analytic, a most uncommon situation indeed.

13.6   MULTILEVEL DESCRIPTION

Multilevel description is an extension of the practice of describing both a bibliographic whole and each of its parts. Multilevel description is the converse of "In" analytics; in multilevel description the larger whole precedes the part rather than vice versa. Although the examples given in AACR2 suggest that multilevel description is applicable to up to three levels, in principle any number of levels may be described, depending on the value of each description to the cataloging agency.

PART 2

Headings

21/   Choice of Access Points

Chapter 21 advises the cataloger about which entities involved in the existence of a publication should be given access points. Choice of access points is important in the cataloging of government documents because documents usually have many entities involved in their existence, including persons as well as corporate bodies.

The roles of human participants in the preparation of a publication are often easier to determine than those of corporate bodies. Corporate bodies perform a variety of functions in the creation of a publication such as issuing, preparing, sponsoring or cosponsoring, contracting, supporting with money or staff, collecting information, coordinating, publishing, and distributing.

It is important to remember that the users of government documents are interested in retrieving the document through the access point they know and/or prefer. A scientist or researcher may look for a person known to be an authority; a government regulator or business may look for the agency known to be active in an area; others may look for a corporation involved with the work. In order to accommodate all types of searchers, as many access points as possible should be assigned.

AACR2 does not acknowledge the existence of a corporate author. The basic rule refers to "Works of personal authorship" (21.1A) and "Entry under corporate body" (21.1B). AACR2 says that a personal author is "responsible for the creation of the intellectual or artistic content of a work" (21.1A1), whereas a work emanates from a corporate body (21.1B2). Footnote 2 defines the term *emanating* as follows: "Consider a work to have emanated from a corporate body if it is issued by that body or has been caused to be issued by that body or if it originated with that body."

The cataloger must decide which entities are to be designated as main and added entries. Many publications, particularly serial publications will be entered under title.

In cataloging government documents, make every attempt to include as many corporate bodies in the descriptive portion of the cataloging record as possible, so that it is possible to make all the added entries needed by the user.

21.0   INTRODUCTORY RULES

21.0A Main and added entries
The rules in this chapter help the cataloger choose the access points for a biblio-

graphic record. Regardless of the choice of main entry, as many other access points should be provided as possible.

21.0B Sources for determining access points
The LC rule interpretation says:

> Generally determine access points for an item from its chief source (or chief source substitute) and from statements appearing prominently (cf. 0.8). When statements appearing in the chief source, or statements appearing prominently, are ambiguous or insufficient, use information appearing in the contents of the item or appearing outside the item for determining access points. Note that for works entered under certain rules (e.g., 21.4 and 21.6C1), it does not matter where the information appears.

For guidance in the use of data found on bibliographic data sheets, see 2.0B in this manual. Added entries can be made from data on the bibliographic data sheet.

21.0C ———

21.0D *Optional addition.* **Designations of function**
LC/GPO are generally not exercising this option. One of the results of this decision is that the designation *joint author* will not be used at all.

The Joint Steering Committee for Revision of AACR has approved the addition of the following as the final paragraph in rule 21.0D in printed text of AACR2:

> In specialist or archival cataloguing, when desirable for identification or file arrangement, add designations from standard lists appropriate to the material being catalogued.

21.1 BASIC RULE

The cataloger must decide which entities require main or added entries. The task is easier for personal name entries since these rules are largely unchanged. For entry under corporate body, however, the cataloger finds a completely new rule. The "emanators" of AACR2 hoped that implementation of the rules would lead to many more title entries for publications, particularly serial publications. Library users will still be able to find publications under the heading for the corporate body with which the publications are primarily associated, but it will now be an added entry, not the main entry. This is particularly true for government documents, which are so frequently associated with an agency's name, and which, except for certain legal works, so seldom satisfy the criteria of 21.1B2 for main entry under corporate body.

21.1A Works of personal authorship

21.1A1 Definition. As an example of personal authorship, AACR2 originally stated that "cartographers are the authors of their maps." The paragraph has been revised to delete the entire second and third sentences, with a generalization substituted that sends catalogers to the special rules for more advice. Cartographers *may* be the authors of their maps. This understanding of a possibility rather than a certainty is necessary since the intellectual responsibility of cartographers can vary from map to map. A cartographer may have complete responsibility for the cartographic item as a whole or may have only limited responsibility that in some cases is no more than photographic/mechanical duplication or the tracing of an existing base map.

21.1A2 General rule. LC rule interpretation says:

Consider the entire run of a serial before entering it under the heading for a personal author. If different issues of the serial are known to have been or are likely to be created by different persons, do not enter the work under the heading for a personal author.

Enter a serial under the heading for a personal author only in instances in which one person is so closely connected to or involved with the serial that the publication seems unlikely to continue without that person. Some types of serials that might sometimes be considered to be unlikely to continue without the person named as author are:

a) serials for which the same person is named as both author and publisher
b) serials that carry the whole name or part of the name of the personal author in the title
c) serials that do not emanate from a corporate body which might see that the serial is continued.

Always lean toward *not* entering a serial under the heading for a personal author.

21.1B Entry under corporate body

21.1B1 Definition. LC rule interpretation says:

Include in the definition of a conference in footnote 1 any named meeting that is entered directly under its own name and any named meeting that is entered subordinately to a heading for a corporate body.

When determining whether a conference has a name, cases arise that exhibit conflicting evidence insofar as two of the criteria in the definition of a corporate body are concerned (capitalization and the definite article). When the phrase is in a language that normally capitalizes each word of a name, even in running text, consider a capitalized phrase a name even if it is preceded by an indefinite article. (This statement does not apply to other languages.)

Named: In July of 1977 a Conference on Management Techniques in Libraries was held . . .

123

> *Unnamed:* Late last year the Retail Manufacturers Association of the Greater Houston area sponsored the national conference on losses by theft at the . . .

Another important point to bear in mind when deciding whether a phrase is a name is that the phrase must include a word that connotes a meeting ("symposium," "workshop," "congress," "colloquium," etc., are some examples; the particular word is not important). (Note: Some notable sequential conferences that lack such a term are nevertheless considered to be named, e.g., Darmstadter Gesprach.)

> *Unnamed:* A symposium titled "Coal Geology and the Future," sponsored by . . .

When a generic-term name of a meeting designates a meeting *of* a body (as opposed to one merely sponsored by a body), the meeting may be considered as named, whether or not the generic term is strengthened by the name or abbreviation of the body. For example, "annual meeting" in relation to the Human Factors Society is named whether it appears as

    Annual Meeting
or HFS Annual Meeting
or Annual Meeting of the Human Factors Society

N.B. If such a meeting is one of two or more bodies, reject its designation as a name:

> Sixteenth annual United Kingdom Civil Aviation Authority/United States Federal Aviation Administration meeting

On the other hand, such generic-term designation for *sponsored* meetings are considered as named only if the name, the abbreviation of the name, or some other distinctive noun or adjective, strengthens the generic term.

> Symposium no. 95 = *not named*
> IAU Symposium no. 95 = *named*

Named

Annual Conference of the American Academy of Advertising

First Constitutional Convention of the Congress of Industrial Organizations

5th Annual Conference of the Nigerian Political Science Association

Human Factors Society 1979 Annual Meeting

Annual Meeting || Society of Christian Ethics

42nd Annual Scientific Meeting || Committee on Problems of Drug Dependence, Inc.

Unnamed

Seventh meeting of the Coordinating Committee for the Regional English
   Language Centre

21.1B2 General rule. Before deciding that a work may be entered under a corporate
main entry heading, consider first whether the document emanates from the body in
question and second, whether the publication fits one of the categories of rule 21.1B2.

The LC rule interpretation says:

> In determining whether a work should be entered under the name of a
> corporate body, the cataloger makes two determinations, keeping in mind that
> in many instances information appearing only in the content of the work will
> have to be taken into account in order to ascertain if the second determination
> particularly applies (cf. 21.0B, last sentence):
>
> 1) Does the work emanate from the corporate body involved? As indicated
> in footnote 2 to chapter 21, a work emanates from a corporate body if one of
> the following conditions applies:
>
> a) The corporate body has issued (published) the work. Normally this means
> that the name of the corporate body appears in a position indicative of publica-
> tion (e.g., for books, the imprint position) in the chief source of information or
> appears elsewhere as a formal publication statement.
>
> b) Corporate body A has caused the work to be issued (published). Generally
> the name of a different body, corporate body B, appears on the chief source of
> information (cf. above) or elsewhere as a formal publisher statement. Body A
> has arranged for body B, named as publisher, to issue the work because body A
> has no facilities for publishing. The arrangement between the two bodies is in
> some cases explicitly stated, e.g., Published for the Historical Association by
> Routledge & Paul. In other cases it must be inferred from evidence in the
> publication. For example, the name of body A at head of title (the name of a
> commercial publisher appears in publisher position) commonly indicates that
> body A has caused the item to be issued (published), or, if the work appears in
> a series for which body A has editorial responsibility but is published by a
> commercial publisher, body A has caused the work to be issued (published).
>
> c) The corporate body, although the originator of the work, does not meet
> the test of issuing (publishing) in either category (a) or (b) above. In this case,
> body B, which has no responsibility for the content, issues (publishes) a work
> whose content originates with body A. For example, a work is prepared by
> corporate body A which functions as a consulting body, commissioned by body
> B for that purpose; the completed work is published by body B. In this case the
> content of the work originates with body A although it has no responsibility for
> publication of the work. A similar situation occurs when a commercial pub-
> lisher arranges to publish the card catalog of a library in book form. The library
> has no real responsibility for publication; it has only given permission to the
> commercial publisher to undertake publication. However, since the content of
> the catalog has been prepared by the library's cataloging staff, the content of
> the publication originates with the library. In all those cases, consider that
> ''originates with'' is equivalent to ''emanates from.''

d) If there is doubt that the work emanates from the corporate body, assume that the corporate body is involved with the work.

2) Does the work fall into one or more of the categories listed in 21.1B2? In answering this question, the following points should be kept in mind:

a) Judge that a work falls into a particular category if that category accounts for the predominant content, or the purpose, of the work. That is, there may be some material that does not fall into one of the categories; that material may be ignored for the purpose of making the determination. For example, a work may contain factual data to support a statement of official position (21.1B2c), when the official position is the chief purpose of the work.

b) If there is any doubt as to whether a work falls into one or more of the categories, enter it either under personal author or title as appropriate; that is, ignore the involvement of a corporate body in determining the main entry heading. (Make an added entry for the corporate body, however, even if not prominently named.)

c) See comments under categories.

3) There is no rule comparable to AACR 1 rule 17 A-B for making a determination of whether the main entry heading for a work is to be under the name of a person or of a corporate body. When a work emanating from a corporate body bears the name of one or more persons as authors, it is necessary, first of all, to determine if the work falls under the provisions of 21.1B2. If the work does not meet the two conditions imposed by 21.1B2, or if there is doubt that it does, it is necessary next to determine if the work may be entered under the heading for a person named, according to the provisions of the appropriate rule, e.g., 21.4A, 21.6. If entry under the name of a person is not permitted, by default the entry is under title (21.1C3). Make an added entry under the heading for the corporate body if the main entry is under the name of a person or under title.

AACR2 rule says:

Enter a work emanating from one or more corporate bodies under the heading for the appropriate corporate body if it falls into one or more of the following categories:

a)   those of an administrative nature dealing with the corporate body itself
or   its internal policies, procedures, and/or operations
or   its finances
or   its officers and/or staff
or   its resources (e.g., catalogues, inventories, membership directories)

Category *a* includes such publications as:

Internal policies, procedures, and/or operations: The United States Government manual, rules and practices of the House of Representatives, the Social Security handbook, the Department of State newsletter, statistical bulletins reflecting statistics of the agency (like the monthly statement of the public debt of the United States), Congressional legislative calendars and journals.

Finances: The Budget of the United States.

Officers and/or staff: The diplomatic list of the State Department.

Resources (e.g., catalogs, inventories, membership directories): The House of
Representatives and Senate telephone directories, the catalog of the Interior
Department Library, the Congressional directories.

Many publications may satisfy more than one subcategory of 21.1B2a.
LC interpretation says:

> To belong to this category the work must deal with the body itself. The
> words "administrative nature" indicate works dealing with the management or
> conduct of the affairs of the body itself, including works that describe the
> activities of the body either in general terms or for a particular period of time,
> e.g., minutes of meetings, reports of activities for a particular period. Nor-
> mally, such works are intended in the first instance for internal use, although
> they may be available to others. Some, particularly reports of activities, pro-
> gress, etc., may be required by superior or related bodies. Other works,
> particularly general descriptions of objectives and/or activities, may be gener-
> ally available for purposes of public relations.
>
> *Internal policy* is limited to policies formulated for the conduct of the affairs
> of the body itself. For works concerned with policies relating to topics of wider
> concern to a body, see category c.

United States. Office of the Federal Register.
United States government manual / Office of the Federal Register, National
Archives and Records Service, General Services Administration. —
1973/74– . — Washington, D.C. : The Office : For sale by the Supt. of
Docs., G.P.O., 1974–
v. ; 25 cm.

Annual.
Continues: United States. Office of the Federal Register. United States
government organization manual.
Includes indexes.
Supt. of Docs. class no.: GS 4.109:(year)
Supt. of Docs. S/N: 022-003-00982-5
ISSN 0092-1904 = United States government manual.

I. Title.

United States. Congress.
Official congressional directory. — Washington : U.S. G.P.O.
v. : ill. ; 24 cm.

Compiled under the direction of the Joint Committee on Printing.
Continues: United States. Congress. Congressional directory.

Description based on: 1979.
Supt. of Docs. class no.: Y 4.P93/1:
Supt. of Docs. S/N : 052-070-04810-7 (cloth) 0052-070-04811-5 (cloth indexed) 0052-070-04809

I. Title.

New York (State). Governor (1975– : Carey) State of New York/
five year projection of income and expenditures : general fund, fiscal years
1979– 80 through 1983– 84. Hugh L. Carey, Governor, Howard F. Miller,
Director of the Budget — [Albany?] : State of New York, [1979]
36 p. ; 28 cm.

"March 2, 1979"– P. [3]
"Submitted as a supplement to the 1979– 80 Executive Budget"– P. [3]

I. Title. II. Title: Five year projection of income and expenditures.

Susquehanna River Basin Commission.
Proposed amendment to comprehensive plan establishing a water supply
management policy : background report / Susquehanna River Basin Commission. Harrisburg, Pa. : The Commission, 1979.
5, 3 leaves, [1] leaf of plats : 1 map ; 28 cm.

Title from cover.
"October 18, 1979."

I. Title.

United States. Forest Service.
Streamside management zone status and ordinances : criteria and institu-
tional arrangement serving water quality objectives on state and private
forest lands — [Washington, D.C.?] : U.S. Dept. of Agriculture : U.S.
Environmental Protection Agency, [1978]
42 p.: ill., 1 map; 27 cm.

Title from cover.
Bibliography : p. 28.

I. United States. Environmental Protection Agency. II. Title.

New York (State). Legislature. Senate Select Committee on the Handicapped.
Report of the Select Committee on the Handicapped. — Albany : The
Committee. 1982.
123 p. ; 28 cm.

"March 1982"

I. Flyn, John E. II. Title.

Note that under AACR1 the *United States Government Manual* and the *Official
Congressional Directory* were entered under title rather than corporate body.
AACR2 says:

b) some legal and governmental works of the following types:
laws (see 21.31)
decrees of the chief executive that have the force of law (see 21.31)
administrative regulations (see 21.32)
treaties, etc. (see 21.35)
court decisions (see 21.36)
legislative hearings

Examples for everything but legislative hearings are under the appropriate rule.
AACR2 says:

c) those that record the collective thought of the body (e.g., reports of commissions, committees, etc.; official statements of position on external policies)

This includes the work of committees and commissions which advise governments of
all types as well as those which advise business, universities and colleges, and other
private groups or institutions.

United States. Congress. Ad Hoc Advisory Committee on Revision of Title 44.
Federal government printing and publishing : policy issues : report of the Ad
Hoc Advisory Committee on Revision of Title 44 to the Joint Committee on
Printing, United States Congress. — Washington : Joint Committee on
Printing : U.S. G.P.O. ₁distributor₁, 1979.
xii, 120 p. : ill.; 24 cm.

At head of title: Committee print.
Bibliography: p. 89–120.
Supt. of Docs. Class. No.: Y 4.P 93/1:P 93/6

I. United States. Congress. Joint Committee on Printing. II. Title.

National Research Council (U.S.). Diesel Impacts Study Committee.
Diesel cars : benefits, risks, and public policy : final report of the Diesel
Impacts Study Committee, Assembly of Engineering, National Research
Council. — Washington, D.C. : National Academy Press, 1982.

xx, 142 p. : ill. ; 25 cm. — (Impacts of diesel-powered light-duty vehicles)
Includes bibliographies.

I. Title. II. Series.

Sierra Leone. Faulkner Commission of Inquiry into the Finance and Administration of the Transport and General Workers' Union.
    Report of the Faulkner Commission of Inquiry into the Finance and Admin-
istration of the Transport and General Workers' Union, and Government
statement thereon. — ₁Freetown₁ : Sierra Leone Govt., ₁1971₁ (₁Freetown?₁ :
Govt. Print. Dept.)
    102 p. ; 35 cm.

Cover title.
Caption title: Government statement on the Report of the Commission of
Inquiry into the Finance and Administration of the Transport and General
Workers' Union / by M.C. d'Alves Faulkner, sole Commissioner.

I. Faulkner, M. C. d'Alves. II. Sierra Leone. III. Title.

LC rule interpretation says:

This category is best characterized by saying that it deals with those works
that present official statements of position of a body on matters other than the
affairs of the body itself. Note the following points particularly:

i)   The body does not have to be a committee or a commission; it may be a
     department or section of a body, or even the whole body.
ii) The subject on which a position is taken normally bears a close relation to
     the body's objectives and activities, which may be explicitly or implicitly
     expressed.
iii) The material dealing with the subject consists primarily of policy state-
     ments, recommendations for policy, or opinions; it is never merely a
     reporting of facts, events, research, investigations, etc.

Organisation for Economic Co-operation and Development.
    Construction of roads on compressible soils : a report / prepared by an
OECD Road Research Group, December 1979. — Paris : Organisation for
Ecomonic Cooperation and Development ; ₁Washington, D.C. : OECD
Publications and Information Center, distributor₁, 1979, c1980.
    148 p. : ill., plans ; 27 cm. — (Road Research)

Includes bibliographical references.
ISBN 926-412-0629

I. Series.

United States. Task Force on Tenant Participation in the Management of
Low-Income Housing.
  Final report of the Task Force on Tenant Participation in the Management of
  Low-Income Housing. — Washington, D.C. : U.S. Dept. of Housing and
  Urban Development, ₁1979₁
  v, 55 p. ; 26 cm.

  Cover title.
  "November 1978."
  "December 1979"—P. ₁4₁ of cover.
  "HUD-H-457 (2)—P. ₁4₁ of cover.
  "The Task Force was an advisory group, established by the Secretary to
  develop recommendations for HUD policy on the subject of tenant participa-
  tion in public housing management"—Transmittal letter (bound in).

I. United States. Dept. of Housing and Urban Development. II. Title.

Committee on Science, Engineering, and Public Policy (U.S.). Panel on Scien-
tific Communication and National Security.
  Scientific communication and national security : a report / prepared by the
  Panel on Scientific Communication and National Security, Committee on
  Science, Engineering, and Public Policy, National Academy of Sciences,
  National Academy of Engineering, Institute of Medicine. — Washington,
  D.C. : National Academy Press, 1982.
  xv, 188 p. ; 28 cm.

  "The Committee on Science, Engineering, and Public Policy is a joint
  committee of the National Academy of Sciences, the National Academy of
  Engineering, and the Institute of Medicine. It includes members of the
  councils of all three bodies"—T.p. verso.
  Bibliography: p. 78–89.

I. Title.

Mexico. Comisión de Estudios del Territorio Nacional.
  Estudio de gran visión para la colonización de ₁sic₁ valle de Edzna, Campeche. : proyecto El-5-2. — Mexico, D.F. : Secretaria de la Presidencia,
  Comisión de Estudios des Territorio Nacional, ₁1976₁ 82 p. : ill. ; 21 cm. +
  7 maps (col. ; 77 × 58 cm. folded to 40 × 30 cm. in portfolio)

I. Title. II. Title: Proyecto El-5-2. III. Title: Colonización del valle de Edzna,
Campeche.

LC rule interpretation expands on 21.1B2c:

> Enter a work prepared by a *consultant* under the heading for the body that
> hired the consultant if the hiring body takes the consultant's document and
> adopts it in some clear way that fits a category of 21.1B2, category c being the
> most likely possibility. One of the clearest ways for the hiring body to do this is
> for it to make explicit recommendations or policy statements *of its own* super-
> imposed on the consultant's material (no matter that the original material is
> copied, even if verbatim). Another clear way is for the hiring body to represent
> as its very own the recommendations that originated with the consultant—
> perhaps even without adding any new material.
>
> If the hiring body does not take the stand described above and simply passes
> on the material without position statements of its own, then enter the work
> under the heading for the consultant if this is a person or persons not constitut-
> ing a corporate body, i.e., apply 21.4A or 21.6. If the consultant is a corporate
> body, test the case under 21.1B2 in relation to the consultant in the same way
> as was done in relation to the hiring body. If the work simply reports on a
> subject without making the consultant's own definite recommendations, it is
> most likely that the work will not fit any of the categories of 21.1B2 and
> therefore main entry would be under title. If the work instead contains the
> policy statements or definite recommendations of the consultant, then main
> entry will probably be under the heading for the consultant.

Independence Avenue, Constitution Avenue : special street plans, phase 1
study : a National Capital Planning Commission urban design study,
    December 1980 / EDAW Inc., Consultants. — Washington, D.C. : Na-
    tional Capital Planning Commission : ₁For sale by the Supt. of Docs., U.S.
    G.P.O., 1981?₁
78 p. : ill. (some col.) ; 25 × 38 cm.

Cover title: Constitution Avenue, Independence Avenue.
Bibliography: p. 78.
S/N 034-000-00009-3
Item 831-A

I. United States. National Capital Planning Commission. II. EDAW Inc.
III. Title: Constitution Avenue, Independence Avenue.

AACR2 says:

> d) those that report the collective activity of a conference (proceedings, col-
>   lected papers, etc.), of an expedition (results of exploration, investigation,
>   etc.), or of an event (an exhibition, fair, festival, etc.) falling within the
>   definition of a corporate body (see 21.1B1), provided that the conference,
>   expedition, or event is prominently named in the item being catalogued.

LC rule interpretation says:

> This category requires little comment, since it may not be applied to any
> type of body other than those stated. Note that the name of the conference,
> expedition, etc., must appear prominently (cf. 0.8) in the publication being
> cataloged in order for the body to be considered as the main entry heading.
> Note also the emphasis upon the collective aspect of the work. It must deal with
> the activities of many persons involved in a corporate body covered by the
> category, not with the activities of a single person.

Governor's Conference on Alcohol Problems (1971 : New York, N.Y.)
  Report on the Governor's Conference on Alcohol Problems held November
  10, 1971, Americana Hotel, New York, New York. — ₁Albany₁ : New York
  State Dept. of Mental Hygiene, ₁1972?₁
  156 p. ; 28 cm.
  Cover title.

  I. New York (State). Dept. of Mental Hygiene.

World Conference for Action Against Apartheid (1977 : Lagos, Nigeria).
  Report of the World Conference for Action Against Apartheid, Lagos, 22–
  26 August 1977. — New York : United Nations, 1977.
  2 v. ; 28 cm.

  Contents: 1. Report, including Lagos declaration for action against apartheid
  —2. Annexes.
  "A/CONF.91/9."
  "United Nations publication. Sales no. E.77. XIV. 2-3."

Conference on Computer Security and the Data Encryption Standard (1977 :
Gaithersburg, Md.).
  Computer security and the data encryption standard : proceedings of the
  Conference on Computer Security and the Data Encryption Standard held at
  the National Bureau of Standards in Gaithersburg, Maryland, on February
  15, 1977 / Dennis K. Branstad, editor ; sponsored by the National Bureau of
  Standards and the U.S. Civil Service Commission. — Washington, D. C. :
  The Bureau : For sale by the Supt. of Docs., U.S. G.P.O., 1978.
  viii, 124 p. : ill. ; 27 cm. — (Computer science & technology) (NBS special
  publication / U.S. Dept. of Commerce, National Bureau of Standards ;
  50027)

  Supt. of Docs. Class. No.: C13.10:50027
  Supt. of Docs. S/N: 003003018911

I. Branstad, Dennis K. II. United States. **National Bureau** of Standards.
III. **United States**. Civil Service Commission. **IV. Title.** V. Series. VI. Series :
NBS special **publication** ; 50027.

United Nations Sugar Conference (1973 : Geneva, **Switzerland)**.
United **Nations** Sugar Conference, 1973 — New York : **United Nations,**
1974.
iii, 23 p. ; 28 cm.

''T/Sugar.8/6.''
United Nations publication. Sales no. : E.74.II.D.16.

AACR2 says:

> e) sound recordings, films, and videorecordings resulting from the collective
> activity of a performing group as a whole where the responsibility of the
> group goes beyond that of mere performance, execution, etc. (For corporate
> bodies that function solely as performers on sound recordings, see 21.23.)

LC rule interpretation says:

> This category emphasizes that the responsibility of a performing group must
> go beyond ''mere performance, execution, etc.'' This means that the group
> must be responsible to a major degree for the artistic content of the work being
> performed. A typical example is an acting group that performs by means of
> improvisation. The group collectively ''plans'' the drama, that is, determines
> the broad outline of the plot, the nature of the characters, etc., in the absence of
> a written dialogue. The development of the drama proceeds entirely on the
> basis of improvised dialogue. The performance is recorded and it is the
> recording that is being cataloged.

Under the original text of AACR2, rules for choice of entry would have required most
cartographic materials to be entered under title. Since the titles of cartographic items are
often so nondistinctive as to be inappropriate for main entry headings, the Joint Steering
Committee for Revision of AACR has approved a rule addition that provides for a new
category *f* under 21.1B2, to allow cartographic materials to be entered under corporate
body.
AACR2 says:

> f) cartographic materials emanating from a corporate body other than a body
> that is merely responsible for the publication or distribution of the materials

The judgment that a corporate body is the producer of the work (i.e., responsible for
the intellectual content, design, and creation of a cartographic item) should normally be

134

based on statements in the chief source of information. The name of the corporate body in question, however, may not always be printed prominently on the item and may not always be accompanied by an explicit statement of responsibility. When there is difficulty determining the degree of responsibility for the cartographic item such a corporate body may have had, consider what is known about the publication history of the body. If it is known to be a map-making organization which normally originates and issues maps, make an entry under the corporate body. If principal responsibility for the production of the cartographic item is clearly attributed to a personal author, do not consider applying this category.

21.1B3 If a corporate body does not qualify for the main entry under 21.1B2, then treat the work as if no corporate body is involved and enter it under title or personal author. This is a drastic change in practice and will mean that many works will not be entered under corporate body, even if no personal author is involved. Instead such works will be entered under title. Catalogers, however, are encouraged to make any and all corporate added entries they believe are necessary. See 21.29D.

21.1B4 Choosing between the parent body and the subordinate body for main entry can result in the cataloging of similar publications under different corporate names, for example if part one of a publication gives prominence to the parent body and part two to the subordinate body.

LC rule interpretation says:

> When a work falling into one or more of the categories given in 21.1B2 involves a parent body and one of its subordinate bodies, with the subordinate body responsible for the preparation of the contents of the work, enter the work under the heading for subordinate body if it is named prominently. Exception: If the name of the parent body appears on the chief source but the subordinate body does not, enter the work under the heading for the parent body alone.
>
> If the name of the subordinate body is not stated prominently, or if the subordinate body has no name, enter the work under the heading for the parent body.

If these rules require main entry under the parent body, according to 21.29D, an added entry can be made for the subordinate body.

21.1C Entry under title
AACR2 says:

> Enter a work under its title when:
>
> 1) the personal authorship is unknown (see 21.5), diffuse (see 21.6C2), or cannot be determined, and the work does not emanate from a corporate body

A typical example of diffuse authorship where the publication is not defined as emanating from a corporate body is a subject bibliography done by four reference librarians at a state university.

Mister President : a biography of Shehu Aliyu Shagari, first Executive President of Nigeria.
— Lagos : Dept. of Information, Executive Office of the President, ₍1980₎
(Lagos : Academy Press)
23 p. : ill., ports. ; 24 cm.

Cover title: Meet Mister President.

I. Nigeria. Office of the President. Dept. of Information. II. Title: Meet Mr. President.

AACR2 says:

2) it is a collection or a work produced under editorial direction (see 21.7)

A typical example of this type of government work is the Bureau of the Census publication *Reflections of America, Commemorating the Statistical Abstract Centennial*. To celebrate the 100th anniversary of the *Statistical Abstract of the United States*, a collection of essays by well-known experts in the field was published with a preface by the honorary editor, Norman Cousins. This publication would be entered under title with added entries for each of the essay authors, depending on the library's practice.

Serving handicapped children in home-based Head Start : a guide for home visitors and others working with handicapped children and their families in the home / edited by Richard D. Boyd, Julia Herwig ; cover and illustrations by Louy Danube ; photographs by Jon Jallings. — Washington, D.C. : U.S. Dept. of Health and Human Services, Office of Human Development Services, Administration for Children, Youth, and Families, Head Start Bureau : For sale by the Supt. of Docs., U.S. G.P.O., ₍1982?₎
v, 287 p. : ill ; 28 cm. — (DHHS publication ; no. (OHDS) 82-31169)

"This manual was developed by the staff of the Portage Project, Cooperative Education Service Agency 12, Portage, Wisconsin, under Grant 5001 G/H/O . . ."
Supt. of Docs. Class. No.: HE 23.
Supt. of Docs. S/N:
Includes bibliographies.

I. Boyd, Richard D. II. Herwig, Julia. III. United States. Head Start Bureau. IV. Series.

AACR2 says:

3) it emanates from a corporate body but does not fall into one or more of the categories given in 21.1B2 and is not of personal authorship

The Canadian minerals yearbook. — 1962–
  Ottawa : Mineral Resources Division, Dept. of Mines and Technical
  Surveys: Available by mail from the Queen's Printer, 1964–.
  v. : ill. ; 25 cm. — (Mineral report)

  Annual.
  Continues: The Canadian mineral industry.
  Each issue individually numbered in series.

I. Canada. Mineral Resources Division. II. Series.

Nutrient requirements of warmwater fishes /
  Subcommittee on Warmwater Fish Nutrition, Committee on Animal Nutrition, Board on Agriculture and Renewable Resources, National Research
  Council. — Washington, D.C. : National Academy of Sciences, 1977.
  vii, 78 p. : ill. ; 20 cm. — (Nutrient requirements of domestic animals ; [12])

  Bibliography: p. 71–78.
  ISBN 0-309-02616-4.

I. National Research Council (U.S.). Subcommittee on Warmwater Fish Nutrition. II. Title: Warmwater fish nutrition. III. Series: Nutrient requirements of
domestic animals ; no. 12.

Nutrient requirements of swine / Subcommittee on Swine Nutrition, Committee
  on Animal Nutrition, Board on Agriculture and Renewable Resources,
  National Research Council. — 8th rev. ed., 1979. — Washington, D.C. :
  National Academy of Sciences, 1979.
  ix, 52 p. ; 28 cm. — (Nutrient requirements of domestic animals ; no. 2)

  Bibliography: p. 33–52.
  ISBN 0-309-02870-1.

I. National Research Council (U.S.). Subcommittee on Swine Nutrition.
II. Series.

1980 U.S. directory of substate planning and development organizations : a
  guide to addresses and jurisdictions. — Montgomery, Ala. (3734 Atlanta
  Hghwy., Montgomery, Ala. 36130) : Office of State Planning and Federal
  Programs, State Planning Division, [1980]
  1 v. (loose-leaf) : maps ; 28 cm.

  "An interim document."
  "ALA-ADO-X996-1011-02"—T.p. verso.

I. Alabama. State Planning Division. II. Title: U.S. Directory of substate planing and development organizations. III. Title: United States directory of substate planning and development organizations.

The conversion of rental housing to condominiums
    and cooperatives : a national study of scope, causes and impacts / Division of Policy Studies. — Washington, D.C. : U.S. Dept. of Housing and Urban Development, Office of Policy Development and Research : For sale by the Supt. of Docs., U.S. G.P.O., ₍1980₎.
    331 p. in various pagings : ill. ; 28 cm.

    "June, 1980."
    "HUD-PDR-554-3"—P. ₍4₎ of cover.
    Includes bibliographical references.
    Supt. of Docs. Class No. : HH
    Supt. of Docs. S/N:

I. United States. Dept. of Housing and Urban Development. Office of Policy Development and Research. Division of Policy Studies.

Report on a survey of manpower requirements in the telecommunication services of the region.
    — ₍Addis Ababa, Ethiopia₎ : United Nations Economic Commission for Africa, ₍1980₎
    187, ₍43₎ p. : ill. ; 29 cm.

    "Distr. restricted."
    "E/CN.14/TEL/80/1."
    "DEC/TRANSCOM/WP/XIII/Rev. 7 November 1980."
    "M80–3074."
    Includes bibliographical references.

I. United Nations. Economic Commission for Africa. II. Title: Manpower requirements in the telecommunication services of the region.

Départment de l'Ouest : grande potentialité économique et humaine à peine entamée. — ₍Abidjan? Ivory Coast₎ : République de Côte d'Ivoire, Conseil économique et social, [1969] (Abidjan : Impr. nationale)
    70 p. : maps ; 27 cm.

    Title from half title page: Grande potentialité économique et humaine à peine etamée.
    Includes bibliographical references.

I. Ivory Coast. Conseil économique et social. II. Title: Grande potentialité
économique et humaine à peine entamée.

An LC rule interpretation adds one additional category of title main entry as follows:

or   5) it consists of contributions of more than one kind (textual, graphic, aural,
etc.), *and* the statement of responsibility in the chief source includes a word
or phrase denoting the particular contribution of each individual named, *and*
such statement of responsibility, by presentation (e.g., typography and position) in the chief source, diminish the importance of the persons named in
relation to the title, so that these persons seem to be receiving technical
credit only, as opposed to credit for the artistic and intellectual content of the
whole item.

The important thing to remember in deciding whether a work issued or published by a
corporate body should be entered under title is whether or not it qualifies under 21.1B2
for entry under corporate body. Only after that determination has been made can one
decide whether to enter the work under personal author or title.

Proposed Bryce Canyon Wilderness Area, Bryce Canyon National park, Utah :
final environmental statement
/ prepared by Bryce Canyon National Park, Midwest Region, National Park
Service, Department of the Interior. — ₍Utah?₎ : The Region, 1974.
47 p. : maps (1 col.) ; 27cm.
"Jan. 10, 1974."
"FES 74–1."

I. United States. National Park Service. Midwest Region. II. Title: Bryce
Canyon Wilderness Area, Bryce Canyon National Park, Utah.

21.2   CHANGES IN TITLES PROPER

21.2A   Definition
AACR2 says:

Consider a title proper to have changed if:
1) any change occurs in the first five words (other than an initial article in the
nominative case)
or 2) any important words (nouns, proper names or initials standing for proper
names, adjectives, etc.) are added, deleted, or changed (including changes
in spelling)
or 3) there is a change in the order of words.

21.2B Monographs

21.2B1 Monographs in one physical part. AACR2 says: "If the title proper of a monograph in one physical part changes between one edition and another, make a separate main entry for each edition. Follow the instructions in 25.2 in deciding whether to use uniform titles to assemble all the editions."

21.2B2————

21.2C Serials

AACR2 says: "If the title proper of a serial changes, make a separate main entry for each title."

> Federally coordinated program of highway research and development / Federal
> Highway Administration, U.S. Dept. of Transportation. — 1974/75– . —
> Washington, D.C. : The Administration : For sale by the Supt. of Docs.,
> U.S. G.P.O.
> v. : ill. ; 28 cm.
>
> Annual.
> Report year ends June 30.
> Continues: Research and development program / Federal Highway Adminis-
> tration, U.S. Dept. of Transportation.
> ISSN 0361-4204= Federally coordinated program of highway research and
> development.
> Supt. of Docs. Class No.: TD. 2: 42:
> Supt. of Docs. S/N:
>
> I. United States. Federal Highway Administration.

> Research and development program
> Federal Highway Administration, U.S. Dept. of Transportation. —
> 1953/54– 1973/74. — Washington, D.C. : The Administration : For sale
> by the Supt. of Docs., U.S. G.P.O.
> v. : ill. ; 28 cm.
>
> Annual.
> Report year ends June 30.
> Continued by: Federally coordinated program of highway research and devel-
> opment / Federal Highway Administration, U.S. Dept. of Transportation.
> ISSN 0098-0234= Research and development program.
> Supt. of Docs. Class No.: TD 2.2:R31/3/year
> Supt. of Docs. S/N: 5000-00091
>
> I. United States. Federal Highway Administration.

21.3 CHANGES OF PERSONS OR BODIES RESPONSIBLE FOR A WORK

21.3A ———

21.3A1– 21.3A2 ———

21.3B Serials

The original text of AACR2 said:

> Make a new entry for a serial when one or more of the following conditions arise, even if the title proper remains the same:
>
> 1) if the name of a person or corporate body under which a serial is entered changes (see 22.2B or 24.1B)
> 2) if the main entry for a serial is under a personal or corporate heading and the person or corporate body responsible for the serial changes.

The LC rule interpretation says:

> The opening statement to make a "new entry" has been interpreted to apply only to cases where multiple entries (i.e., records) will result. Therefore, "new entry" in this case means that an *additional* entry (record) should be created, with at least two records resulting: one for the old form of entry and one for the new form of entry. Given this interpretation, in subpart (1) of the rule, the words ". . . person or . . ." have been omitted by the Joint Steering Committee for Revision of AACR. While the existing serial record may be *replaced* when the form of a personal name is changed, an *additional* entry (record) will not be created.

New York (State). Drug Abuse Control Commission.
  Annual report / New York State Drug Abuse Control Commission. —
  1973– 1974. — Albany (Executive Park South, Albany, New York 12203)
  : New York State, Office of Drug Abuse Services, 1973– 1974.
  v. : ill. ; 22 cm.

  Continued by : Annual report/New York State, Office of Drug Abuse
  Services.

New York (State). Office of Drug Abuse Services.
  Annual report / New York State Office of Drug Abuse Service. — 1975–
  1977. — Albany (Executive Park South, Albany, New York 12203) : The
  Office, 1975– 1977.
  v. : ill. ; 28 cm.

  Continues : Annual report / New York State Drug Abuse Control Commission.
  Continued by: Annual report / New York State, Office of Alcoholism and
  Substance Abuse.

21.4   *Works for which a single person or corporate body is responsible*

If a serial is entered under title/statement of responsibility and there is a change in the statement of responsibility, do not make a new entry for the serial. The cataloger simply adds a note to the existing record to indicate a change in the body's name. Refer to rules 1.1F, 12.1F, 12.7B6, and 12.7B7.

> Personnel literature
> / U.S. Civil Service Commission Library. — Vol. 1, no. 1 (Jan. 1941) —
> Washington, D.C. : The Library : For sale by the Supt. of Docs., U.S.
> G.P.O.
> v. ; 27 cm.
>
> Monthly.
> Issued by: Office of Personnel Management Library, 1979—
> Item 300-D
> Supt. of Docs. class no.: CS 1.62:(v.nos. and nos.)
> Supt. of Docs. S/N: 006-000-80002-5
> ISSN 0031-5753 = Personnel literature.

I. United States. Civil Service Commission. Library. II. United States. Office of Personnel Management. Library.

21.4 WORKS FOR WHICH A SINGLE PERSON OR CORPORATE BODY IS RESPONSIBLE

> Moore, Norman R.
> Improvement of the lower Mississippi River and Tributaries, 1931– 1972 /
> ₁Norman R. Moore₁. — Vicksburg, Miss. : Mississippi River Commission,
> 1972.
> xii, 241 p. : ill. (some col.), col. maps ; 27 cm.
>
> At head of title: Department of the Army Corps of Engineers, U.S. Army.

I. United States. Mississippi River Commission. II. United States. Army. Corps of Engineers. III. Title.

21.4A Works of single personal authorship

> White, Gilbert Fowler, 1911–
> Nonstructural floodplain management study : overview / ₁Gilbert F. White₁.
> — Washington, D.C. : U.S. Water Resources Council ; ₁Springfield, Va.₁ :
> U.S. Dept. of Commerce, National Technical Information Service, ₁1979₁
> 10 p.; 28 cm.

Title from cover.
"Oct. 79."
"PB 80– 158538."

I. Water Resources Council (U.S.). II. Title.

Hicks, Jesse L.
Limestone-Muddy Creek watershed, Duplin County, North Carolina : draft
watershed plan and environmental impact statement / prepared by sponsoring local organizations, Duplin Soil and Water Conservation District . . . ₍et
al.₎, Jesse L. Hicks. — ₍North Carolina₎ : U.S. Dept. of Agriculture, Soil
Conservation Service, ₍1979₎
iii, 36, ₍35₎ p. ₍2₎ folded leaves of plates : 2 col. maps ; 27 cm.

"July 1979."
"USDA-SCS-EIS-WS(ADM)-79-1(D)-NC."
Bibliography: p. 35 (2nd group)

I. Duplin Soil and Water Conservation District (N.C.) II. United States. Soil
Conservation Service. III. Title.

21.4B Works emanating from a single corporate body
AACR2 says: "Enter a work, collection of works, or selections from a work or works
emanating from one corporate body (or any reprint, reissue, etc., of such a work) under
the heading for the body if the work or collection falls into one or more of the categories
given in 21.1B2."

Spain. Ministerio de Educación Nacional.
Catalogo de la Biblioteca de Iniciación Cultural / Ministerio de Educación
Nacional, Comisaria de Extensión Cultural. — Madrid : El Ministerio,
1965.
78 p. cm.

I. Title.

21.4C ———

**21.4D Works by heads of state, other high government officials, popes, and
other high ecclesiastical officials**
The examples given under this rule are good, therefore no added examples are
needed. An official communication is usually one which is required by law or is an
integral part of the responsibilities of the office. For example, the economic report of the
President to Congress is required by law. It is a new practice to give an added entry for
a personal heading when the work is entered under an official heading.

21.5   WORKS OF UNKNOWN OR UNCERTAIN AUTHORSHIP OR BY UNNAMED GROUPS

21.5A AACR2 says: "If a work is of unknown or uncertain personal authorship or if it emanates from a body that lacks a name, enter it under title."

> Laboratory animal housing : proceedings of a symposium held at Hunt Valley, Maryland, September 22–23, 1976 / [sponsored by] Institute of Laboratory Animal Resources, Division of Biological Sciences, Assembly of Life Sciences. — Washington, D.C. : National Academy of Sciences, 1978.
> vii, 230 p. : ill. ; 28 cm.
>
> I. National Research Council (U.S.). Institute of Laboratory Animal Resources.

> Final environmental impact statement (EIS) for 106-mile ocean waste disposal site designation
> / prepared under contract 68-01-4610 for U.S. Environmental Protection Agency, Oil and Special Materials Control Division, Marine Protection Branch ; T.A. Wastler, project officer. — Washington, D.C. (20460) : EPA, [1980].
> 481 p. in various pagings : ill., maps ; 28 cm.
>
> "February 1980."
> Bibliography: p. 7/19–7/42.
>
> I. United States. Environmental Protection Agency. Oil and Special Materials Control Division. Marine Protection Branch. II. Wastler, T.A. III. Title: Environmental impact statement (EIS) for 106-mile ocean waste disposal site designation.

21.5B AACR2 says: "If a work falling into one or more of the categories given in 21.1B2 probably emanates from a particular corporate body, enter under the heading for that body."

Often federal libraries catalog government documents that do not have title pages or information in the publication indicating responsibility. The cataloger then may base the choice of a main entry heading on information gained from other sources; perhaps the cataloger knows the author of the publication personally.

21.5C ———

21.6   WORKS OF SHARED RESPONSIBILITY

21.6A Scope

AACR2 says:

Apply this rule to:

1) works produced by the collaboration of two or more persons
2) works for which different persons have prepared separate contributions
3) works consisting of an exchange between two or more persons (e.g., correspondence, debates)
4) works falling into one or more of the categories given in 21.1B2 that emanate from two or more corporate bodies
5) works listed in 1–3 above that also contain contributions emanating from one or more corporate bodies
6) works resulting from a collaboration or exchange between a person and a corporate body.

21.6B Principal responsibility indicated

21.6B1 AACR2 says: "If, in a work of shared responsibility, principal responsibility is attributed (by the wording or the layout of the chief source of information) to one person or corporate body, enter under the heading for that person or body. If the name of another person or corporate body appears first in the chief source of information, make an added entry under the heading for that person or body. Make added entries under the headings for other persons or bodies involved if there are not more than two."

Even though this rule puts a limit on added entries, note that rule 21.29 permits the cataloger to make all the added entries the user might find useful.

> Hale, Robin C.
> Gold deposits of the Coker Creek District, Monroe County, Tennessee / by Robin C. Hale ; prepared in cooperation with the Tennessee Valley Authority. — Nashville : State of Tennessee, Dept. of Conservation, Division of Geology, 1974.
> 93 p. : ill., maps ; 28 cm. — (Bulletin / State of Tennessee, Division of Geology ; 72)
>
> 3 folded maps in pocket.
> Bibliography : p. 87–88.
>
> I. Tennessee Valley Authority. II. Title. III. Series: Bulletin (Tennessee. Division of Geology) ; 72.

> United States. Interagency Regulatory Liaison Group.
> Hazardous substances summary and full development plan / by Interagency Regulatory Liaison Group, U.S. Consumer Product Safety Commission, U.S. Environmental Protection Agency, Food and Drug Administration, Occupational Safety and Health Administration. — Washington : United States Environmental Protection Agency, 1978.
> iv, 236 p. ; 28 cm.
>
> Supt. of Docs. no.: Y3.C76/3:H34/13

I. United States. Environmental Protection Agency. II. U.S. Consumer Product Safety Commission. III. United States. Food and Drug Administration. IV. United States. Occupational Safety and Health Administration. V. Title.

On the title page it is indicated that the four agencies are part of the group, therefore the group gets main entry.

> Marlatt, William E.
>   Applications of remote sensing to emergency management : final report / for Federal Emergency Management Agency by William E. Marlatt (Department of Earth Resources, Colorado State University), E. Bruce Jones. ₁S.l. : s.n.₁, 1980.
>   vi, 41, ₁10₁ leaves : ill., 1 map ; 28 cm.
>
>   "February 1980."
>   "Contract #DCPA01–79-C-0268, work unit H"
>   Bibliography : leaves 36–41.
>
>   I. Jones, E. Bruce. II. United States. Federal Emergency Management Agency. III. Colorado State University. Dept. of Earth Resources. IV. Title.

21.6B2 AACR2 says: "If principal responsibility is attributed to two or three persons or bodies, enter under the heading for the first named of these. Make added entries under the headings for the others. If a work is by two principal persons or corporate bodies and one collaborating person or body, make an added entry also for the third person or body."

> Southwestern Illinois Metropolitan and Regional Planning Commission.
>   Model code : basic ordinances for municipalities in Southwestern Illinois / prepared by Southwestern Illinois Metropolitan and Regional Planning Commission. — Collinsville (203 West Main St., Collinsville, Ill. 62234) : The Commission, 1977.
>   680 p. in various paging ; 28 cm.
>
>   Final report financed in part through a comprehensive planning grant from the Dept. of Housing and Urban Development under a contract with the Illinois Dept. of Local Government Affairs.
>   Also distributed by the Southwestern Illinois Council of Mayors.
>   Report No.: SWIL-MAPC 77-09.
>   Contract Grant No.: CPA-IL-05-00-1083 (and -275).
>
>   I. United States. Dept. of Housing and Urban Development. II. Illinois. Dept. of Local Government Affairs. III. Southwestern Illinois Council of Mayors.

21.6C. Principal responsibility not indicated

21.6C1 AACR2 says: "If responsibility is shared between two or three persons or bodies and principal responsibility is not attributed to any of them by wording or layout, enter under the heading for the one named first. Make added entries under the headings for the others."

> Bingham, J. W. (James William), 1925–
> Hydrogeologic data for the Lower Connecticut River Basin, Connecticut / by J.W. Bingham, F.D. Paine, and L.A. Weiss ; prepared by the U.S. Geological Survey in cooperation with the Connecticut Department of Environmental Protection. — ₁Hartford₁ : Connecticut Dept. of Environmental Protection, 1975.
> 59 p. ; map ; 28 cm. — (Connecticut water resources bulletin ; no. 30)
> Folded col. map in pocket
>
> Bibliography: p. 6.
>
> I. Paine, F. D. II. Weiss, L. A. III. Geological Survey (U.S.). IV. Connecticut. Dept. of Environmental Protection. V. Series.

> Storfer, Miles D.
> Characteristics of the indigent aged population in New York City, 1980 / by Miles Storfer and Edward Jove (Office of Policy and Economic Research). —₁New York, N.Y.₁ : City of New York, Human Resources Administration, Office of Policy and Program Development, ₁1982₁
> vii, 41 leaves ; 28 cm.
>
> Cover title.
> "July 1982."
> "AR-12."
> Includes bibliographical references.
>
> I. Jove, Edward. II. New York (N.Y.). Human Resources Administration. Office of Policy and Program Development. III. New York (N.Y.). Human Resources Administration. Office of Policy and Economic Research. IV. Title.

21.6C2 AACR2 says: "If responsibility is shared between more than three persons or corporate bodies and principal responsibility is not attributed to any one, two, or three, enter under title. Make an added entry under the heading for the first person or corporate body named."

Even though the recommendation here for added entries is restrictive, rules 21.29D and 21.30A do allow added entries for all the bodies and persons involved.

Manual sobre elaboración de libraros de texto
/ preparado por Samuel Eduardo Quenza . . . ₁et al.₁ — El Macaro :
Departamento de Materiales Educativos del Centro de Capacitacion Docente
"El Macaro" del Ministerio de Educación, 1971.
iii , 101 p. ; 20 cm.

Preparado por Samuel Eduardo Quenza, Haydee Bracho de Cortez, Luis
Tejada Hernandez, Florencia Salazar Zabaia, Jesus Nunez Meneses.
"Trabajo realizado . . . para el Departamento de Asuntos Educativos de la
Organizacion de los Estados Americanos, dentro del Programa Regional de
Desarrollo Educativo."

I. Quenza, Samuel Eduardo. II. Centro de Capacitación Docente "El Macaro".
Departamento de Materiales Educativos (Venezuela). III. Organization of
American States. Dept. of Educational Affairs. IV. Bracho de Cortez, Haydee.
V. Hernandez, Luis Tejada. VI. Zabaia, Florencia Salazar. VII. Meneses,
Jesus Nunez.

Transport of oily pollutants in the coastal waters of Lake Michigan
/ by D.L. McCowan . . . ₁et al.₁ (Energy and Environmental Systems
Division, Argonne National Laboratory) ; prepared for U.S. Environmental
Protection Agency, Office of Research and Development, Office of Energy,
Minerals, and Industry and U.S. Dept. of Energy, Assistant Secretary for
the Environment, Office of Health and Environmental Research. —
Washington : United States Dept. of Energy, 1978.
45 p. ; 24 cm.

Prepared by D. L. McCowan, K. D. Saunders, J. H. Allender, J. D.
Ditmars, and W. Harrison.
"EPA/DOE interagency agreement no. IAG-D6-E681."
Dept. of Energy no. ANL/WR-78-1.
EPA-600/7-78-230.
Supt. of Docs. no.: E 1.28:ANL/WR-78-1.

I. McCowan, D. L. II. Saunders, K. D. III. Allender, J. H. IV. Ditmars, J. D.
V. Harrison, W. VI. Argonne National Laboratory. Energy and Environmental
Systems Division. VII. United States. Environmental Protection Agency. Of-
fice of Energy, Minerals, and Industry. VIII. United States. Dept. of Energy.
Office of Health and Environmental Research.

The LC rule interpretation covering rule 1.1F7 says that a corporate body to which the
personal authors are connected can be added in parentheses after the personal name or
quoted in a note if an added entry is required for the body.

21.6D ———

21.7 COLLECTIONS AND WORKS PRODUCED UNDER EDITORIAL DIRECTION

21.7A Scope
AACR2 says:

Apply this rule to:

1) collections of independent works by different persons or bodies
2) collections consisting of extracts from independent works by different persons or bodies
3) works consisting of contributions by different persons or bodies, produced under editorial direction
4) works consisting partly of independent works by different persons or bodies and partly of contributions produced under editorial direction.

Do not apply this rule to works emanating from a corporate body that fall into one or more of the categories given in 21.1B2. For papers or proceedings of named conferences, see 21.1B2.

Remember to review the types of publications that fall under rule 21.1B2, such as a group of works which reflect the official position of the body.

21.7B With collective title
Remember that 21.35F and 21.36C9 deal with particular types of law collections.

21.7C ———

21.8–21.12 ———

21.13   TEXTS PUBLISHED WITH COMMENTARY

21.13A ———

21.13B Commentary emphasized
AACR2 says: "If the chief source of information presents the item as a commentary, enter it as such (see 21.1–21.7). Make an added entry under the heading appropriate to the text."

Oppenheim, S. Chesterfield (Saul Chesterfield), 1897–
   Unfair trade practices : cases and comments / by S. Chesterfield Oppenheim. — 2nd ed. — St. Paul : West Pub. Co., 1965.
   xxix, 783 p. ; 27 cm. — (American Casebook series)

Includes legislation.

I. United States. Laws, etc. II. Title. III. Series.

149

Rothstein, Paul F., 1938–
Rules of evidence for the United States courts and magistrates : practice
comments / by Paul F. Rothstein. — 2nd ed. — New York : C. Boardman
Co., c1978.
1v. (loose-leaf) ; 26 cm. — (Federal practice)

Cover title : Federal rules of evidence.
Includes index.

I. United States. Laws, etc. II. Title. III. Title: Federal rules of evidence.

Blaine, Charles G.
Federal regulation of bank holding companies : an analysis of the Bank
holding company act of 1956, as amended / by Charles G. Blaine of the
New York Bar. — Washington : Bureau of National Affairs, Inc., c1973.
1v. (loose-leaf) ; 30 cm.

Includes bibliographical references.

I. United States. Bank Holding Company Act of 1956. II. Title.

21.13C Edition of the work emphasized

AACR2 says: ''If the chief source of information presents the item as an edition of
the original work, enter it as such (see 21.1– 21.7). Make an added entry under the
heading appropriate to the commentary.''

United States.
₁Laws, etc.₁
Special federal food and drug laws : statutes, regulations, legislative history,
annotations / by Thomas W. Christopher and Charles Wesley Dunn. —
Chicago : Commerce Clearing House, ₁1954₁
xiii, 1334 p. ; 26 cm. — (Food Law Institute series)

I. Christopher, Thomas W., 1917– . II. Dunn, Charles Wesley, 1885– .
III. Title. IV. Series.

21.13D ———

21.14– 21.22 ———

21.23 ENTRY OF SOUND RECORDINGS

Sound recordings are produced by government agencies and include such examples as the talking books by the Library of Congress, Division For the Blind; the Nixon tapes; folklore music by the Library of Congress; jazz and other types of music by the Smithsonian Institution; and band music by Marine, Air Force, Navy and Army bands.

21.24   COLLABORATION BETWEEN ARTIST AND WRITER

Government agencies occasionally produce coloring books, story books, cartoons, and other works with the joint creative efforts of both an artist and a writer.

21.25   REPORTS OF INTERVIEWS OR EXCHANGES

Government agencies often conduct open meetings to provide for the exchange of information between the agency and various segments of the public or selected experts. Examples are public hearings on the building of highways, dams, nuclear plants, and the issuance of various environmental permits.

Government officials are often interviewed and sometimes the agency publishes the interview.

21.26–21.27 ———

21.28   RELATED WORKS

21.28A Scope·
AACR2 says: "Apply this rule to separately catalogued works (see also 1.9) that have a relationship to another work."

Continuations and sequels, supplements, indexes, subseries, special numbers of serials, and collections of extracts from serials are of particular concern in documents cataloging. Some examples of these types of publications are the *Serials Supplement to the Monthly Catalog of United States Government Publications, Government Reports Announcements and Index,* and the many subseries published by the Census Bureau.

21.28B General rule[1]

    New York (State). Dept. of Labor.
        Statistics on operations : supplement to the annual report of the New York
        State Dept. of Labor. — Albany : State of New York, Dept. of Labor.
        v. ; 28 cm.

        Description based on: 1972.

      I. New York (State). Dept. of Labor. Annual report. II. Title.

---

1. This rule eliminates the "dash" entry practice provided on page 242 in AACR1.

New York (State). Dept. of Social Welfare.
New York State social statistics. — 1953– 1966. — Albany (112 State St., Albany, N.Y.) : State Dept. of Social Welfare, 1954– 1967.
14v. : ill. ; 23– 28 cm. — (Legislative document)

Annual.
A statistical supplement to the Annual report of the New York State Dept. of Social Welfare.
Continued by: New York State social statistics / New York State Dept. of Social Services.

I. New York (State). Dept. of Social Welfare. Annual report. II. Title. III. Series: State of New York legislative document.

LC rule interpretation says:

> If the item is a collection of *excerpts from a serial,* generally make a related work added entry for the serial only if the serial is mentioned in the chief source of information and all the items in the collection would not be entered under the same heading. If two or more serials are mentioned, make an added entry only for the latest if the titles represent a succession of changes (cf. 21.2C, 21.3B). If the titles represent different serials, make added entries for each if there are no more than three. If four or more different serials are mentioned, generally do not make an added entry for any of them.

Added entries

21.29 GENERAL RULE

This rule is very important because it allows as many additional entries as are needed to serve the user. Although some rules covered earlier in this chapter limit the number of added entries a cataloger may make, the permissiveness of this rule allows additional access points. Notes should be added to the cataloging record to justify added entries if they are not justified by expressions within the bibliographic description (areas 1– 4).

The LC rule interpretation says:

> *Order of added entries.* Give added entries in the following order:
>
> 1) Personal name;
> 2) Personal name/title;
> 3) Corporate name;
> 4) Corporate name/title;
> 5) Uniform title (all instances of works entered under title);
> 6) Title traced as Title-period;
> 7) Title traced as Title-colon, followed by a title;
> 8) Series.
>
> For arrangement within any one of these groupings, generally follow the

order in which the justifying data appears in the bibliographic description. If such a criterion is not applicable, use judgment.

Even though a general material designation (GMD) is given in the title and statement of responsibility area (RI 1.1C), do not use a GMD in added entries, including added entries for titles, series, related works, etc.

21.30 SPECIFIC RULES

21.30A Two or more persons or bodies involved

Although this rule limits the number of added entries by saying "If four or more persons or bodies are involved in a particular instance, make an added entry under the heading for the first named in the source from which the names are taken," rules 21.29D and 21.30F permit additional added entries.

21.30B–21.30D ———

21.30E Corporate bodies

This rule allows added entries for corporate bodies which participate in the creation of works, such as cooperative publications (e.g., a water study done by the United States and Canada), contract reports (e.g., a contract done by a laboratory), sponsors of symposiums, conferences, etc., This rule is important because many studies, contract reports, etc. will be entered under the personal author or title.

LC rule interpretation says:

> If a corporate body is a sponsor of a conference, make an added entry for the body in the following cases:
> 1) when the work is entered under the heading for the conference (21.1B2d) and the body is prominently named;
> 2) when the work is entered under title and the body is named anywhere in the item.
>
> If a prominently named corporate body functions as the issuing body for the series, make an added entry for the body only if it has responsibility for work in addition to its responsibility for the series. In case of doubt, make the added entry.

For items cataloged according to chapters 7 and 8, generally make an added entry for the corporate body named in the publication, distribution, etc., area. /

21.30F Other related persons or bodies
LC rule interpretation says:

> When considering added entries for institution(s) in which an exhibition is held, make an added entry under the heading for each institution if there are three or less, or under the first if there are four or more.

21.30G Related works

LC rule interpretation says:

> Note that an unnumbered supplement or "special number" to a serial is not treated as a series (cf. RI 1.6H) even if it appears in a formal series-like statement. Instead, mention it in a note (if not already recorded in the body of the entry) and make an added entry for the serial itself on the bibliographic record for the analyzable title.
>
> If the supplement or special number relates to the serial as a whole, formulate an added entry consisting of the name of the serial followed by two spaces and either "Supplement" or "Special number" in English:

> Balliol College record. Supplement.

> If a supplement relates to a particular number of a serial, formulate an added entry consisting of the name of the serial, the number (preceded by two spaces), and the qualifier "(Supplement)":

> Actualites-Service. No 306 (Supplement)
> Bulletin (Association francaise pour l'etude du quaternaire). No 50 (Supplement)
> Mondo. N. 33 (Supplement)
> Regione Trentino-Alto Adige. N. 8, 1976 (Supplement)

> If the supplement is to a title for which a series authority record exists, give the numbering in the form specified on the series authority record. This will insure that the added entry for the supplement to a particular number will file in proper relation to any series added entry for that number.

> Actualités-Service ; no 306.
> Actualités-Service. No 306 (Supplement)

> If the supplement relating to a particular number of a serial is itself numbered (in relation to the number of the serial, not the whole serial), formulate the added entry as described above but include the number in the qualification:

> Actualités-Service. No 306 (Supplement 1)
> Actualités-Service. No 306 (Supplement 2)

21.30H– 21.30K ———

21.30L Series

AACR2 says: "Make an added entry under the heading for a series for each separately catalogued work in the series if it provides a useful collocation." LC/GPO will follow the option "adding the numeric or other designation of each work in the series."

LC will follow these guidelines for tracing series:

1. Trace all series in the following categories:
   a) those published before the 20th century, including contemporary reprints of the same, without regard to the type of publisher

    b) those entered under a personal author (note that this means ignoring the third category listed at the top of p. 325 of AACR2)—whether these are monographic series or multipart items, without regard to the type of publisher

    c) those published by any corporate body that is not a commercial publisher. (For this purpose, treat a university press as a noncommercial publisher.)

    d) those published by small or "alternative" presses, i.e., small printing/publishing firms that, though commercial, are devoted to special causes or to branches of literature, usually without a mass audience.

2. Do not trace series in the following categories:

    a) series in which the items are related to each other only by common physical characteristics

    b) series in which the numbering suggests that the parts have been numbered primarily for stock control or to benefit from lower postage rates

    c) series published by a commercial publisher in which the title indicates *primarily* a literary genre, with or without the name of the publisher. (If, however, the title includes words that significantly narrow the focus of the literary genre or that indicate that the series is intended for a specialized audience (e.g., children), it is not primarily indicative of literary genre and should be traced.)

    d) series published by a commercial publisher in which the title conveys little or no information about the content, genre, audience, or purpose of the works in the series.

3. Trace also series:

    a) that fall into both categories 1 and 2 above

    b) in special cases in which the cataloger feels that a useful collocation would be served by creating added entries for the series despite the lack of informative words in the series title

    c) in any case of doubt.

21.30M Analytical entries

Many government publications contain several works. Some catalogers may wish to provide an analytical entry for such works (e.g., law within a hearing, a special report, or bibliography within a larger report).

21.31 LAWS, ETC.

21.31A ———

21.31B Laws of modern jurisdiction

21.31B1 Laws governing one jurisdiction. AACR2 says: "Enter laws governing one jurisdiction under the heading for the jurisdiction governed by them. Make added entries under the headings for persons and corporate bodies (other than legislative bodies) responsible for compiling and issuing the laws. Add a uniform title as instructed in 25.15A to the main entry.''

Argentina.
[Código de comercio (1889)]
Código de comercio de la República Argentina. — Nueva ed. / actualizada y revisada por Apolinar E. García. — Buenos Aires : Sainte Claire Editora, 1979.
462 p. ; 23 cm.

Includes related legislation.

I. Garcia, Apolinar E. II. Title.

United States.
[Federal Insecticide, Fungicide, and Rodenticide Act]
The Federal Insecticide, Fungicide, and Rodenticide Act as amended :
Public Law 92-516, October 21, 1972, as amended by Public Law 94-140, November 28, 1975 / United States Environmental Protection Agency. — Washington, D.C. : EPA, 1976.
22 p. ; 23 cm.

Cover title.
Supt. of Docs. no.: EP 1.5:In7

I. United States. Environmental Protection Agency. II. Title.

California.
[Library Laws]
California library laws 1977 : selections from the California Administrative Code, Education Code, Government Code, and others, relating to public libraries, county law libraries and the State Library / edited by Cy H. Silver, Chief, Library Development Services Bureau, California State Library. — Sacramento (Library and Courts Building, P.O. Box 2037, Sacramento, Calif. 95809) : The Library, 1977.
113 p. ; 23 cm.

Appendix title: California court decisions and attorney generals' opinions relative to libraries.
Distributed under the Library Depository Act.
Includes index.

I. Silver, Cy H., II. California State Library. Library Development Services Bureau. III. Title.

Kansas.
  ₍Discrimination Laws₎
  Kansas Act Against Discrimination (1978). — ₍Topeka?₎ : State of Kansas,
  Commission on Civil Rights, ₍1978?₎.
  29 p. ; 23 cm.
  Cover title.

  I. Kansas. Commission on Civil Rights. II. Title.

Illinois.
  ₍Vehicle Code₎
  1978 Illinois Vehicle Code : as amended through Public Act 80-1055 : under
  same classification as Illinois Revised Statutes, State Bar Association edition
  and Smith-Hurd Illinois Annotated Statutes / ₍issued by₎ Alan J. Dixon,
  Secretary of State. — ₍Springfield, Ill.₎ : Secretary of State, 1978.
  xxii, 270 p. ; 25 cm.

  Reprinted from Chapter 951/2 of the Illinois Revised Statutes 1977.
  Includes index.

  I. Dixon, Alan J. II. Illinois. Secretary of State. III. Title. IV. Title: Illinois
  Vehicle Code.

21.31B2 Laws governing more than one jurisdiction. AACR2 says: "Enter a compilation of laws governing more than one jurisdiction as a collection (see 21.7)."

Compendium of state licensing laws regulating motor vehicle manufactures,
  dealers and salesmen.
  — Washington : National Automobile Dealers Association, ₍1968₎.
  57 p. ; 28 cm.

  Cover title.
  Includes texts of licensing laws of Wisconsin, Tennessee, North Carolina,
  California, and Ohio.

  I. National Automobile Dealers Association.

Canadian occupational safety and health law.
  — ₍Toronto₎ : Corpus, —₍1978₎.
  11 v. (loose-leaf) : ill. ; 30 cm.

  Cover title.
  Includes indexes.
  Contents: ₍1–2₎ Canada — ₍3₎ Alberta— ₍4–5₎ British Columbia — ₍6₎ New

Brunswick — ₍7₎ Nova Scotia — ₍8₎ Ontario — ₍9₎ Prince Edward Island
Newfoundland — ₍10₎ Quebec — ₍11₎ Saskatchewan, Manitoba.

I. Corpus Information Services Limited.

Digest of motor laws. — ₍Washington₎ : American Automobile Association.
v. ; 19 cm.

"Summary of regulations governing registration and operation of passenger
cars in the United States, Canal Zone, Guam, Puerto Rico, Virgin Islands,
and Provinces of Canada."
Description based on: 1973.

I. American Automobile Association.

21.31B3 Bills and drafts of legislation. AACR2 says: "Enter legislative bills under
the heading for the appropriate legislative body (see 24.21). Enter other drafts of
legislation as instructed in 21.1–21.7."

United States. Congress. Senate.
₍Bill 95th Congress, S.1437₎
A bill to codify, revise and reform title 18 of the United States Code, and for
other purposes / introduced by Mr. McClellan for himself and Mr. Kennedy. — Washington : United States Congress Senate, 1977.
308 p. ; 28 cm.

Citation title: Criminal Code Reform Act of 1977.

I. McClellan, John L. II. Kennedy, Edward M. III. Title. IV. Title: Criminal
Code Reform Act of 1977.

21.31C ———

21.32   ADMINISTRATIVE REGULATIONS, ETC.

21.32A   Administrative regulations, etc., promulgated by government agencies

21.32A1 AACR2 says: "If administrative regulations, rules, etc., are from jurisdictions
in which such regulations, etc., are promulgated by government agencies or agents
under authority granted by one or more laws (as is the case in the United States), enter
them under the heading for the agency or the agent. If the regulations, etc., are issued
by an agency other than the promulgating agency, make an added entry under the
heading for the issuing agency. If the regulations, etc., derive from a particular law,
make an added entry under the heading and uniform title (see 25.15A) for that law."

New Mexico. Mining and Minerals Division.
　　State of New Mexico surface coal mining regulations. Rule 80-1 / adopted
　　by the New Mexico Coal Surface Mining Commission, May 15, 1980 ;
　　administered and enforced by the Mining and Minerals Division of the
　　Energy and Minerals Dept. — Santa Fe, N.M. : The Division, [1980].
　　xvi, 262 p. ; 28 cm.

　　"Rule 80-1 supersedes Rule 79-1 filed July 11, 1979, by the Mining and
　　Minerals Division of the Energy and Minerals Department."
　　"July 1980."

I. New Mexico Coal Surface Mining Commission. II. Title.

Iowa. State Dept. of Health.
　　Rules governing Radiation Emitting Equipment, State Department of
　　Health : 136C, the Code. — Des Moines : State of Iowa, 1980.
　　vii, 45 p. ; 28 cm.

　　Issued by: Radiological Health and Work-related Disease Section, Division
　　of Disease Prevention, Iowa State Dept. of Health.

I. Iowa. Radiological Health and Work-related Disease Section. II. Iowa.
Radiation Emitting Equipment. III. Title.

New Mexico. Construction Industries Division. Mechanical Bureau. 1979 New
　　Mexico Uniform solar energy code. — [Santa Fe, N.M.] : Commerce and
　　Industry Dept., Construction Industries Division, Mechanical Bureau,
　　[1980?].
　　[35] leaves ; 28 cm.

　　Cover title.

I. Title. II. Title: New Mexico Uniform solar energy code.

Kansas. Commission on Civil Rights.
　　Rules and regulations. — Topeka (535 Kansas Ave., Topeka, Kan. 66603) :
　　State of Kansas, Commission on Civil Rights, [1978 or 1979].
　　65 p. ; 22 cm.

　　Authorized by Kansas Statutes Annotated, Chapter 44 Article 10: Kansas
　　Acts Against Discrimination.

I. Kansas. Kansas Act Against Discrimination.

21.32A2 AACR2 says: "If a law or laws and the regulations, etc., derived from it are
published together, enter the item under the heading appropriate to whichever is
mentioned first in the title elements. Make an added entry under the heading for the

other. If only the law(s) or only the regulations, etc., are named in the title proper, enter under the heading appropriate to the one mentioned. Make an added entry under the heading for the other. If the evidence of the chief source of information is ambiguous or insufficient, enter under the heading for the law(s) and make an added entry under the heading for the regulations, etc.''

> Oregon.
> ₁Revenue and Taxation Laws₁
> 1965 State of Oregon personal income and corporation income and excise tax laws and regulations / regulations promulgated by the Oregon State Tax Commission. — Salem, Or. : Oregon State Tax Commission, 1965.
> x, 175, ₁128₁ p. ; 28 cm.
>
> Chapters 305, 314, 316, 317 and 318, Oregon Revised Statutes, including all amendments through Oregon Laws, 1965.
> Includes index.
>
> I. Oregon State Tax Commission. II. Title. III. Title: Personal income and corporate income and excise tax laws and regulations.

21.32B ———

21.32C AACR2 says: "Enter a collection of regulations enacted by more than one agency or agent as a collection (see 21.7)."

> Federal consumer protection : laws, rules, and regulations / compiled and edited by Bernard D. Reams, Jr., and J. Ray Ferguson. — Dobbs Ferry, N.Y. : Oceana Publications, 1978– .
> 2 v. (loose-leaf) ; 27 cm.
>
> I. Reams, Bernard D. II. Ferguson, J. Ray. III. United States. Laws, etc.

> 1974 administrative rules of South Dakota : comprised of administrative rules of a general and permanent nature filed with the Secretary of State on or before July 31, 1974. — ₁Pierre₁ : South Dakota Code Commission, ₁1974– ₁.
> v. ; ill. ; 26 cm.
>
> Kept up to date by cumulative supplements and loose-leaf vols.
>
> I. South Dakota Code Commission. II. Title: Administrative rules of South Dakota.

> Ohio administrative code : rules of the administrative agencies of the state of Ohio. — Approved ed. — Cleveland : Banks-Baldwin Law Pub. Co., c1977– .
> v. (loose-leaf) ; 28 cm.
>
> Includes indexes.
>
> I. Banks-Baldwin Law Publishing Company.

21.33 CONSTITUTIONS, CHARTERS, AND OTHER FUNDAMENTAL LAWS

21.33A AACR2 says: "Enter the constitution, charter, or other fundamental law of a jurisdiction under the heading for that jurisdiction."

> Honolulu (Hawaii).
> Revised charter of the city & county of Honolulu 1973. — Honolulu : Dept. of the Corporation Counsel, c1973.
> v, 92 p. ; 23 cm.
>
> ". . . revised by the Charter Commission in 1972 and approved at the General Election on November 7, 1972. Practically all of the provisions became effective as of the second day of January 1973" — Foreword. Includes a table of opinions pertaining to the original Charter (Act 261, Session Laws of Hawaii 1959).
> Includes index.
>
> I. Honolulu (Hawaii). Dept. of the Corporation Counsel. II. Honolulu (Hawaii). Charter Commission. III. Title.

> New Mexico.
> ₁Constitution₁
> The Constitution of the state of New Mexico : as adopted January 21, 1911, and as subsequently amended by the people in general and special elections, 1912 through 1980. — ₁Santa Fe₁ : Shirley Hooper, Secretary of State, ₁1981₁.
> 98 p. ; 16 cm.
>
> "January, 1981."
>
> I. New Mexico. Secretary of State. II. Title.

> Kansas.
> ₁Constitution₁
> Constitution of the state of Kansas : with amendments / issued by Elwill M. Shanahan, Secretary of State. — Topeka, Kan. : Secretary of State, 1977.
> 38 p. ; 23 cm.
>
> List of amendments arranged chronologically: p.31–38.
>
> I. Shanahan, Elwill M. II. Kansas. Secretary of State. III. Title.

21.33B ———

21.33C Drafts

AACR2 says: "If a draft of a constitution, charter, etc., is a legislative bill, enter it under the heading for the appropriate legislative body (see 24.21). Enter all other drafts of such documents as instructed in 21.1–21.7."

> New York (State). Constitutional Convention (1967)
> Text, abstract and highlights of proposed Constitution of the state of New York to be submitted to the electors of the state on November 7, 1967 / 1967 New York State Constitutional Convention — ₁Albany? N.Y.₁ : The Convention, 1967.
> xv, 73 p. ; 28 cm.
>
> Cover title: Your proposed new constitution : text, abstract and highlights.
>
> I. Title. II. Title: Your proposed new constitution.

21.34 COURT RULES

21.34A AACR2 says: "Enter court rules governing a single court (regardless of their official nature, e.g., laws, administrative regulations) under the heading for that court."

> Illinois. Appellate Court (3rd District)
> Rules of practice of the Appellate Court, Third District, State of Illinois : adopted April 12, 1928. — ₁S.l. : s.n., 1928?₁ (₁Girard : Goode Printshops₁) 60 p., ₁1₁ ; 15 cm.
>
> "List of attorneys in Third District of Illinois": p. 29–₁61₁
>
> I. Title.

> Hawaii. Supreme Court.
> District Court rules of civil procedure / adopted and promulgated by the Supreme Court of the State of Hawaii, November 8, 1971, effective January 1, 1972. — Honolulu : Supreme Court, ₁1972₁.
> xiii, 53 p. ; 25 cm.
>
> I. Title.

21.34B– 21.34C ———

21.35 TREATIES, INTERGOVERNMENTAL AGREEMENTS, ETC.

21.35A International treaties, etc.

21.35A1 AACR2 says:

> Enter a treaty, or any other formal agreement, between two or three national governments under (in this order of preference):

  a) the heading for the government on one side if it is the only one on that
     side and there are two governments on the other
  b) the heading for the government whose catalogue entry heading (see
     24.3E) is first in English alphabetic order.

Make added entries under the headings for the other government(s). Add a uniform
title (see 25.16B1) to the main and added entries.

    Brazil.
      ₍Treaties, etc., Canada, 1975 Apr. 2₎
      Economic co-operation : agreement between Canada and Brazil, Brazilia,
      April 2, 1975 = Cooperation economique : accord entre le Canada et le
      Brasil, Brasilia, le 2 avril 1975. — Ottawa : Queen's Printer for Canada,
      1976.
      12 p. ; 25 cm. — (Treaty Series = Recueil des Traites / Canada ; 1976 No.
      10)

      English and French.
      Instruments of ratification exchanged January 6, 1976; in force January 6,
      1976.
      ISBN 0-660-00541-7 : $0.50 ($0.60 in other countries)
      Catalogue no.: E3-1976/10

      I. Canada. Treaties, etc. Brazil, 1975 Apr. 2. II. Title. III. Series: Treaty series
      (Canada); 1976, No. 10.

21.35A2 AACR2 says: "Enter a treaty, or any formal agreement, between more than
three national governments under title . . . ."

      International Convention for the Prevention of Pollution of the Sea by Oil,
         Revision, 1962. French & English.
      International Convention for the Prevention of Pollution of the Sea by Oil,
      1954 : including the amendments adopted in 1962 = Convention internatio-
      nale pour la prevention de la pollution des eaux de la mer par les hydrocar-
      bures, 1954, y compris les amendements adoptés en 1962. — London :
      Inter-governmental Maritime Consultative Organization, ₍1972₎.
      77 p. ; 24 cm.

      English and French.
      Contains the text of the international convention for the prevention of
      pollution of the sea by oil, 1954, and the annexes thereto as amended by the

International Conference on Prevention of Pollution of the Sea by Oil 1962, together with the resolutions adopted by that Conference.

I. International Conference on Prevention of Pollution of the Sea by Oil (1962 : London, England). II. Great Britain. Treaties, etc., 1954, Mar. 3. Protocols, etc., 1954 Mar. 3. III. United States. Treaties, etc., 1954, Mar. 3. Protocols, etc., 1954 Mar. 3.

21.35B Agreements contracted by international intergovernmental bodies

UNICEF.
ₗTreaties, etc., United States, 1977 May 4, 11ₗ
Agricultural commodities : transfer under Title II : agreement between the United States of America and the United Nations Children's Fund, signed at Washington and New York, May 4 and 11, 1977
75 p. ; 25 cm. — (Treaties and other international acts series ; 9100)

Supt. of Docs. class no.: S9.10:9100

I. United States. Treaties, etc., UNICEF, 1977 May 4, 11. II. Title. III. Series.

Austria.
ₗTreaties, etc., European Economic Community, 1972 July 22ₗ
Agreement between the European Economic Community and the Republic of Austria with final act and exchange of letters, Brussels, 22 July 1972 / Presented to Parliament by the Secretary of State for Foreign and Commonwealth Affairs by command of Her Majesty. — London : H.M.S.O., 1972. 124 p. ; 25 cm. (Miscellaneous ; no. 49 (1972)) (Cmnd. 5159)

"The agreement is not in force."

I. European Economic Community. Treaties, etc., Austria, 1972 July 22.
II. Title. III. Series: Miscellaneous (Great Britain. Foreign and Commonwealth Office); 1977, No. 49.

21.35C ———

21.35D Agreements contracted by jurisdictions below the national level

21.35D1 AACR2 says: "Enter an agreement between two or more jurisdictions below the national level, or between a national government and one or more jurisdictions within its country, as instructed in 21.6C."

France.
ₗTreaties, etc., Great Britain, 1973 Nov. 17ₗ

Treaty between the United Kingdom of Great Britain and Northern Ireland
and the French Republic concerning the construction and operation of a
railway tunnel system under the English Channel (with exchanges of notes
and letters and agreements No. 2, 17 November 1973. — London ;
H.M.S.O., 1973.
xxxv, 192 p. ; 25 cm. — (France No. 1, 1973) (Cmd. 5486)

English and French.
"Instruments of ratification have not been exchanged."

I. Great Britain. Treaties, etc., France, 1973 Nov. 17.

21.35D2 ———

21.35D3 ———

21.35E Protocols, amendments, etc.

Universal Postal convention (1964). Protocols, etc., 1974 July 5
Universal Postal Union : second additional protocol to the constitution,
convention, and related documents between the United States of America
and other governments done at Lausanne July 5, 1974, with English text of
the constitution signed at Vienna July 10, 1964, as amended, and final
protocol. — Washington : U.S. Dept. of State : For sale by the Supt. of
Docs., U.S. G.P.O., 1976.
[2], 450 p. ; 24 cm. — (Treaties and other international acts series ; 8231)

English and French.
"Entered into force Jan. 1, 1976."
Item 899.

I. United States. Dept. of State. II. United States. Treaties, etc., 1974 July 5.
III. Title. IV. Series.

21.35F Collections

21.35F1 AACR2 says: "If a collection of treaties, etc., consists of those contracted
between two parties, enter it in the same way as a single agreement between those two
parties . . . ."

Soviet Union.
[Treaties, etc., United States]
U.S.-Soviet commercial agreements, 1972 : text, summaries, and supporting
papers. — Washington : U.S. Dept. of Commerce, Domestic and Interna-

tional Business Administration, Bureau of East-West Trade : For sale by the
Supt. of Docs., U.S. G.P.O., 1973.
v, 107 p. ; 26 cm.

Supt. of Docs. Class. No.: C 57.402:So8/972.

I. United States. Treaties, etc., Soviet Union. II. United States. Bureau of
East-West Trade. III. Title.

Add a uniform title (see 25.16A) to the main and added entries for the two parties.

European Economic Community.
   ₁Treaties, etc., Greece.₁
   Association between the European Economic Community and Greece :
   collected acts. — ₁Luxembourg₁ : Secretariat of the Council of the European
   Communities, ₁1973?— ₁
   v. (loose-leaf) ; 31 cm.

I. Greece. Treaties, etc., European Economic Community. II. Title.

21.35F2 AACR2 says: ''If a collection of treaties, etc., consists of those contracted
between one party and two or more parties, enter it under the heading for the one
party.''

European Economic Community.
   ₁Treaties, etc.₁
   Association between the European Economic Community and the United
   Republic of Tanzania, the Republic of Uganda and the Republic of Kenya:
   collected acts. — ₁Luxembourg₁ : Secretariat of the Council of the European
   Communities ₁1970?— ₁
   1 v. (loose-leaf) ; 31 cm.

I. Tanzania. Treaties, etc. II. Uganda. Treaties, etc. III. Kenya. Treaties, etc.
IV. Council of the European Communities.

United States.
   ₁Treaties, etc.₁
   Treaties and other international agreements on fisheries, oceanographic resources, and wildlife involving the United States / prepared at the request of
   Warren G. Magnuson for the use of the Committee on Commerce, Science,
   and Transportation, United States Senate, by the Congressional Research
   Service, the Library of Congress. — Washington : U.S. G.P.O., 1977.
   xv, 1201 p. ; 24 cm.

At head of title: 95th Congress, 1st session. Committee print.
"October 31, 1977."
Supt. of Docs./class no.: Y 4.C73/7:F53

I. United States. Congress. Senate. Committee on Commerce, Science, and
Transportation. II. Library of Congress. Congressional Research Service.
III. Title.

United States.
  ₍Treaties, etc.₎
  Tax treaties : full texts of U.S. treaties with foreign countries covering
  income and estate taxes, alphabetically arranged, including annotations and
  regulations, current reports of new developments, finding lists : fully indexed. — Chicago, Ill. : Commerce Clearing House, c1965.
  2 v. (loose-leaf) ; 25 cm. — (Topical law reports)

I. Title.

21.36   COURT DECISIONS, CASES, ETC.

21.36A Law reports

21.36A1 Reports of one court
New Jersey Tax Court reports.
  — Vol. 1, no. 1 (Oct. 1980)— — St. Paul, Minn. : West Pub. Co.,
  ₍C1980– ₎
  v. ; 23 cm.

Bimonthly.
Title from cover.
ISSN 0279-6481 = New Jersey Tax Court reports.

I. New Jersey. Tax Court. II. West Publishing Company.

21.36A2 Reports of more than one court

Reports of cases in criminal law argued and determined in all the courts in
England and Ireland, 1843/46– 1939/40 / edited by Edward W. Cox. —
London : J. Crockford, Law Times Office, 1846– . (London : Butterworth's)
  v. ; 24 cm.

I. Cox, Edward William, 1809– 1879

21.36B Citations, digests, etc.

> West's New York digest, 3d. — St. Paul, Minn. :
> West Pub. Co., c1979–
> v. ; 26 cm.
>
> "Key number digest covers new York State and Federal cases decided since
> 1961."
> Previous editions published under title: Abbott New York digest.
> Kept up to date by Pocket Supplements.
>
> I. West Publishing Company. II. Title: Abbott New York Digest.

> West's Pacific digest, beginning 367 P.2d. — St. Paul, Minn. : West Pub. Co.,
> c1979–c1981.
> 60 v. ; 26 cm.
>
> Supplements the Pacific digest, covering v. 101–366, Pacific reporter, 2nd
> ser., 1940–1962, the Pacific digest, Covering v. 1–100, Pacific reporter,
> 2nd ser., 1931–1940, and the Pacific digest, covering v. 1–300, Pacific
> reporter; and the pre-reporter decisions, 1850–1931.
> Kept up to date by pocket parts and cumulative supplements.
>
> I. West Publishing Company. II. Title: Pacific digest. III. Title: Pacific re-
> porter, 2nd ser.

> West's California digest, 2d. — St. Paul, Minn. : West Pub. Co., c1981–
> v. ; 27 cm.
>
> "Covers state and federal cases decided since 1950" — Pref.
> "West key number system."
> Includes bibliographical references.
>
> I. West Publishing Company. II. Title: California digest, 2d.

21.36C Particular cases
AACR2 says: "Optionally, add the appropriate legal designation (e.g., *defendant,
libelee*) to headings for persons or bodies prosecuted."
LC/GPO are not exercising this option under rules 21.36C1 to 21.36C5.

21.36C1 Proceedings in the first instance. Criminal proceedings

> Anthony, Susan Brownell, 1820–1890.
> An account of the proceedings on the trial of Susan B. Anthony on
> the charge of illegal voting at the presidential election in Nov., 1872. —

New York : Arno Press, 1974.
vii, 212 p. ; 23 cm. — (Women in America : from colonial times to the 20th century)

Reprint. Originally published: Rochester, N.Y.: Daily Democrat and Chronicle Book Print, [1874]

I. Title. II. Series: Women in America.

Bryant, Stephen A.
    The trial of Dr. Stephen A. Bryant, William Bryant,and James Dobbins, for the murder of Shelby Butler, tried in Circuit Court, March term, 1860, Hon. Wm. S. Mudd, judge / stenographically reported by M. H. Wood. — Tuskaloosa : Printed at the "Observer" office, 1860.
    95 p. ; 22 cm.

I. Bryant, William. II. Dobbins, James. III. Wood, M. H. IV. Alabama. Circuit Court (3rd District). V. Title.

Jenrette, John W.
    Excerpts from the transcript of trial proceedings in the case of the United States of America v. John W. Jenrette, Jr., in the United States District Court for the District of Columbia, Crim No. 80-289 / prepared for the use of the Committee on Standards of Official Conduct, House of Representatives, 96th Congress, second session. — Washington : U.S. G.P.O., 1980.
    5 v. ; 24 cm.

Supt of Docs. class no.: Y 4.St2/3:T73/pt.1-5

I. United States. Congress. House. Committee on Standards of Official Conduct. II. United States. District Court (District of Columbia).

21.36C2 Proceedings in the first instance. Other proceedings

Weisberg, Harold, 1913–
    The legal proceedings of Harold Weisberg v. General Services Administration, civil action 2051-73 : together with the January 22 and 27 Warren Commission transcripts / David R. Wrone, editor. — Stevens Point, Wis. : Foundation Press, c1978.
    xii, 249 p. ; 23 cm. — (The Freedom of Information Act and political assassinations ; v. 1)

Suit filed in the U.S. District Court for the District of Columbia, Nov. 13, 1973.

Bibliography: p. 239–240.
Includes index.

I. Wrone, David R. II. United States. General Services Administration, defendant. III. Warren Commission. IV. United States. District Court (District of Columbia) V. Title. VI. Series.

Prigg, Edward.
Report of the case of Edward Prigg against the Commonwealth of Pennsylvania : argued and adjudged in the Supreme Court of the United States, at January term, 1842 . . . / by Richard Peters. — Westport, Conn. : Negro Universities Press, ₍1970₎.
140 p. ; 213 cm.

Reprint. originally published: 1842.

I. Peters, Richard, 1780–1848. II. United States. Supreme Court. III. Pennsylvania. IV. Title.

21.36C3 Appeal proceedings

New York Times Company.
New York Times Company v. United States : a documentary history of the Pentagon papers litigation / compiled and with an introd. by James C. Goodale, general counsel. — ₍New York₎ : Arno Press, ₍1971₎.
2 v. (xiv, 1298 p.) : facsims. ; 32 cm.

"A complete record of this case, arranged chronologically, starting with the motion by the Government on June 15, 1971, in Federal Court, for a temporary restraining order and ending with the opinion of the Supreme Court on June 30, 1971. Contains all the legal papers and briefs filed in the District Court, as well as transcripts of all arguments except for those proceedings held in camera. Also included are reprints of articles in the Times covering this case and the companion case, United States v. The Washington Post Company et al."

I. Goodale, James C., 1933– . II. New York Times. III. United States. IV. United States. District Court (New York (State) V. United States. Court of Appeals (2nd Circuit). VI. United States. Supreme Court. VII. Title.

Bakke, Allan.
Regents of the University of California v. Allan Bakke : complete case record. — Englewood, Colo. : Information Handling Services, c1978.
3 v. ; 24 cm. — (United States Supreme Court records & briefs, landmark cases)

Includes bibliographical references and index.
ISBN 0-910972-91-5 : $160.00

I. University of California, Berkeley. II. United States. Supreme Court.
III. Title. IV. Series.

21.36C6 Judicial decisions

European Court of Human Rights.
Affaire Luedicke, Belkacem et Koc : arrêt du 10 mars 1980, article 50 =
Case of Luedicke, Belkacem and Koc : judgment of 10 March 1980, article
50. Affaire König : arrêt du 10 mars 1980, article 50 = König case :
judgment of 10 March 1980, article 50. — Strasbourg : Greffe de la Cour,
Conseil de l'Éurope ; Koln : C. Heymanns, 1980.
20, 20 p. ; 24 cm. — (Publications de la Cour européenne des droits de
l'homme. Série A, Arrêts et décisions ; v. 36 = Publications of the European Court of Human Rights. Series A, Judgments and decisions ; v. 36)

French and English.

I. Luedicke, Gerhard W. II. Belkacem, Mohamed, 1954– . III. Koc, Arif,
1940– . IV. Konig, Eberhard, 1918– . V. European Court of Human Rights.
Affaire Konig. VI. Title. VII. Title: Case of Luedicke, Belkacem, and Koc.
VIII. Title: Affaire Konig. IX. Series: Publications de la Cour européenne des
droits de l'homme. Series A, Arrêts et décisions ; v. 36.

21.37–21.39 ———

23/ Geographic Names

Chapter 23 contains the rules for establishing geographic names. Although geographic names can be added to corporate bodies as qualifiers or be used as the names of headings for governments, these rules are covered in chapter 24.

Chapter 23 provides instructions for choosing the correct form of geographic name. This form is based mainly on language. The English form of a place name is preferred if there is one in general use. Since AACR2 does not recommend any English-language geographical reference sources for librarians to use, a list of gazetteers and atlases has been included in this manual.

Chapter 23 also provides detailed instructions for making modifications and additions to geographic names. Special provisions apply for qualifying names of places in the United States, Canada, Australia, the British Isles, the Soviet Union, Malaysia, Yugoslavia, and on islands that are jurisdictions. These instructions have been further expanded in this manual with numerous examples to show clearly how LC/GPO are applying the options.

The rules and examples in chapter 23 apply only to geographic names which can be used as the names of political jurisdictions (e.g., countries, administrative regions, cities, etc.). Chapter 23, and AACR2 in general, does not cover other types of geographic headings (e.g., continents, mountains, rivers, lakes, etc.). Because these geographic names are not capable of authorship but can only be used as subject headings, their treatment in a descriptive cataloging manual like AACR2 is not appropriate. For establishing physical features and other similar geographic headings, librarians should consult a comprehensive subject cataloging manual (e.g., *Library of Congress Subject Cataloging Manual*) for guidance.

23.1———

23.2   GENERAL RULES

23.2A   English form
Use the English form of a place name if there is one in general use. Determine this by consulting English-language gazetteers and other geographical reference sources. The following gazetteers and atlases are recommended.

172

Gazetteer of Conventional Names : Names Approved by the United States
Board on Geographic Names. 2nd ed. Washington, D.C. : Defense Mapping
Agency, 1977

National Geographic Society (U.S.). Cartographic Division. National Geographic Atlas of the World. 5th ed. Washington, D.C. : National Geographic
Society, 1981

Rand McNally and Company. The New International Atlas. Chicago : Rand
McNally & Company, c 1983

The Times Atlas of the World. Comprehensive ed. New York : Times Books,
c 1983

The Times Index-Gazetteer of the World. London : Times Publishing Co.,
1965

Webster's New Geographical Dictionary. Springfield, Mass. : G. & C. Mer-
riam Co., c 1980

For verifying place names in the United States (e.g., cities, counties, townships,
etc.), consult a recent edition of the *Rand McNally Commercial Atlas & Marketing
Guide*. LC/GPO are using this source for establishing U.S. place names.

For foreign place names, LC/GPO are using the form of name approved by the
United States Board on Geographic Names (BGN). For the following place names,
however, LC/GPO are using the English form of the name even though BGN approves
only a vernacular form.

Amoy *(China)*	**Heilungkiang Province** *(China)*
Anhwei Province *(China)*	**Hesse** *(Germany)*
Bavaria *(Germany)*	**Hokkaido** *(Japan)*
Bruges *(Belgium)*	**Honan Province** *(China)*
Canton *(China)*	**Hopeh Province** *(China)*
Carinthia *(Austria)*	**Hunan Province** *(China)*
Chekiang Province *(China)*	**Hupeh Province** *(China)*
Crete	**Inner Mongolia** *(China)*
Dairen *(China)*	**Istanbul** *(Turkey)*
East Flanders *(Belgium)*	**Jaffa** *(Israel)*
Fukien Province *(China)*	**Kalgan** *(China)*
Ghent *(Belgium)*	**Kansu Province** *(China)*
Harbin *(China)*	**Kiangsi Province** *(China)*

Kiangsu Province *(China)*

Kirin *(China)*

Kwangsi Chuang Autonomous Region *(China)*

Kwangtung Province *(China)*

Kweichow Province *(China)*

Kyoto *(Japan)*

Liaoning Province *(China)*

Louvain *(Belgium)*

Lower Austria *(Austria)*

Lower Saxony *(Germany)*

Malacca *(Malacca)*

Mantua *(Italy)*

Mexico City *(Mexico)*

Ningsia Hui Autonomous Region *(China)*

North Brabant *(Netherlands)*

North Holland *(Netherlands)*

North Rhine-Westphalia *(Germany)*

Nuremberg *(Germany)*

Osaka *(Japan)*

Padua *(Italy)*

Peking *(China)*

Piraeus *(Greece)*

Port Arthur *(China)*

Rhineland-Palatinate *(Germany)*

Saint Gall *(Switzerland)*

Seville *(Spain)*

Shanghai *(China)*

Shansi Province *(China)*

Shantung Province *(China)*

Shensi Province *(China)*

Sian *(China)*

Sicily

Sinkiang Province *(China)*

South Holland *(Netherlands)*

Styria *(Austria)*

Swatow *(China)*

Syracuse *(Sicily)*

Szechwan Province *(China)*

Tehran *(Iran)*

Tibet *(China)*

Tientsin *(China)*

Tsinan *(China)*

Tsinghai Province *(China*

Tsingtao *(China)*

Tsitsihar *(China)*

Turin *(Italy)*

Upper Austria *(Austria)*

West Flanders *(Belgium)*

Yunnan Province *(China)*

Zurich *(Switzerland)*

LC/rule interpretation says: "If a foreign place name is established in an English form, use the same form whenever the name is used by more than one jurisdictional level or is used as part of another place name."

> **Venice** *(Italy)*
> **Venice** *(Italy : Province)*
>
> *not*   Venezia *(Italy : Province)*

> **Warsaw** *(Poland)*
> **Warsaw** *(Poland : Voivodeship)*
>
> *not*   Warszawa *(Poland : Voivodeship)*

> **Cologne** *(Germany)*
> **Cologne-Deutz** *(Cologne, Germany)*
>
> *not*   Köln-Deutz *(Cologne, Germany)*

LC/GPO are not using *Union of Soviet Socialist Republics* as the English form of the name as indicated in AACR2 rule 23.2A, but are using instead the short form *Soviet Union*. BGN approves both forms.

For the United Kingdom, LC/GPO are continuing to use *Great Britain* as the heading. (The British Library has decided to do the same.)

If a place name contains the abbreviation *St.* for *Saint* or *Mt.* for *Mount*, LC/GPO are using the spelled out form regardless of how the name appears in a reference source or on the item being cataloged (unless BGN approves the abbreviated form).

> **Saint Louis** *(Mo.)*
>
> *not*   St. Louis *(Mo.)*

> **Mount Wellington** *(N.Z.)*
>
> *not*   Mt. Wellington *(N.Z.)*

23.2B Vernacular form

23.2B1 If there is no English form of a place name in general use, or, in case of doubt, use the form in the official language of the country (i.e., vernacular form).

23.2B2 According to AACR2, "If the country has more than one official language, use the form most commonly found in English-language sources." Consult the gazetteers and atlases listed in 23.2A in this manual.

23.3   CHANGES OF NAME

If the name of a place changes, use as many of the names as are required by the various rules in Chapter 24.

23.4 ADDITIONS TO PLACE NAMES

23.4A Punctuation
AACR2 says: ''Make all additions to place names used as entry elements in paren-theses.''

Chicago *(Ill.)*

''If the place name is being used as an addition, precede the name of a larger place by a comma.''

Loyola University *(Chicago, Ill.)*
not   Loyola University *(Chicago (Ill.))*

23.4B General rule
The rule in AACR2 says:

> If it is necessary to distinguish between two or more places of the same name (including place names that are the same when romanized), add to each name the name of a larger place as instructed in 23.4C– 23.4J.

LC rule interpretation says:

> When adding the name of a larger place as a qualifier, use the heading for the current name of the larger place [e.g., Zimbabwe, not Southern Rhodesia; Sri Lanka, not Ceylon; etc.]. If the smaller place existed when the larger place had an earlier name, make a reference from the form that shows the earlier name of the larger place if the qualifier is appropriate for the smaller place. (Do not make such a reference for places in the British Isles.)

Colombo *(Sri Lanka)*
   x Colombo *(Ceylon)*

Porto-Novo *(Benin)*
   x Porto-Novo *(Dahomey)*

If the smaller place has changed its name or has ceased to exist, use as a qualifier the name the larger place had during the period in which the name of the smaller place is applicable.

Tananarive *(Malagasy Republic)*
Antananarivo *(Madagascar)*
   (When the Malagasy Republic changed its name to Madagascar in 1975, the city of Tananarive was renamed Antananarivo.)

LC/GPO are conditionally exercising the first option given in AACR2 23.4B. LC/ GPO are adding the name of a larger place as the qualifier to all cities and towns and other local places, even if there is no need to distinguish between places, and regardless of how large or well-known the city or town is.

> **San Francisco** *(Calif.)*
>
> **Dar es Salaam** *(Tanzania)*
>
> **Paris** *(France)*
>
> **Tallahassee** *(Fla.)*

LC/GPO, however, are not adding a qualifier to cities and other local places that prior to 1967 were in Jordan or Syria and that are currently within the administered territories of Israel. In addition, the city of Jerusalem is not qualified.

> **Jerusalem**

LC/GPO are treating military installations (e.g., forts, bases, camps, airfields, etc.) as local places. LC/GPO are adding the name of the larger place in which the military installation is located as the qualifier. This provision is followed even if the installation is located in a country that does not control it (e.g., a U.S. military base in a foreign country). References are made from the name of the installation as a subheading of the country which controls it and as a subheading of the military branch to which it belongs. (Under AACR1, military installations were treated strictly as corporate bodies and were generally not qualified by a larger place.)

> **Randolph Air Force Base** *(Tex.)*
> *x* United States. *Randolph Air Force Base*
> *x* United States. *Air Force. Randolph Air Force Base*
>
> **Yokosuka Naval Base** *(Japan)*
> *x* United States. *Yokosuka Naval Base*
> *x* United States. *Navy. Yokosuka Naval Base*
> *(U.S. military installation in Japan)*

LC/GPO are also adding the name of a larger place as a qualifier to all other places below the national level *except* to the name of a state, province, or territory in Australia, Canada, or the United States; of a county, region, or islands area in the British Isles (other than the counties of Northern Ireland); of a constituent state of Malaysia, the Soviet Union, or Yugoslavia; or of an island that is a jurisdiction.

> **New South Wales**
> *not*   New South Wales *(Australia)*
>
> **Manitoba**
> *not*   Manitoba *(Canada)*

Tennessee
not   Tennessee *(U.S.)*

Humberside
not   Humberside *(England)*

Kelantan
not   Kelantan *(Malaysia)*

Armenian S.S.R.
not   Armenian S.S.R. *(Soviet Union)*

Serbia
not   Serbia *(Yugoslavia)*

Réunion
not   Réunion *(France)*

LC/GPO are fully exercising the second option given in AACR2 23.4B. If the name of a state, province, or territory of Australia, Canada, or the United States; of a county, region, or islands area in the British Isles (other than the counties of Northern Ireland); of a constituent state of Malaysia, the Soviet Union, or Yugoslavia; or of an island that is a jurisdiction is being used as a qualifier, do not add to it the name of its larger geographic area.

Melbourne *(Vic.)*
not   Melbourne *(Vic., Australia)*

Halifax *(N.S.)*
not   Halifax *(N.S., Canada)*

Austin *(Tex.)*
not   Austin *(Tex., U.S.)*

Tolworth *(Surrey)*
not   Tolworth *(Surrey, England)*

Kuantan *(Pahang)*
not   Kuantan *(Pahang, Malaysia)*

Moscow *(R.S.F.S.R.)*
not   Moscow *(R.S.F.S.R., Soviet Union)*

Ljubljana *(Slovenia)*
not   Ljubljana *(Slovenia, Yugoslavia)*

Fort-de-France *(Martinique)*
not   Fort-de-France *(Martinique, France)*

23.4C Places in Australia, Canada, or the United States
If a place is in a state, province, or territory in Australia, Canada, or the United

States, add the name of the state, province, or territory in which the place is located as the qualifier.

Alice Springs *(N.T.)*

Canberra *(A.C.T.)*

Ottawa *(Ont.)*

Ponce *(P.R.)*

Sacramento *(Calif.)*

Whitehorse *(Yukon)*

23.4D Places in the British Isles

23.4D1 Counties, etc. LC/GPO are not adding the name of a larger place as the qualifier to the name of a county, region, or islands area in the British Isles (other than the counties of Northern Ireland) in accordance with the options in 23.4B. The following examples given in AACR2 are restated here accordingly.

Dorset
not Dorset *(England)*

Clare
not Clare *(Ireland)*

Strathclyde
not Strathclyde *(Scotland)*

Powys
not Powys *(Wales)*

but **Tyrone** *(Northern Ireland)*
not Tyrone
    (Former county in Northern Ireland)

An exception is made for the name of a county in England or a region or islands area in Scotland that is composed entirely of a phrase indicating orientation. The county, region, or islands area is qualified by either *England* or *Scotland* as appropriate.

West Midlands *(England)*
not West Midlands

Central Region *(Scotland)*
not Central Region

179

23.4D2 Other places (other than places in cities). For other places (other than places in cities) in the British Isles, follow the instructions in AACR2. If a place is in England, Wales, or the Republic of Ireland, add the name of the county in which the place is located as the qualifier. If a place is in Scotland, add the name of the region or islands area in which the place is located as the qualifier. If a place is in Northern Ireland, add *Northern Ireland* as the qualifier.

23.4D3 Places that bear the names of jurisdictions in the United Kingdom that have ceased to exist. AACR2 says:

> If a place (other than a county) located in the United Kingdom bears a name that is also that of a jurisdiction that has ceased to exist, add the name of the geographic county in which the place was located when it was a jurisdiction.

When determining if a place bears the name of a jurisdiction in the United Kingdom that has ceased to exist, consult a recent edition of the *Municipal Year Book and Public Services Directory*.[1] If the place name is not listed in the directory as a county, district, London borough, parish, or community (Wales), it no longer exists as a jurisdiction.

For London, England, LC/GPO are using the following headings:

Corporation of London
(As the name of the government that has administrative control over the 677-acre "City of London")

Greater London Council
(As the name of the government that has administrative control over the 32 London boroughs which make up "Greater London" excluding the "City of London")

London *(England)*
(As the location qualifier added to corporate headings, even though the body concerned is located in a borough of "Greater London" or in the "City of London"; as the entry element for cross references from place; and as the subject heading)

23.4E Places in Malaysia, the U.S.S.R., or Yugoslavia
If a place is in a constituent state of Malaysia, the Soviet Union, or Yugoslavia, add the name of the state in which the place is located as the qualifier.

For the constituent republics of the Soviet Union, LC/GPO are using the following headings:

Armenian S.S.R.

Azerbaijan S.S.R.

---

1. Municipal Year Book and Public Services Directory. London, Eng. : Municipal Publications Ltd.

Byelorussian S.S.R.

Estonia

Georgian S.S.R.

Kazakh S.S.R.

Kirghiz S.S.R.

Latvia

Lithuania

Moldavian S.S.R.

Russian S.F.S.R. the
 ("R.S.F.S.R." is the heading when it is used as a qualifier in accordance
 with AACR2, Appendix B.14.)

Tajik S.S.R.

Turkmen S.S.R.

Ukraine

Uzbek S.S.R.

For the constituent republics of Yugoslavia, LC/GPO are using the following headings:

Bosnia and Hercegovina

Croatia

Macedonia *(Republic)*

Montenegro

Serbia

Slovenian

23.4F Places on islands
For places on islands, add the name of the island or island group in which the place is located as the qualifier if it is predominantly associated with the name of the place. If the island or island group is not predominantly associated with the name of the place, or, in case of doubt, add instead the larger jurisdiction.

    Palermo *(Sicily)*
not Palermo *(Italy)*

    Chania *(Crete)*
not Chania *(Greece)*

but **Victoria** *(B.C.)*
not Victoria *(Vancouver Island, B.C.)*

For local places in Hawaii, LC/GPO are always using the name of the state (i.e., Hawaii) as the qualifier rather than the name of the island on which the place is located. If two or more local places in Hawaii have the same name, however, LC/GPO are adding the name of the island in which each place is located as the qualifier in addition to the name of the state.

Honolulu *(Hawaii)*
not   Honolulu *(Oahu, Hawaii)*

Kailua *(Oahu, Hawaii)*

Kailua *(Hawaii Island, Hawaii)*

23.4G Places in cities

For places in cities, add the name of the city in which the place is located as the qualifier.

LC rule interpretation says:

> Establish named parts of cities according to rule 23.4G even though the part may not have a government of its own. Add to the name the qualifier that is appropriate to its current status. Use this one heading for the entire period of the place's existence (including any earlier independent existence it may have had), provided the name remains constant.

Oak Cliff *(Dallas, Tex.)*
    x Dallas *(Tex.). Oak Cliff*
    (Oak Cliff was formerly an independent town before it was annexed to Dallas in 1904.)

If the place once had an independent existence but changed its name when it was absorbed into the larger place, establish a heading for each name.

Endersbach *(Germany)*

Weinstadt-Endersbach *(Weinstadt, Germany)*
    x Weinstadt *(Germany). Weinstadt-Enderbach*
    (When Endersbach was absorbed into Weinstadt in 1975, Endersbach was renamed Weinstadt-Endersbach)

23.4H Other places

For all other places not previously covered by 23.4C–23.4G, add the name of the country in which the place is located as the qualifier.

Ashanti *(Ghana)*

Cundinamarca *(Colombia)*

Quito *(Ecuador)*

Seine-et-Oise *(France)*

Trondheim *(Norway)*

Uttar Pradesh *(India)*

Harare *(Zimbabwe)*

23.4J Further additions

AACR2 says: "If the addition of a larger place as instructed in 23.4B–23.4H is insufficient to distinguish between two or more places with the same name, include a word or phrase commonly used for each place to distinguish them." (LC/GPO are generally using this longer form of the name, if it is supplied by BGN, even if there is no need to distinguish the name from another place.)

Vailly-sur-Aisne *(France)*

Vailly-sur-Sauldre *(France)*

Bruck an der Leitha *(Austria)*

Bruck an der Mur *(Austria)*

If there is no such identifying word or phrase to distinguish two or more places with the same name, add an appropriate narrower geographical qualification (e.g., county, province, or other administrative division) before the name of the larger place in the qualifier.

Valkenburg *(Limburg, Netherlands)*

Valkenburg *(South Holland, Netherlands)*

Middleburg *(Cape of Good Hope, South Africa)*

Middleburg *(Transvaal, South Africa)*

In the example given in AACR2, the headings are not correctly given. The headings should read:

Friedberg *(Bavaria, Germany)*
not   Friedburg *(Bavaria, Germany)*

Friedberg *(Hesse, Germany)*
not   Friedburg *(Hesse, Germany)*

If two or more cities or other local places of the United States with the same name are in the same state, add the name of the county in which each city or other local place is located as the narrower geographical qualification.

Plantation *(Broward County, Fla.)*

Plantation *(Monroe County, Fla.)*

183

If two or more townships of the United States (called "towns" in Connecticut, Maine, Massachusetts, New Hampshire, New York, Rhode Island, Vermont, and Wisconsin) with the same name are in the same state, add the name of the county in which each township is located as the narrower geographical qualification.

> **Spring** *(Berks County, Pa.)*

> **Spring** *(Centre County, Pa.)*

> **Sigel** *(Chippewa County, Wis.)*

> **Sigel** *(Wood County, Wis.)*

If a city or other local place has the same name as a township and both are in the same state, follow the instructions in 24.6 for distinguishing between the two places.

23.5 PLACE NAMES INCLUDING A TERM INDICATING A TYPE OF JURISDICTION

23.5A AACR2 says: "If the first part of a place name is a term indicating a type of jurisdiction and the place is commonly listed under another element of its name in lists published in the language of the country in which it is located, omit the term indicating the type of jurisdiction."

> **Princeton** *(N.J.)*
> *not*   Borough of Princeton *(N.J.)*

"In all other cases include the term indicating the type of jurisdiction."

> **City of Commerce** *(Calif.)*
> *not*   Commerce *(Calif.)*
> *(Listed under "City of Commerce" in most reference sources)*

For District of Columbia, LC/GPO are using the following headings:

> **District of Columbia**
> *(As the heading for the government)*

> **Washington** *(D.C.)*
> *(As the location qualifier added to corporate headings; as the entry element for cross references from place; and as the subject heading)*

For counties of the United States, LC/GPO are including the term *County* as part of the name. *County* is always spelled out in full. In Louisiana, the term *Parish* is used instead.

> **Sarpy County** *(Neb.)*
> *not*   Sarpy Co. *(Neb.)*

> **Caddo Parish** *(La.)*

For townships of the United States (called "towns" in Connecticut, Maine, Massachusetts, New Hampshire, New York, Rhode Island, Vermont, and Wisconsin), LC/GPO are not including the term *Township* (or *Town*) as part of the name. (Under AACR1, many townships were established with the term *township*.)

> **Delta** *(Mich.)*
> *not*   Delta Township *(Mich.)*

> **Ellsworth** *(N.H.)*
> *not*   Ellsworth Town *(N.H.)*

If two or more townships with the same name are in the same state, follow the instructions in 23.4J for distinguishing between the places. If a township has the same name as a city or other local place and both are in the same state, follow the instructions in 24.6 for distinguishing between the two places.

23.5B AACR2 says: "If a place name does not include a term indicating a type of jurisdiction and such a term is required to distinguish that place from another of the same name, follow the instructions in 24.6."

24/ Headings for Corporate Bodies

Chapter 24 is crucial in the cataloging of government documents because it gives guidance on the choice of a corporate name and how that name will be structured for use as a heading (access point). Many kinds of corporate bodies are associated with the existence of government documents and there is always at least one government body involved with a document. Other corporate bodies include such types as consulting firms, research laboratories, universities, and advisory committees. The basic rule discusses the choice of a corporate name and its form as a heading. The subrules of the first rule cover romanization and change of name. The rest of the rules are divided into three general areas: (1) choice from among variant names of a name to be used as a heading, (2) modifications of the name such as additions and omissions, and (3) decision as to subordinate or independent entry. The process is composed of two steps: first choose a name and second determine alterations, additions to the name. For example, in establishing a conference name, a number of rules are used to determine the choice of name and how that name will be modified. There is no one way to choose a name for the various types of corporate bodies discussed in this chapter. There are special rules for choice of name for international bodies, ancient bodies, autocephalous patriarchates and archdioceses, religious orders and societies, governments, meetings, and local churches. The principal concerns of a documents cataloger are the rules for international bodies, governments, and meetings. There are also special rules for the modification of the names for such bodies as institutions, "incorporated" bodies, governments, meetings, exhibitions, fairs, festivals, chapters and branches, local churches, and radio and television stations. The final rules of this chapter cover subordinate or independent entry for all types of bodies. There are three subsections: nongovernment bodies, government bodies, and most religious bodies.

All the examples of headings in this chapter include any necessary qualifiers. This is done to remind users of AACR2 that although many examples of headings in AACR2 are not qualified, they should be qualified in their final form. Note that this is a practice generally followed by both LC and GPO.

24.1 BASIC RULE

The basic rule says, "Enter a corporate body directly under the name by which it is predominantly identified, except when the rules that follow provide for entering it under the name of a higher or related body (see 24.13) or under the name of a government (see 24.18).'' When a government body (e.g., an agency, office, or bureau) is entered under its own name and that name does not include the name of the government or the name of the highest unit in the hierarchy (parent body), confusion may result for the user. The government agency may be confused with a similar name in another government (local, state, federal, foreign, or international) and also with a similar name of private laboratories, research centers, organizations and businesses.

The LC rule interpretation says:

> If the form of the name selected as the heading includes quotation marks around an element or elements of the name, retain them (cf. example in rule 24.7B4). Use American-style double quotation marks in the heading.

Conference ''Systematics of the Old World Monkeys'' (*1969 : Burg Wartenstein, Austria*)

The LC rule interpretation says:

> If the form of name selected as the heading includes a place name at the end, and the place name is enclosed within parentheses or is preceded by a comma-space, retain in the heading the punctuation as found.

Exxon Minerals Company, U.S.A.

SR1 - Washington

Names of corporate bodies are formulated as they appear, including the order of initials.

L. S. Goodfriend Associates
not   Goodfriend (L.S.) Associates

EDWA Inc.

The LC rule interpretation says:

> When the name of a body consists of both a numerical or alphabetical designation and words indicating the body's function, include both in the heading for the body. Separate the two parts with a double hyphen.

source: Abteilung V — Vermessungswesen
heading: **[parent body]**. *Abteilung V —Vermessungswesen*

source: Social and Economic Sciences (Section K)
heading: **[parent body]**. *Social and Economic Sciences —Section K*

source: Sub-task Force I, Gas Dissolved in Water
heading: **[parent body]**. *Sub-task Force I —Gas Dissolved in Water*

24.1A Romanization

LC/GPO do not use the alternative rule in footnote 4. This means always using systematic romanization in the heading for a body with a name written in a nonroman script. LC states that the option is not used because "for corporate names a consistent policy of systematic romanization results in a more predictable practice."

Chuo Denpa Kansokujo
> *x* Japan. *Central Radio Wave Observatory*

Japan. *Naimusho. Eiseikyoku*
> *x* Japan. *Central Sanitary Bureau*

Japan. *Sen'in Chuo Rodo Iinkai*
> *x* Japan. *Central Seamen's Labor Relations Commission*

Korea (*South*). *Nongnimbu*
> *x* Korea (*South*). *Ministry of Agriculture and Forestry*

Korea (*South*). *Sanggongbu*
> *x* Korea (*South*). *Ministry of Commerce and Industry*

Korea (*South*). *Munhwa Kongbobu*
> *x* Korea (*South*). *Ministry of Culture and Information*

Korea (*South*). *Chaemubu*
> *x* Korea (*South*). *Ministry of Finance*

Han'guk Haengjong Kwahak Yon'guso
> *x* Korea Administrative Science Research Institute

Han'guk T'uja Kongsa
> *x* Korea Investment Corporation

Jāmi'at Banghāzī
> *x* University of Benghazi
> *x* Bengazi (*Libya*). *Jami'at Banghazi*
> *x* Bengazi (*Libya*). *University of Benghazi*
> *xx* Jami'ah al-Libiyah
> *xx* Jami'at Tarabulus
> *xx* Jami'at Qaryunis
> *xx* Jami'at al-Fatih

Nihon Kisha Kurabu
> *x* Japan National Press Club

Kazanskii nauchno-issledovate'skii insitut travmatologii i ortopedii s
> *x* Kazan (*R.S.F.S.R.*). *Nauchno-issledovatel'skii institut travmatologii i ortopedii*

Han'guk Chungkwondan
> *x* Korea Securities Group

Nihon Genshiryoku Kenkyujo
> *x* Japan. *Atomic Energy Research Institute*

188

24.1B Changes of name

AACR2 specifies: "If the name of a corporate body has changed (including change from one language to another), establish a new heading under the new name for items appearing under that name. Refer from the old heading to the new and from the new heading to the old (see 26.3C)."

A number of examples follow. A copy of the same explanatory text appears under each heading.

United States. *National Technical Information Service.*

The name U.S. Office of the Publication Board, established in 1945, was changed in 1964 to U.S. Clearinghouse for Scientific and Technical Information; and in 1970 to U.S. National Technical Information Service.

Works by this body are found under the following headings according to the name used at the time of publication.

United States. *Office of the Publication Board.*

United States. *Clearinghouse for Scientific and Technical Information.*

United States. *National Technical Information Services.*

United States. *Dept. of Health and Human Services.*

The name of the U.S. Dept of Health, Education, and Welfare was changed to U.S. Dept. of Health and Human Services by Public Law 96-88, signed Oct. 17, 1979, effective date May 4, 1980.

Works by this body are found under the following headings according to the name used at the time of publication.

United States. *Dept. of Health, Education and Welfare.*

United States. *Dept. of Health and Human Services.*

United States. *Office of National Narcotics Intelligence.*

The U.S. Federal Narcotics Control Board was created in Feb. 1900. In July 1930 it was replaced by the Bureau of Narcotics. The Bureau of Drug Abuse Control was created in 1965. In 1968 the Bureau of Narcotics and the Bureau of Drug Abuse Control were merged to form the Bureau of Narcotics and Dangerous Drugs. In 1973 the Drug Enforcement Administration was created to replace the Bureau of Narcotics and Dangerous Drugs, the Office for Drug Abuse Law Enforcement and the Office of National Narcotics Intelligence.

Works by these bodies are found under the following headings according to the name used at the time of publication.

United States. *Bureau of Drug Abuse Control.*

United States. *Bureau of Narcotics.*

United States. *Bureau of Narcotics and Dangerous Drugs.*

United States. *Drug Enforcement Administration.*

United States. *Federal Narcotics Control Board.*

United States. *Office for Drug Abuse Law Enforcement.*

United States. *Office of National Narcotics Intelligence.*

Canada. *Dept. of Industry, Trade, and Commerce.*

The Dept. of Trade and Commerce, established in 1892, and the Dept. of Industry, established in 1963, merged in 1969 to form the Dept. of Industry, Trade, and Commerce.

Works by these bodies are found under the following headings according to the name used at the time of publication.

> **Canada.** *Dept. of Trade and Commerce.*
> **Canada.** *Dept. of Industry.*
> **Canada.** *Dept. of Industry, Trade, and Commerce.*

California. *Dept. of Health.*

The California State Board of Health was succeeded in 1927 by the Dept. of Public Health. The Dept. of Institutions was established in 1921 and the name changed to Dept. of Mental Hygiene in 1945. In 1973 the Dept. of Public Health, Dept. of Mental Hygiene, and the Dept. of Health Care Services merged to become the Dept. of Health.

Works by these bodies are found under the following headings according to the name used at the time of publication.

> **California.** *Dept. of Mental Hygiene.*
> **California.** *Dept. of Institutions.*
> **California.** *State Board of Health.*
> **California.** *Dept. of Public Health.*
> **California.** *Dept. of Health Care Services.*
> **California.** *Dept. of Health.*

New York *(State). Drug Abuse Control Commission.*

For works by this body see also the earlier heading:

> **New York** *(State). Narcotic Addiction Control Commission.*

New York *(State). Narcotic Addiction Control Commission.*

For works by this body see also the later heading:

> **New York** *(State).* Drug Abuse Control Commission.

New York *(State). Legislature. Select Committee on Consumer Protection.*

For works by this body see also under the earlier heading:

> **New York** *(State). Legislature. Joint Committee on Consumer Protection.*

New York *(State). Legislature. Joint Committee on Consumer Protection.*

For works by this body see also the later heading:

> **New York** *(State). Legislature. Select Committee on Consumer Protection.*

24.2 VARIANT NAMES. GENERAL RULES

Sometimes each issue of an agency's documents will carry a different version of the agency's name. Consult reference sources to determine the official form and use it, rather than change the form of the name each time the agency uses a variant name on a document.

LC rule interpretation says:

> If a heading is needed for a proposed body, use the name found in the available sources. If the body is actually established later, and the established name differs from the proposed name, use the established name in the heading and treat the proposed name as a variant form. . . .

> Universities of North America frequently have main library buildings named in honor of someone, e.g., "The Joseph S. Regenstein Library of the University of Chicago," while the library complex itself is called by a generic term instead of the honorific, e.g., "The Libraries of the University of Chicago." When the distinction between the building's name and the library's name can be made in this way, use the library's name as the basis for the heading even if it can be found only off the chief source or outside the item altogether. Limit research, however, to the most obvious reference sources.

24.2A–24.2B ———

24.2C Variant forms

AACR2 says:

> If variant spellings of the name appear in items issued by the body, use the form resulting from an official change in orthography, or, if this does not apply, use the predominant spelling. In case of doubt, use the spelling found in the first item catalogued.

LC rule interpretation says:

> In the case of names of corporate bodies that are located in countries where orthographic reform has taken place (e.g., Indonesia/Malaysia, the Netherlands, Russia), if the first item received gives the name of the corporate body in the old orthography, establish the name in that form; make a reference from the form in reformed orthography. When, subsequently, the first item with the name in the reformed orthography is received, change the heading to reflect the reformed orthography; make a reference from the earlier form. Note that variant names resulting from orthographic reform are treated as such rather than as a change of name.

24.2D If variant forms appear in the chief source of information, use the form that is presented formally. If no form is presented formally, or if all forms are presented formally, use the predominant form.

The following examples from Corps of Engineers publications illustrate the problem.

Wording on chief source of information:

> *example 1*
> *title page: 1*
>> U. S. Army Engineer District, St. Louis Corps of Engineers St. Louis, Missouri

title page: 2
> Dept. of the Army, St. Louis Corps of Engineers. St. Louis, Missouri

> *use:* **United States.** *Army. Corps of Engineers. St. Louis District.*

example 2
title page: 1
> U.S. Army Engineers District Corps of Engineers Sacramento, California

title page: 2
> United States Army Corps of Engineers Sacramento District Office

> *use:* **United States.** *Army. Corps of Engineers. Sacramento District Office.*

example 3
title page: 1
> U. S. Army Corps of Engineers Huntington District

title page: 2
> Department of the Army Huntington District Corps of Engineers Huntington,
> West Virginia

> *use:* **United States.** *Army. Corps of Engineers. Huntington District.*

AACR2 says: "If there is no predominant form, use a brief form (including an initialism or an acronym) that would differentiate between the body and others with the same or similar brief names."

Since corporate bodies are so often known by initialisms and acronyms, it is important in choosing among variant forms of the name to remember the caution in this rule: "If the variant forms do not include a brief form that would differentiate two or more bodies with the same or similar brief names, use the form found in reference sources or the official form, in that order of preference." The following examples illustrate why it is often wiser to give the fuller name. (Note, however, that this leaning toward the fuller form is appropriate only in the situations covered by the LC rule interpretation quoted below.)

> **Capital District Library Council** (*N.Y.*)
> > *x* CDLC
> > *x* Capital District Library Council for Reference and Research Resources

> **American Institutes for Research**
> > *x* American Institutes for Research in the Behavioral Sciences

> **American Medical Joggers Association**
> > *x* AMJA

North Atlantic Treaty Organization
 x NATO

World Meteorological Organization
 x WMO

Organisation for Economic Co-operation and Development
 x O.E.C.D.

OECD Nuclear Energy Agency
 x Organisation for Economic Co-operation and Development. Nuclear
  Energy Agency
 x Nuclear Energy Agency
 x Organization for Economic Cooperation and Development. Agence pour
  l'energie Nucleaire

Royal Ontario Museum
 x ROM
 x Toronto (Ont.). *Royal Ontario Museum*
 x University of Toronto. *Royal Ontario Museum*

Organisation Armee Secrete
 x OAS

Organization of American States
 x OAS

Initialisms not pronounceable as words, e.g., "AFL-CIO," may also now be used as headings.[1]

The LC rule interpretation says:

> If in a body's publications its full form of name and its initials appear together formally, choose the full form for use in the heading. (Change the heading if later evidence shows a clear pattern of predominant usage that differs from the heading chosen.)
>
> When a corporate name must be established for an item not issued by the corporate body, treat the item being cataloged as a reference source. If the item provides both the body's full form of name and its initials, choose the full form for use in the heading (even if the initials appear prominently and the full form does not).
>
> If variant forms appear formally in chief sources of the body's publications, choose the predominant form. If an initial form (including an acronym) appears predominantly, check the catalog to see if there is a reference or a heading for another body already under the same initials. If there is, this means the initials do not "differentiate" and thus the full form must be adopted as the AACR2 form.

---

1. AACR1 allowed as headings only those initialisms presented as words where the first letter alone was capitalized, such as Unesco, or where the letters represented syllables.

24.3 VARIANT NAMES. SPECIAL RULES

24.3A Language. Noninternational bodies

AACR2 states: "If the name appears in different languages, use the form in the official language of the body."

LC/GPO are not applying the alternative rule found in footnote 8: "Use a form of name in a language suitable to the users of the catalogue if the body's name is in a language which is not familiar to those users."

LC rule interpretation says:

> If the name of a corporate body appears in different languages in formal presentations in the chief sources of the body's own items, apply the following:
>
> 1) If one of these is in the official language of the body, use it.
> 2) If the body has two or more official languages, one of which is English, use the English form.
> 3) If the body has two or more official languages, none of which is English, use the form in the language predominantly used in items issued by the body.
> 4) If the official language of the body is not known, use the form in the official language of the country in which the body is located if the country has a single official language.
> 5) If categories 1–4 are not applicable, use the English, French, German, Spanish, or Russian form, in this order of preference. If none of these applies, use the form in the language that comes first in English alphabetic order.

Daichōgan Kenkyūkai
> *x* Japanese Research Society for Cancer of Colon and Rectum

Costa Rica. *Ministerio de Obras Públicas y Transportes*
> *x* Costa Rica. Ministry of Public Works and Transportation

National Research Council of Canada
> *x* Conseil national de recherches du Canada

LC rule interpretation continues:

> If the body is an international one and its name appears in English in formal presentations in the chief sources of its own items, use the English form (24.3B). If there is no English form, apply the above provisions.

International Finance Corporation
> *x* IFC
> *x* Societe financiere internationale
> *x* Mezhdunarodnaia finansovaia korporatsiia
> *x* Miedzynarodowe Towarzystwo Finansowe

Congressus Internationalis Fenno-Ugristarum
> *x* International Finno-Ugric Congress

LC rule interpretation says:

> For countries that have only one official language, follow the above provisions in constructing headings for non-government bodies and government bodies that are entered under their own names. For government bodies entered under the name of the jurisdiction, construct the heading in the official language of the country whenever possible. This means taking the name from reference sources when it does not appear in the body's own publications. If the form in the official language is not found, establish the heading according to the above provisions and mark it "provisional." Change the heading to the official language when that is known.

24.3B Language. International bodies

AACR2 specifies: "If the name of an international body appears in English on items issued by it, use the English form. In other cases follow 24.3A."

World Bank
>*x* International Bank for Reconstruction and Development
>*x* Banque internationale pour la reconstruction et le developpement
>*x* Mezhdunarodny bank dlia rekonstruktsii i razvitiia
>*x* Sekai Ginko
>*x* Kokusai Fukko Kaihatsu Ginko
>*x* Welt Bank
>*x* Internationale Bank fur Wiederaufbau und Entwicklung
>*x* Banco Internacional de Reconstruccion y Fomento
>*x* IBRD
>*x* Kukche Puhung Kaebal Unhaeng
>*x* Segye Unhaeng
>*x* International Bank for Reconstruction and Development
>*x* Banco Mundial
>*x* B.I.R.D.
>*x* Banca Internationala pentru Reconstructie si Dezvoltare
>*x* Verdensbanken
>*x* Miedzynarodowy Bank Rozwoju i Obbudowy
>*x* al-Bank al-Dawli lil-Insha wa-al-Ta'mir etc.

European Federation of Productivity Services
>*x* Federation européenne pour l'accroissement de la productivité

Permanent International Committee of Linguists
>*x* Comite international permanent des linquistes

24.3C Conventional name

24.3C1   General rule. If a body is frequently identified by a conventional form of name in reference sources in its own language, use this conventional name.

This is rare for government bodies. A case can be made for keeping "United States. Congress. House of Representatives." under "United States. Congress. House." because of this rule. The term *House* is conventionally used in place of *House of Representatives*.

24.3C2–24.C3 ———

24.3D ———

24.3E Governments

AACR2 says: "Use the conventional name of a government, unless the official name is in common use. The conventional name of a government is the geographic name (see chapter 23) of the area (country, province, state, county, municipality, etc.) over which the government exercises jurisdiction." In many cases, this will be the English-language form of the name (see 23.2).

Italy
x Repubblica italiana (1946–   )
x Italian Republic (1946–   )

Argentina
x Argentine Repúblic
x Republica Argentina
x Provincias Unidas del Río de la Plata
x Provincias Unidas en Sud-América
x United Provinces of Río de la Plata
x Río de la Plata (*United Provinces*)
x United Provinces in South America

South Africa
x Union of South Africa
x Suid-Afrika
x Unie van Suid-Afrika
x Republic of South Africa
x Republiek van Suid-Afrika

Korea (*North*)
x Korea (People's Democratic Republic)
x Korean People's Republic
x People's Democratic Republic of Korea
x Korea (North Korean Government)
x Democratic People's Republic of Korea
x North Korea
x Ch'ao-hsien min chu chu i jen min kung ho kuo
x Korea (Democratic People's Republic)
x Korean Peoples' Democratic Republic
x Chōsen Minshushugi Jimmin Kyōwakoku
x Chosŏn Minjujuui Inmin Konghwaguk

Bellefonte *(Pa.)*
   x Borough of Bellefonte (Pa.)

AACR2 continues: "If the official name of the government is in common use, use it." The official name of the District of Columbia is in common use, so LC has decided to use it as the heading for the government, even though the conventionalized name *Washington (D.C.)* is used as the location qualifier added to corporate headings, as the entry element for cross references from place, and as the subject heading.

For the Union of Soviet Socialist Republics, LC/GPO are using *Soviet Union* as the heading.

For the United Kingdom, LC/GPO are continuing to use *Great Britain* as the heading for the government.

For London, England, LC/GPO are using the following headings:.

Corporation of London
   (As the name of the government that has administrative control over the 677-acre "City of London")

Greater London Council
   (As the name of the government that has administrative control over the 32 London boroughs which make up "Greater London" excluding the "City of London")

London *(England)*
   (As the location qualifier added to corporate headings even though the body concerned is located in a borough of "Greater London" or in the "City of London"; as the entry element for cross references from place; and as the subject heading)

24.3F Conferences, congresses, meetings, etc.

24.3F1. AACR2 says: If the variant forms of a conference name appearing in the chief source of information include a form that includes the name or abbreviation of the name of a body associated with the meeting, use this form."

IFIP Working Conference on Decision Making and Medical Care

EPA Noise Technology Research Symposium *(1979: : Dallas, Tex.)*

Dept. of Energy Workshop on Energy Conservation in the Textile Industry *(1978 : North Carolina State University)*

Maryland's State-wide Conference on Day Care Services for Children

National Conference on Degree Sandwich Courses *(1975 : University of Bath)*

Alabama White House Conference on Aging *(1981 : Montgomery, Ala.)*

Alabama White House Conference on Aging Committee

> **Alabama Governor's Conference on Library & Information Services**
> *(1979 : Montgomery, Ala.)*

> **Australian Conference on Coastal Engineering**

"If, however, the name or abbreviation of a name is of a body to which the meeting is subordinate (e.g., the annual meeting of an association), see 24.13."

> **American Library Association.** *Meeting*

Some conferences do not have a formal name in the chief source of information. Refer to 21.1B1, footnote 1 for the definition of a conference.

24.4 ADDITIONS

24.4A General rule

AACR2 says: "Make additions to the names of corporate bodies as instructed in 24.4B–24.4C."

Additions to a corporate name are placed within a single set of parentheses, multiple qualifiers within the one set of parentheses each being separated by a space-colon-space.[2]

24.4B Names not conveying the idea of a corporate body

AACR2 says: "If the name alone does not convey the idea of a corporate body, add a general designation in English." There are many contracting and grantee bodies associated with the creation of government documents. Unless some very general term comes to mind, follow what is on the document, work, or item.

> **Gilbert/Commonwealth** *(Firm)*

> **Innovative Programming Systems** *(Firm)*

> **Pyramid** *(Firm)*

> **Courses by Newspaper** *(Project)*

> **Gambier Bay** *(Ship)*

> **David & Catherine Zinn Spahr Reunion** *(Organization)*

> **Trade Research Publications** *(Firm)*

> **Gulf Maps** *(Firm)*

> **Historic Urban Plans** *(Firm)*

The LC rule interpretation says:

> Generally do not add a general designation qualifier to a corporate name containing two or more surnames (without forenames or without forename initials . . . .
> When establishing a heading for a ship, add a general designation in English

---

2. AACR1 provided for parentheses in some cases and for a comma in other cases as the means of linking the qualifier to the name.

if the name alone does not convey the idea of a corporate body. If there is any question as to whether there is an appropriate general term, take the term from the item being cataloged. If there is more than one ship with the same name, add a term as specific as neccessary to resolve the conflict.

Ulua *(Ship)*
 (Unique name; qualifier added to clarify the meaning of the heading)

Franklin *(Aircraft carrier)*
Franklin *(Steamship)*
 (Two ships of the same name but each of a different type)

Lexington *(Aircraft carrier : CV6)*
Lexington *(Aircraft carrier : CVA(N) 65)*
 (Two aircraft carriers with the same name)

LC rule interpretation says:

> If the name chosen for the heading for a corporate body is composed of letters written in all capital letters (with or without periods between them), add a 24.4B qualifier to the name (unless 24.5C is applicable). Do not add such a qualifier when the capitalized form is used in a ''see'' reference.

CAST *(Group)*
 x C.A.S.T.

If the name is eligible for another qualifier (as when the name conflicts or when the body is a directly entered government agency that is not an institution), add the 24.4B qualifier first. Separate the qualifiers by a space-colon-space.

BANAS *(Organization : Indonesia)*
 x B.A.N.A.S. *(Indonesia)*

24.4C Two or more bodies with the same or similar names

24.4C1 General rule. AACR2 says: ''If two or more bodies have the same name or names so similar that they may be confused, add a word or phrase to each name as instructed in 24.4C2–24.4C10.''
Most federal agencies whose names begin with ''National'' or ''Center'' are part of another agency. If these agencies or offices are to be entered directly under their own names, then it is important to remember that they need to be modified with an addition which clearly shows that they are part of a government.

National Center for Chronic Disease Control *(U.S.)*

National Heart and Lung Institute *(U.S.)*

National Research Council *(U.S.). Diesel Impacts Study Commission*

The LC rule interpretation says:

When two or more bodies have the same name, 24.4C requires the addition of a qualifier to each name. Determine that a conflict exists when the AACR2 name or heading for one body is the same as the AACR2 name or heading for another body. "Conflict" is restricted to headings already established or being established in the catalog. It includes headings for earlier names that are covered by "see" references to later names but excludes names treated as variants; if a variant name used in a reference conflicts with a form used in the heading for another body, apply the provisions for resolving conflicts only to the variant name. Ignore the conflict that is only between names used as variants.

Arlington Development Center *(Tex.)*
   (Independent nongovernment body)

Arlington Development Center *(Calif.)*
   (Government body belonging to Arlington)

Arlington Development Center *(Infodata, Inc.)*
   (Subordinate nongovernment body)

Arlington Development Center *(S.D.)*
   (Government body belonging to South Dakota)

LC rule interpretation continues:

NONCONFLICTS

Nongovernment bodies
If a nongovernment body is entered under its own name, add a qualifier unless one or more of the following apply:

1) In effect, the qualifier is already present.
2) The body is a business firm. If there is *any* doubt whatsoever as to whether a body is a business firm, consider that it is not so.
3) The body is an international one. If, however, the name comes to conflict, use your own judgment of the case in hand: founding dates, some geographical qualifier, or something else that may occur to you as appropriate.
4) The name of the body is a very distinctive one. In many cases distinctiveness characterizes a name because of the presence of proper nouns or adjectives, as when a body is named in honor of a person or named after a place. The assessment of the name, however, primarily remains in terms of repeatability. Thus for example, a proper noun or adjective may not help at all in making the name unlikely to be repeated, e.g., "Center for Latin American Studies" (this being the name of one higher body's center devoted to the subject) or "Esso Research Centre" (this being the name of one of the several Esso companies' research units, which units are not themselves business firms).

Note: The phrase "Nongovernment bodies" includes directly entered subordinate or related units or directly entered government bodies; cf. 24.17, second sentence.

Government bodies

If a government body other than an institution (see below) is entered under its own name, add a qualifier unless the government's name (or an understandable surrogate of the government's name) is already present in the name. The qualifier is required even if the name includes a proper noun or adjective (other than the name or the surrogate of the name of the government).

If, however, the body is an institution (school, library, laboratory, hospital, archive, museum, prison, etc.) do not qualify its name when it is a very distinctive one (cf. point 4 above under "Nongovernment bodies"). If one of these names comes to conflict or the nonconflicting name is not distinctive, add a qualifier.

LC rule interpretation continues:

FORMS OF QUALIFIERS

Geographic names

If a geographic name (place or jurisdiction) is the appropriate qualifier, use its catalog-entry form. Whenever the heading for a place name is qualified by the name of a larger place, retain the qualification when the heading for the smaller place is itself used as a qualifier. For the form of this qualifier and its punctuation see the following example:

name of body needing qualifier: Conference on Astrophysics
heading for qualifier: Chicago (Ill.)
heading: **Conference on Astrophysics** *(1978 : Chicago, Ill.)*

For the insertion of the comma between "Chicago" and "Ill.," see rule 23.4A. Note that other qualifications, e.g., "(Province)," "(East)," "(West)," "(North)," "(South)," "(Republic)," are not retained (cf. the second paragraph of rule 24.4C1).

Corporate names

If a corporate name is the appropriate qualifier, use the name in the form and language on which the heading for the body is (not necessarily its catalog-entry form).

Center for Materials Science *(U.S.) National Measurement Laboratory*
not Center for Materials Science *(National Measurement Laboratory) (U.S.)*

LC rule interpretation continues:

CHOICE OF QUALIFIERS

Independent nongovernment bodies

24.4C provides for various additions to corporate names as qualifiers. This rule emphasizes place names as t appropriate qualifier. Certainly other categories of qualifiers are possible (note especially 24.4C8). Considering solely the issue of qualifying by place name, one notes that even after having made the decision to apply 24.4C2–24.4C5, a decision remains as to *which* place name should serve as the qualifier. In sum, the direction contained in the rule is to use a local place name unless the body has a non-local character, in which case the direction is to use the name of the country for bodies national in character, the name of the province for bodies provincial in character, etc. This leaves it very much up to the cataloger to decide which place name to use, depending on an assessment of the body's character (or activities), based on the cataloger's experience and whatever knowledge or hints are available for the case in hand. There are no rules or rule interpretations for this assessment.

Once the cataloger has assessed the body's character, etc., then there are at least three situations in which catalogers need advice:

1. The cataloger knows precisely the range of activities of the body, but the extent of these activities corresponds to no jurisdiction, district, etc. For example, the body covers 4 counties of one of the U.S. states. Then qualify by the name of the jurisdiction just above those involved, e.g., the state if counties are involved, the nation if states are involved, etc.
2. The cataloger has only certain clues as to the body's character, etc. One obvious clue is the presence of words such as "national," "state," "provincial," etc. Generally choose the qualifier that matches these words, if you really are in doubt about the body's character. (If you *know* that a body called "national" is actually local, this paragraph does not apply.) In other cases, if the clues indicate that the body is either one or the other of two possibilities, e.g., it must be either municipal or county-wide, generally use the broader of the two possible qualifiers, e.g., the county instead of the city.
3. The cataloger has no knowledge or clues as to the body's character, etc., and therefore the assessment mentioned at the outset results in "I do not know and cannot guess." In this situation, qualify by the local place (cf., in the opening paragraph under "Choice of Qualifiers," the statement about the rule's emphasizing local place name)—unless, for whatever reason, the name of the country seems appropriate. Use this solution as a genuine last resort, however, not as a substitute for the assessment required.

Subordinate [or] related nongovernment bodies
If a qualifier is needed for a directly entered subordinate or related unit of a nongovernment body or of a government body entered directly under its own name, add the name of a higher or related body, unless a geographic qualifier (place or jurisdiction) seems more appropriate.

Annenberg School of Communications (University of Pennsylvania)
Annenberg School of Communications (University of Southern California)

National Museum of American History (U.S.)
not   National Museum of American History (Smithsonian Institution)

If the immediately higher or related body is entered subordinately, use in the qualifier the name of the next higher body in the hierarchy that is directly entered.

202

Institut avtomatiki i elektrometrii (Akademiĩa nauk SSSR)
not   Institut avtomatiki i elektrometrii (Sibirskoe otdelenie)
not   Institut avtomatiki i elektrometrii (Akademiĩa nauk SSR. Sibirskoe otdelenie)

Government bodies

If a qualifier is needed for a directly entered government body, add the name of the government. *EXCEPTION:* For the various forest and range experiment stations of the U.S. Forest Service that are independently entered, use the local place as the qualifier if the name if not distinctive.

LC rule interpretation continues:

CONFLICTS IN QUALIFIERS

Geographic names

If the addition of nonlocal geographic name (place or jurisdiction) does not resolve the conflict, use the name of the local place instead.

Environmental Research Laboratory (Duluth, Minn.)
Environmental Research Laboratory (Gulf Breeze, Fla.)
(Pre-conflict form: Environmental Research Laboratory (U.S.))

EXCEPTION: If the name of the government is the appropriate qualifier for two bodies that have the same name, and one body is located in the People's Republic of China and the other is in the Republic of China, or one is located in East Germany and the other is in West Germany, or one is located in North Korea and the other is in South Korea, use as qualifiers:

(name) (Germany : East)
(name) (Germany : West)
(name) (Korea : North)
(name) (Korea : South)
(name) (China)
(name) (China : Republic : 1949–)

If two bodies have the same name, and one is located in East Berlin and the other is in West Berlin, and the local place qualifier is appropriate to both bodies, use as qualifiers:

(name) (Berlin, Germany : East)
(name) (Berlin, Germany : West)

Corporate names

In exceptional cases, such as the institutes of branches of the Akademiia nauk SSSR, catalog entry form for the corporate name may be used.

Institut geologii (Akademiĩa nauk SSSR. Komi filial)
Institut geologii (Akademiĩa nauk SSSR. Karel'skiĭ filial)

AACR2 says: *"Optionally,* apply rules 24.4C2– 24.4C10 even if there is no need to distinguish between bodies."
The GODORT Committee urges that the cataloger always use the option for govern-

ment bodies since there are thousands of government agencies on every level and the chance of similar names is very high.

There is a trend in government to establish unusual new government groupings. For example, the United States Department of Housing and Urban Development and other agencies are funding regional groups which include counties or other government units. In Indiana, Owen and Monroe Counties have been formed into the Region Ten Planning Commission. A heading for this commission would have to include the state as a qualifier since there are Region Ten Planning Commissions in other states (even though the commission is under a federal agency).

Region Ten Planning Commission *(Ind.)*

24.4C2 Names of countries, states, provinces, etc. It is important to always provide an addition because a number of government agency names will be entered independently under what the cataloger has decided are their names. The decision as to what the agency's name is will vary from cataloger to cataloger. The following names were established by LC catalogers under AACR2. As you can see, no hierarchy was included in the name. Without the qualifier giving the jurisdiction (government) there would be no clue that these are all government bodies.

Fish Disease Control Center *(U.S.)*

National Diabetes Information Clearinghouse *(U.S.)*

Agricultural Research Council *(Pakistan)*

National Research Council *(U.S.)*

National Research Council *(U.S.). Subcommittee on Swine Nutrition*

National Research Council *(U.S.). Subcommittee on Warm-Water Fish Nutrition*

Water Resources Council *(U.S.)*

LC, following AACR2, changed the heading ''United States. Bureau of Indian Affairs. Missouri River Basin Investigations Project'' to ''Missouri River Basin Investigations Project (U.S.).'' The complete hierarchy for this name is: United States, the Department of the Interior, Bureau of Indian Affairs, Missouri River Basin Investigations Project. It is important to the researcher to know that this project is being done by the Bureau of Indian Affairs, which presumably wishes to preserve the river for fishing and wildlife purposes versus another Interior bureau which may wish to use it for other purposes. This agency name was qualified by the addition *(U.S.)*. Another addition, as allowed in 24.4C10, would be helpful in clearly identifying this agency.

24.4C3 Local place names

Flagstaff *(Ariz.)*

Florence *(Italy)*

Gorham *(N.H. : Town)*

Porter *(Huntingdon County, Pa.)*

Springfield State Hospital *(Md.)*

Springfield State Hospital *(Mass.)*

24.4C4 Bodies located outside the British Isles AACR2 says: "In the case of bodies located outside the British Isles (The United Kingdom and the Republic of Ireland), add the name of the smallest or most specific local political jurisdiction in which the body is located or that is commonly associated with its name (e.g., the name of the city, town, borough)."

In the case of the United States, LC/GPO always add the state to the city. For other jurisdictions see rule 23.4B. This is based upon the option in footnote 11: "The examples shown in rules 24.4C4– 24.5, 24.7– 24.11, and elsewhere, with a few exceptions, omit the name of the larger geographic area in which the local place is located. The construction of these headings by a particular cataloguing agency will depend on the application of the options in chapter 23 or on the actual need for differentiation in a particular catalogue."

Loyola University *(Chicago, Ill.)*

St. Mary's College *(Morga, Calif.)*

24.4C5 Bodies located in the British Isles. For help in structuring these names refer to rule 23.4D.

24.4C6 ———

24.4C7 Corporate names including a local place name. The rule says to qualify with the state name, etc., as necessary.

Montgomery County Planning Commission *(Md.)*

Greater Greenville Chamber of Commerce *(S.C.)*

24.4C8 Institutions. LC rule interpretation says:

When adding the name of a corporate body to a corporate name, give the name of the body in the form and language on which the heading for the body is *based* (not necessarily the catalog-entry for the institution). Nevertheless, if the combination of corporate name plus qualifier actually conflicts in the file being searched against, then give the qualifier in catalog-entry form. Use in the qualifier the body's current name. However, if a qualifier is added to the name of a body that no longer exists, use in the qualifier the name of the body that was appropriate at the time the body ceased.

Newman Club *(Southern State College)*

not   Newman Club *(Southern State College (Springfield, S.D.)*

but   **Newman Club** *(St. Joseph's College (Brooklyn, New York, N.Y.)*
Newman Club *(St. Joseph's College (Philadelphia, Pa.)*

LC rule interpretation continues:

Change an established heading whenever the existing qualifier becomes inappropriate (as when the name used in the qualifier changes or when the name used in the qualifier is no longer associated with the body being qualified). . . .

Documentations-Leitstelle Afrika *(Institut fur Afrika-Kunde)*

x Documentations-Leitstelle Afrika *(Deutsches Institut fur Afrika-Forschung)*
(The name of the parent body changed from Deutsches Institut fur Afrika-Forschung to Institut fur Afrika-Kunde.)

24.4C9 Year(s). AACR2 says: "Add the year of the founding or the inclusive years of existence if the name has been used by two or more bodies that cannot be distinguished by place."
The LC rule interpretation says:

Always use dates as qualifiers to headings for expeditions, even if there is no current conflict. For the form of the qualifier, see rule 24.4C9. Follow 24.7 when the date appears in the name of the expedition.

Also add the state to the examples in AACR2.

Lewis and Clark Expedition *(1804 – 1806)*

Committee of Fifteen *(New York, N.Y. : 1900)*

Massachusetts Agricultural Experiment Station *(1888 –)*

National Dental Association *(1897 – 1922)*

24.4C10 Other additions. AACR2 says: "If the place, name of institution, or date(s) is insufficient or inappropriate for distinguishing between two or more bodies, add an appropriate general designation in English."

24.5   OMISSIONS

24.5A Initial articles
LC has directed its catalogers to "ignore the provision for retention of the initial

article for grammatical reasons and continue to delete it unless the intent is to file on the initial article.''

The Citadel would be: **Citadel** *(Charleston, S.C.)*

24.5B ———

24.5C Terms indicating incorporation and certain other terms

24.5C1 AACR2 says: ''Omit adjectival terms indicating incorporation (*incorporated, E.V., ltd.,* etc.) or state ownership of a corporate body, and words or phrases designating the type of incorporated entity (*Aktiebolaget, Gesellschaft mit beschrankter Haftung, Kabushiki Kaisha, Societa per azione,* etc.) unless they are an integral part of the name or are needed to make it clear that the name is that of a corporate body.''

ABAM Engineers Incorporated

Physical Sciences Inc.

ARA, Inc.

Energy Utilization Systems, Inc.

Levitt and Sons
  without Inc.

Springborn Laboratories
  without Inc.

Do not abbreviate words in the heading except for those actually used by the body. Refer to AACR2, Appendix B for help in determining when abbreviations are permissible.

Incorporated and *Limited* are abbreviated to *Inc.* and *Ltd.* See Appendix A.18E Other Corporate Bodies, and B.9, General Abbreviations, in AACR2. Note that unlike AACR1, *Inc.* and *Ltd.* are always capitalized regardless of punctuation.

24.5C2–24.5C4 ———

24.6 GOVERNMENTS. ADDITIONS

24.6A If governments with the same name are not differentiated by 23.4, make a further addition as instructed in AACR2 with the following special provisions.

LC rule interpretation says:

> When a sovereign nation and another place of the same name that is not a sovereign nation exist at the same time, do not qualify the name of the sovereign nation.

Italy *(Tex.)*

Italy

not Italy *(Republic)*

LC rule interpretation says:

> When a succession of jurisdictions would be entered under the same name, use one heading for all, no matter what differences there are between the jurisdictions.

North Carolina

not North Carolina *(Colony)*
not North Carolina *(State)*

Texas

not Texas *(Republic)*
not Texas *(State)*

Hawaii

not Hawaii *(Kingdom)*
not Hawaii *(Republic)*
not Hawaii *(State)*

India

not India *(Dominion)*
not India *(Republic)*

LC rule interpretation continues:

> However, when the geographical qualifier added to a name to reflect its current status is not appropriate for the earlier entity, use two headings and qualify each.

Brabant *(Belgium)*
Brabant *(Duchy)*
not Brabant *(Belgium)*

Venice *(Italy)*
Venice *(Republic)*
not Venice *(Italy)*

Tuscany *(Italy)*
Tuscany *(Grand Duchy)*
not Tuscany *(Italy)*

Aragon *(Spain)*
Aragon *(Kingdom)*
not Aragon *(Spain)*

LC rule interpretation says:

When the name of a state, province, or territory in Australia, Canada, or the United States; of a British county, region, or islands area; of a constituent state of Malaysia, the U.S.S.R., or Yugoslavia; or of an island that is a jurisdiction conflicts with the name of a place within the same larger jurisdiction, add the type of government as a qualifier to the larger geographic entity.

New York *(N.Y.)*
New York *(State)*
not New York

Durham *(Durham)*
Durham *(County)*
not Durham

Malacca *(Malacca)*
Malacca *(State)*
not Malacca

LC rule interpretation says:

When the name of a state, province, or territory in Australia, Canada, or the United States; of a British county, region, or islands area; of a constituent state of Malaysia, the U.S.S.R., or Yugoslavia; or of an island that is a jurisdiction conflicts with the name of a place in another jurisdiction, qualify the latter only.

Virginia *(Minn.)*
Virginia
not Virginia *(State)*

Alberta *(Va.)*
Alberta
not Alberta *(Province)*

Victoria *(Tex.)*
Victoria
not Victoria *(State)*

Dorset *(Vt.)*
Dorset
not Dorset *(County)*

Corsica *(S.D.)*
Corsica
not Corsica *(Dept.)*

An exception will be made for the State of Washington.

Washington *(State)*
not Washington

If a township of the United States (called ''town'' in Connecticut, Maine, Massachussetts, New Hampshire, New York, Rhode Island, Vermont, and Wisconsin) has the same name as a city or other local place and both are in the same state, add *Township* (or *Town*) to the qualifier of the township. Do not further qualify the city or other local place.

> **Passaic** *(N.J. : Township)*
> **Passaic** *(N.J.)*
> *not*   Passaic *(N.J. : City)*

> **Rutland** *(Vt. : Town)*
> **Rutland** *(Vt.)*
> *not*   Rutland *(Vt. : City)*

If a township has the same name as both a city or other local place and another township and all are in the same state, add *Township* (or *Town*) and the name of the county in which each is located to the qualifier of township. Do not further qualify the city or other local place.

> **Greenfield** *(Lagrange County, Ind. : Township)*
> **Greenfield** *(Orange County, Ind. : Township)*
> **Greenfield** *(Ind.)*
> *not*   Greenfield *(Ind. : City)*

> **Berlin** *(Green Lake County, Wis. : Town)*
> **Berlin** *(Marathon County, Wis. : Town)*
> **Berlin** *(Wis.)*
> *not*   Berlin *(Wis. : City)*

If two or more townships with the same name are in the same state, follow the instructions in 23.4J for distinguishing between the places.

LC rule interpretation says:

> Add a 24.6 qualifier to the heading for a jurisdiction that does not conflict with the heading for another jurisdiction in the following cases:
>
> 1) When the heading for the jurisdiction is the same as the name of a geographic area, but the territory governed by the jurisdiction varies significantly from the geographic area.
>
> **West Indies** *(Federation)*
> *(The heading for ''Federation of the West Indies,'' which consisted only of some of the British possessions in the Caribbean; ''West Indies'' is a subject heading that covers all the islands in the Caribbean.)*
>
> **Pacific Islands** *(Trust Territory)*
> *(The heading for ''Trust Territory of the Pacific Islands,'' which consists of the Caroline, Marshall, and Mariana Islands; without the qualifier the heading could mean the subject heading for all the islands of the Pacific Ocean.)*

2) When the heading for the jurisdiction is the same as the name of a geographic area but the name of the jurisdiction has ceased.

New Guinea *(Territory)*
(The heading for "Territory of New Guinea," which ceased in 1942; "New Guinea" is a subject heading for the island which contains the current jurisdictions "Papua New Guinea" and "Propinsi Irian Jaya.")

24.6B The following examples given in AACR2 are revised in accordance with how LC/GPO are applying the options in 23.4B.

Cork *(Cork)*
not Cork *(Cork, Ireland)*

Cork *(County)*
not Cork *(Ireland : County)*

New York *(State)*
not New York *(U.S. : State)*

Québec *(Province)*
not Québec *(Canada : Province)*

24.6C For the two republics of Germany, LC/GPO are using the following forms and not those given in AACR2.

Germany *(East)*
(For the German Democratic Republic)

Germany *(West)*
(For the Federal Republic of Germany)

For the two republics of Korea, LC/GPO are using the following forms:

Korea *(North)*
(For the Democratic People's Republic of Korea)

Korea *South)*
(For the Republic of Korea)

24.6D For the various governments of China, LC/GPO are using the following forms:

China
(For all governments in all periods that have controlled the mainland of China for all periods except 1931–1945; for the government headquartered in Nanking, 1931–1937; and for the government headquartered in Chungking, 1937–1945)

> **China** *(Soviet Republic, 1931–1937)*
> *(For the government headquartered in Jui-chin, 1931–1937)*

> **China** *(Provisional government, 1937–1940)*
> *(For the government headquartered in Peking, 1937–1940)*

> **China** *(Reformed government, 1938–1940)*
> *(For the government headquartered in Nanking, 1938–1940)*

> **China** *(National government, 1940–1945)*
> *(For the government headquartered in Nanking, 1940–1945)*

> **China** *(Republic : 1949–)*
> *(For the government on Taiwan since 1949)*

> **Taiwan**
> *(For the province of Taiwan)*

24.7 CONFERENCES, CONGRESSES, MEETINGS, ETC.

In formulating the headings for meetings, consult both rules 24.3F1 and 24.3F2 before determining what omissions and additions are to be made. Rule 24.7 provides guidance for the modification of, or an addition to, that name.

24.7A Omissions
AACR2 says: "Omit from the name of the conference, etc., words that denote its number, frequency, or year of convocation."

> **Nutrition Conference**
> *not*   Annual Nutrition Conference

> **National Assembly on the Jail Crisis**
> *not*   Second National Assembly on the Jail Crisis

24.7B Additions

24.7B1 General rule. Headings for conferences, meetings, etc., are qualified by the addition of number (if any), date, and place in that order.[3]

24.7B2 Number. AACR2 says:

> If a conference, etc. is stated or inferred to be one of a series of numbered

---

3. Under *AACR1*, the order was number (if any), place, and date. The elements are separated by space-colon-space, e.g., 2nd : 1958 : New Orleans, La. Dates were considered more important than location and therefore the order is different from that in AACR1.

meetings of the same name, add the abbreviation of the ordinal number in English.

If the numbering is irregular, omit it from the heading. *Optionally,* provide an explanation of the irregularities in an appropriate form (e.g., a note, an information reference.

LC/GPO are exercising this option.

24.7B3 Date

24.7B4 Location. Here are a number of complete examples showing both date and location. "Location" means both place names and names of the institution, as in the first and fifth examples.

Missouri Governor's Conference on Education *(1976 : University of Missouri)*

International Conference on Production Engineering *(1974 : Tokyo, Japan)*

Seattle Conference on Continuing Medical Education *(1975)*

Automated In Situ Water Quality Sensor Workshop *(1978 : Las Vegas, Nev.)*

ERDA Workshop on Mid-Atlantic Coastal Oceanographic Research *(1977 : Brookhaven National Laboratory)*

Finite Beta Theory Workshop *(1977 : Varenna, Italy)*

AACR2 says: "If the sessions of a conference, etc., were held in two places, add both names." Add those names in the order in which the conferences were held.

LC rule interpretation says:

In deciding between using local place or institution, etc. (24.7B4) when establishing the heading for a named conference, add as the qualifier the local place or institution, etc., that appears with the conference name in the source for the conference name (cf. 21.1B2(d)) as opposed to other locations within the item where the conference name is repeated. If an institution's name appears in the source, transcribe the institution's name as the qualifier, or if a local place name appears, transcribe that. If both such names appear, prefer to use the name of the institution, etc., generally without the name of the local place unless the name of the institution is a very "weak" one (use judgment in this respect and do not be concerned about a high degree of consistency).

If the item being cataloged contains the proceedings, etc., of two meetings of the same conference, and main entry under the heading for the conference is appropriate (cf. 21.1B2(d)), enter the item under the specific heading for the first conference (i.e., the name and its 24.7B additions) and make an added entry under the specific heading for the second conference even if the meetings are consecutively numbered.

If the item contains the proceedings, etc., of three or more meetings, enter the item under the heading for the conference without any 24.7B additions.

24.8   EXHIBITIONS, FAIRS, FESTIVALS, ETC.

An LC rule interpretation says that names of exhibitions, fairs, festivals, etc., are to be treated in the same way as names of meetings with regard to the matter of qualifiers added to the name.

24.9   CHAPTERS, BRANCHES, ETC.

AACR2 says: "Add to the name of a chapter, branch, etc., that carries out the activities of a corporate body in a particular locality, the name of that locality. If the locality is part of the name of the chapter, branch, etc., do not add it.

This rule can be applied to government agencies which have field offices (e.g., "United States. Environmental Protection Agency. Region 7," "United States. Forest Service. Alaska Region"). The United States Veterans Administration lists in the *United States Government Manual* the following types of chapters or branches: centers, domiciliaries, medical centers, medical and regional offices, supply activities, and data processing centers."

United States. *Bureau of Land Management. Oregon State Office*

Special Libraries Association. *Heart of America Chapter (Kansas City, Mo.)*

24.10 ———

24.11   RADIO AND TELEVISION STATIONS

24.11A   AACR2 says: "If the name of a radio or television station consists solely or primarily of its call letters or if its name does not convey the idea of a radio or television station, add the words *Radio station* or *Television station* and the name of the place in which the station is located."

WGEM-TV *(Television station : Quincy, Ill.)*

Notice that *Television station* is added even though we may assume that the initials *TV* means television station.

24.11B   AACR2 says: "Add to the names of any other radio and television stations the place in which it is located unless it is an integral part of the name."

Radio New Zealand

Radio Clube Portugues
  x R.C.P.

Radio RSA, Johannesburg
  x South African Broadcasting Corporation. Radio RSA, Johannesburg

Radio Free Europe

Subordinate and related bodies

24.12   GENERAL RULE

There are two major sequences of rules for subordinate and related bodies: rule 24.13 for all bodies not entered under jurisdiction (government), and rule 24.18 for bodies entered under jurisdiction (government). These sequences list the types of names or bodies that should be entered subordinately. The two lists of types are similar in the beginning. The first three types in both lists are practically the same and emphasize the body's name, rather than its nature: (1) "department," etc., names, (2) "committee," etc., names, and (3) "empty" names or names indicating location, numerical, or alphabetical designation.

The types after number three are quite different. In the nonjurisdiction list, type 4 is for faculties, etc., of universities, provided the name of the entity indicates no more than the field of study. This type is a combination of the two criteria, kind of name and kind of body. Type 5 is for names of subordinate or related bodies that contain the higher body's name, and this type is absent from the jurisdiction list. There are only five types in the nonjurisdiction list.

The jurisdiction (government) list contains ten types and types 4–10 are dependent upon the criterion of function, no matter what the name, and are for ministries (type 4), legislatures (type 5), courts (type 6), armed services (type 7), chiefs of state (type 8), embassies (type 9), and delegations to international entities (type 10).

AACR2 embodies a major change of philosophy in these rules. In addition to now treating subordinate and related bodies identically, AACR2 also requires the cataloger to place more emphasis on the name of the body than on the body's function. How does the name of the body sound? Does the name sound as if it implies subordination? While the rules may still require that the cataloger determine what the body is (i.e., government versus nongovernment body), the cataloger is much less often than before concerned with what the corporate body actually does.

Rules 24.20–24.26 provide special provisions for some of the bodies entered under jurisdiction. These special provisions are concerned with language, qualifiers, hierarchy, the choice of a jurisdiction when there is more than one, etc. Taking the armed services as an example, one should note that there are several provisions in this sequence of rules that require arbitrary direct entry under the jurisdiction, with no possibility of using intervening hierarchy, if there is any. The bodies covered here all require some kind of special treatment.

Note that rules 24.17–24.26 do not contain anything corresponding to type 5 in rule 24.13, which requires subordinate entry if the subordinate body's name contains the name of the higher body. For the higher body's heading, rule 24.17 calls for direct entry under the name without recourse to rules 24.12–24.16, e.g., "University of British Columbia." If rules 24.12–24.16 were applied to this name, type 5 of rule 24.13 would require "British Columbia. University" as the heading. The "University of British Columbia Library," however, is treated under rules 24.12–24.16. Type 5 of rule 24.13 requires "University of British Columbia. Library" as the heading.

The list of types of bodies not entered under jurisdiction is essentially the same in AACR2 as AACR1. The list of types of bodies entered under jurisdiction in AACR2 shows one major difference. This difference relates to the institutions, installations, banks, etc., for which AACR1 provided automatic independent entry. Under AACR2, none of these government bodies is accorded arbitrary independent entry, and any one might be entered subordinate to the jurisdiction, if the body fits one of the types enumerated for subordinate entry.

East African Society of African Culture
> *x* Society of African Culture. *East African Society of African Culture*

Korean Service Corps
> *x* KSC
> *x* Korea *(South). Yukkun. Korean Service Corps*
> *x* United States. *Army. Korean Service Corps*

SRI-Washington
> *x* SRI International. *SRI-Washington*

Paul D. Merica Research Laboratory
> *x* International Nickel Company. *Paul D. Merica Research Laboratory*

IDH-WHO Working Group on Quality of Water
> *x* International Hydrological Decade-World Health Organization Working Group on Quality of Water
> *x* World Health Organization Working Group on Quality of Water.

Note that rules 24.13–24.16 are used also when dealing with a body that is subordinate to a government body that is entered directly under its own name. Do not use rules 24.17–18 for these cases.

24.13 SUBORDINATE AND RELATED BODIES ENTERED SUBORDINATELY

AACR2 says:

> Enter a subordinate or related body as a subheading of the name of the body to which it is subordinate or related if its name belongs to one or more of the following types. Make it a direct or indirect subheading as instructed in 24.14. Omit from the subheading the name or abbreviation of the name of the higher or related body in noun form unless this does not make sense.

> *name:* Senate Committee on Natural Resources and Wildlife (of the California legislature)
> *heading:* **California.** *Legislature. Senate. Committee on Natural Resources and Wildlife*

LC rule interpretation says:

> If a body is entered subordinately according to types 2, 3, or 4, make a direct reference from the name of the subordinate body only if its name appears without the name of its parent body on the chief source of one of its own publications. When making the reference, generally qualify the name with the

name of the parent body (in the form and language on which the heading for the parent body is based, not necessarily its catalog-entry form).

If the name of a subordinate body lacks a term indicating that it is a corporate body, enter it subordinately if the name of a higher body is required for identification of the subordinate body.

name: Conservation Research and Development

heading: **Minnesota Energy Agency.** *Conservation Research and Development*

name: Adaptive Driver Education

heading: **Human Resources Center** *(Albertson, N.Y.). Adaptive Driver Education*

24.13   TYPE 1

AACR2 says: "A name that contains a term that by definition implies that the body is part of another, e.g., department, division, section, branch."

Babcock & Wilcox Company. *Contract Research Division*

Sanders Associates. *Defensive Systems Division*

American Medical Association. *Resident Physicians Section*

Scandia Laboratories. *Combustion Sciences Dept.*

24.13   TYPE 2

AACR2 says: "A name that contains a word normally implying administrative subordination (e.g., committee, commission), providing the name of the higher body is required for the identification of the subordinate body."

National Research Council *(U.S.). Subcommittee on Swine Nutrition*
National Research Council *(U.S.). Subcommittee on Warm-Water Fish Nutrition*

Committee on Science, Engineering, and Public Policy *(U.S.). Panel on Scientific Communication and National Security*

Colorado State University. *Dept. of Earth Resources*

LC rule interpretation says:
Note that bodies called by terms other than "committee" and "commission" come under this type (cf. fourth example). Some other words are as follows:

24.13   *Type 2*

English

administration	. . . group
administrative . . .	(e.g., work group)
(e.g., administrative office)	office
advisory . . .	panel
(e.g., advisory panel)	secretariat
agency	service
authority	task force
board	working party
bureau	

French

administration	direction
agence	groupe de . . .
bureau	inspection
cabinet	office
comité	secrétariat
commission	service
délégation	

Spanish

administración	gabinete
agencia	gerencia
asesoría	grupo de . . .
comisaría	jefatura
comisión	junta
comité	negociado
coordinación	oficina
delegación	secretaria
diputación	secretariado
direccion	servico
directoria	superintendencia
fiscalía	

Conversely, here are some commonly used words which have been rejected as falling into type 2:

> council
> project
> program

For the type's second criterion, "providing the name of the higher body is required for the identification of the subordinate body," use judgment.

The proviso "providing the name of the higher body is required for the identification of the subordinate body" should be used positively to justify entering the name subordinately since most names of this type need further identification. In the Australian example, the logical question would be, whose national committee?

> **American National Standards Institute.** *Committee X3 – Computers and Information Processing*
>
> **Australian Labor Party.** *National Committee of Inquiry*

but   **ASTM Committee D-1 on Paint and Related Coatings and Materials**

is entered directly because the name of the higher body in its abbreviated form is included as part of the name.

24.13   TYPE 3

AACR2 as revised says: "A name that is general in nature does no more than indicate a geographic, chronological, or numbered or lettered subdivision of the parent body."

> **U.S. Customs Service.** *Region IX*

"In case of doubt, do not enter the body subordinately."

LC rule interpretation says: ". . . 'general in nature' usually means that the name contains neither very distinctive elements (such as proper nouns or adjectives) nor subject words."

For example, enter these names subordinately:

> Technical Information Library
>
> Class of 1880
>
> Friends of the Library
>
> District 330
>
> 42nd Annual Meeting
>
> Scientific Forum
>
> Western Region District
>
> Utah Society
>   *(of the American Institute of Architects)*
>
> Research Institute
>
> Central Region
>
> Orange District
>
> Region 9
>
> Human Resources Center

Otherwise, consider that the name is not "general in nature" and enter it indepen-

24.13   *Type 4*

    Academy of Sciences

    Carnegie Library

    Fine Arts Museum

    Music Archive

with qualifiers as necessary (cf. RI 24.4C).

24.13   TYPE 4

AACR2 says: "A name of a university faculty, school, college, institute, laboratory, etc., that simply indicates a particular field of study."

    University of Nebraska at Omaha. *College of Business Administration*

    Carnegie-Mellon University. *Environmental Studies Institute*

    Moore School of Electrical Engineering

    Universidad Mayor de San Simón (*Cochabamba, Bolivia*). *Editorial Universitaria*

    Universität Wien. *Institut für Österreichische Geschichtsforschung*

    University of California, Berkeley. *University Art Museum*

    University of London. *Southern African Materials Project*

    University of Texas at Austin. *Council on Energy Resources*

24.13   TYPE 5

AACR2 says: "A name that includes the entire name of the higher or related body."
LC rule interpretation says:

    Understand the term "includes" in the rule to apply to any linguistic relationship between the name of the body and its parent (higher or related) body, not just to those shown in the example under type 5.

ENTIRE NAME
    Understand the phrase "entire name" to apply to the name that was selected for use in the heading for the parent body, not necessarily the catalog-entry form of the parent body's heading. For example, disregard cataloger's additions to the parent body's name or the fact that the parent body may be entered subordinately. Note, however, that if the heading for the parent body includes a term indicating incorporation, etc. (24.5C1), the form with the term must also appear in the name of the subordinate body for type 5 to be applicable.

    name of subordinate body: Northwestern University School of Law
    heading for parent body: **Northwestern University** *(Evanston, Ill.)*
    heading for subordinate body: **Northwestern University** *(Evanston, Ill.).*
        School of Law

but   *name of subordinate body:* Hoechst Chemical Society
  heading for parent body: **Hoechst A.G.**
  heading for subordinate body: **Hoechst Chemical Society**
not   Hoechst A.G. Chemical Society

Exceptions: Treat as falling under type 5 a name that fits one of the following categories:

 a) the subordinate body's name contains the entire name of a directly entered U.S. government body except that one body uses "United States" and the other body uses "U.S.";
 b) the subordinate body's name contains the entire name of its parent body except that the form for the parent body in the subordinate body's name is in another language.

 name of subordinate body: South Carolina Advisory Committee to the U.S. Commission on Civil Rights
 heading for parent body: **United States Commission on Civil Rights**
 heading for subordinate body: **United States Commission on Civil Rights.** *South Carolina Advisory Committee*

 name of subordinate body: 10th International Symposium of the Princess Takamatsu Cancer Research Fund
 heading for parent body: **Takamatsu no Miya Hi Gan Kenkyu Kikin**
 heading for subordinate body: **Takamatsu no Miya Hi Gan Kenkyu Kikin.** *International Symposium (10th : 1979 : Tokyo, Japan)*

REFERENCES
 Routinely make a reference from the entire name of a body entered under type 5 unless the name belongs to 24.13, type 1.

American Legion. *Auxiliary*
 x American Legion Auxiliary

Auburn University. *Agricultural Experiment Station.*
 x Agricultural Experiment Station of Auburn University

EXCLUSIONS FROM TYPE 5
 Type 5 is not applicable to a name that falls into one of the following categories:

 a) the subordinate body's name contains the entire name of the parent body except that the name of the subordinate body contains an element of location:

 name: Camden Friends of the Earth
 heading: **Camden Friends of the Earth**
not   Friends of the Earth. *Camden Friends of the Earth*

 b) the name of a U.S. state university that contains the name of the state-wide system:

> *name:* University of Nebraska Medical Center
> *heading:* **University of Nebraska Medical Center**
> *not*   University of Nebraska *(Central administration). Medical Center*

NAMED MEETINGS

If a named meeting (cf. RI 21.1B1) contains the entire name of a corporate body (as defined above), enter the meeting subordinately to the heading for the body if the name contains, in addition to the name of the body, no more than a generic term for the meeting, or no more than a generic term plus one or more of the following elements: the venue of the meeting; number, date, or other sequencing element.

> *name:* First Constitutional Convention of the Congress of Industrial Organizations
> *heading:* **Congress of Industrial Organizations** *(U.S.). Constitutional Convention (1st : 1938 : Pittsburgh, Pa.)*

> *name:* 5th Annual Conference of the Nigerian Political Science Association
> *heading:* **Nigerian Political Science Association.** *Conference (5th : 1978 : University of Ife)*

> *name:* Human Factors Society 1979 Annual Meeting
> *heading:* **Human Factors Society** *(U.S.). Meeting (1979 : Boston, Mass.)*

In all other cases, enter the named meeting directly under its own name.

> *name:* Miami University Conference on Sentence Combining and the Teaching of Writing
> *heading:* **Miami University Conference on Sentence Combining and the Teaching of Writing** *(1978)*
> *not*   Miami University. *Conference on Sentence Combining and the Teaching of Writing (1978)*

> *name:* Unesco International Chemistry Conference
> *heading:* **Unesco International Chemistry Conference** *(1978 : Perth, W.A.)*
> *not*   Unesco. *International Chemistry Conference (1978 : Perth, W.A.)*

24.14   DIRECT OR INDIRECT SUBHEADING

AACR2 says:

> Enter a body belonging to one or more of the types listed in 24.13 as a subheading of the lowest element in the hierarchy that is entered under its own name. Omit intervening elements in the hierarchy unless the name of the subordinate or related body has been, or is likely to be, used by another body entered under the name of the same higher or related body. In that case, interpose the name of the lowest element in the hierarchy that will distinguish between the bodies.

Englehard Minerals and Chemicals Corporation. *Industries Division. Research and Development Dept.*

National Research Council *(U.S.). Subcommittee on Swine Nutrition*

National Research Council *(U.S.). Subcommittee on Warm-Water Fish Nutrition*

Both of these subordinate bodies of the National Research Council are subordinate to the intermediate unit, the Board on Agriculture and Renewal Resources.

AACR2 continues: "Refer from the name in the form of a subheading of the name of its immediately superior body when the heading does not include the name of that superior body."

> **Rockwell International.** *Electronic Systems Group*
>   *x* Rockwell International. *Autonetics Strategic Systems Division. Electronic Systems Group*

24.15   JOINT COMMITTEES, COMMISSIONS, ETC.

24.15A AACR2 says: "Enter a body made up of representatives of two or more other bodies under its own name."

> **IMCO/FAO/UNESCO/WMO/WHO/IAEA/UN Joint Group of Experts on the Scientific Aspects of Marine Pollution**
>   *(A joint committee of Inter-Governmental Maritime Consultative Organization; Food and Agriculture Organization; United Nations Educational, Scientific and Cultural Organization; World Meteorological Organization; World Health Organization; International Atomic Energy Agency; United Nations)*

> **Arkansas-White-Red Basins Inter-Agency Committee**
>   *(Consists of 1 member from the Dept. of the Army, Dept. of Interior, Dept. of Agriculture, Dept. of Commerce, Federal Power Commission, the Governors of Ark., La., Okla., N.M., Kans., and Mo.)*

> **Upper Great Lakes Regional Commission**
>   *(Consists of members from federal, state, and local bodies)*

> **Committee on Science, Engineering, and Public Policy.** *Panel on Scientific Communication and National Security*
>   *(A joint committee of National Academy of Sciences, the National Academy of Engineering, and the Institute of Medicine)*

AACR2 continues: "Omit the names of the parent bodies when these occur within or at the end of the name if the name of the joint unit is distinctive without them."

> **Joint Committee for Stroke Facilities**
> *not* Joint Committee for Stroke Facilities of the American Neurological Association and the U.S. Dept. of Health, Education, and Welfare

24.15B AACR2 says: "If the parent bodies are entered as subheadings of a common higher body, enter the joint unit as a subordinate body as instructed in 24.12–24.14."

> **United States.** *Congress. Joint Economic Committee*
> *(A joint committee of the House and the Senate)*

Even if the subordinate parent bodies are established differently (e.g., American Library Association/Resources and Technical Services Division is entered subordinately, whereas ALA's Public Library Association is entered under its own name), enter the joint unit as a subordinate to the highest parent body.

LC rule interpretation says:

> If a body is made up of representatives of two or more other bodies, and these other bodies are all entered as subheadings of a common higher body, enter the joint unit as a subordinate body as instructed in 24.14 or 24.19 if the name of the joint unit fits one of the types under 24.13 or 24.18.

> **United States.** *Joint Meteorological Committee*
> *x* United States. *Army. Joint Meteorological Committee*
> *x* United States. *Navy. Joint Meteorological Committee*
> *x* United States. *Weather Bureau. Joint Meteorological Committee*

24.16 CONVENTIONALIZED SUBHEADINGS FOR STATE AND LOCAL ELEMENTS OF AMERICAN POLITICAL PARTIES

Include special elements and caucuses of political parties.

> *name:* Democratic Congressional Campaign Committee
> *heading:* **Democratic Party** *(U.S.). Congressional Campaign Committee*

> *name:* National Republican Congressional Committee
> *heading:* **Republican Party** *(U.S.). Congressional Committee*

Government bodies and officials

24.17 GENERAL RULE

AACR2 says:

> Enter a body created or controlled by a government under its own name (see 24.1–24.3) unless it belongs to one or more of the types listed in 24.18. However, if a body is subordinate to a higher body that is entered under its own name, formulate the heading for the subordinate body according to 24.12–24.14. Refer to the name of a government agency entered independently from its name in the form of a subheading of the name of the government (see 26.3A7).

LC will consider the United Nations to be a government body under rules 24.17 and 24.18 when determining the heading for its subordinate and related bodies.

National Hospital Insurance Fund *(Kenya)*

Arctic Environmental Research Station *(U.S.)*

California State Water Resources Control Board

Charleston Naval Shipyard

FAA Interservice Energy Task Force III

New York Public Library

Geological Survey of Alabama

Colorado Geological Survey

British Information Services

Iowa Geological Survey

Maryland Aricultural Experiment Station

Ohio Legislative Service Commission

United Nations Development Programme

Krajske Vlastivedne Muzeum v Olomouci

Board of Governors of the Federal Reserve System *(U.S.)*

National Science Foundation *(U.S.)*

UNICEF

Office of the United Nation's Disaster Relief Coordinator

Unesco

LC rule interpretation says:

> Establish the names of National Unesco Commissions that are agencies of the governments they represent according to 24.17 or 24.18, type 2, not 24.18, type 10.

24.18   GOVERNMENT AGENCIES ENTERED SUBORDINATELY

AACR2 says:

> Enter a government agency subordinately if it belongs to one or more of the following types. Make it a direct or indirect subheading of the heading for the government as instructed in 24.19. Omit from the subheading the name or abbreviation of the name of the government in noun form unless such an omission would result in an objectionable distortion.

All of the examples in 24.18, types 1 to 10 show direct entry under jurisdiction. Avoid the conclusion as indicated in examples like "United States. Division of Wildlife Service" that you always enter these subordinate parts directly under the jurisdiction. Use 24.19 to determine whether the subordinate body will be entered directly or indirectly under the jurisdiction.

A further distinction should be made between words that imply higher versus lower levels of hierarchy. In general, divisions, sections, and branches should be treated as indirect subheadings.

LC rule interpretation says:

> There is no counterpart to rule 24.13, type 5 under 24.18. Therefore, even if the name of a subordinate government agency contains the entire name of its parent body (i.e., the name of the parent body in the form on which the heading of the parent body is based), and the parent body is entered subordinately to the heading for the government, nevertheless enter the subordinate agency directly under its own name unless the name meets one of the following conditions:
>
> a) the name of the subordinate agency itself fits one of the types under 24.18;
>
> b) the name of its parent body occurs at the beginning of the subordinate agency's name and the first word is a 24.18, type 1 term. (Note: If the name meets this condition, do not omit any hierarchy from the heading for the subordinate agency.)

> *name:* Veterans Administration Dental Education Center
> *(The name does not meet either of the two conditions)*
> *heading:* **Veterans Administration Dental Education Center** *(U.S.)*

> *name:* Senate Committee on Natural Resources and Wildlife
> *(The name fits 24.18, type 5)*
> *heading:* **California.** *Legislature. Senate. Committee on Natural Resources and Wildlife*

> *name:* Department of Health and Social Security Library
> *(The parent body's name occurs at the beginning and the first word is a type 1 term.)*
> *heading:* **Great Britain.** *Dept. of Health and Social Security. Library*

If the name of a government agency lacks a term indicating that it is a corporate body, enter it subordinately unless the name contains the name of the government or an understandable surrogate.

> *name:* Naval Oceanography and Meteorology
> *heading:* **United States.** *Naval Oceanography and Meteorology*

> *name:* Landesvermessung
> *heading:* **Lower Saxony** *(Germany). Landesvermessung*

24.18   TYPE 1

AACR2 says: "An agency with a name containing a term that by definition implies that the body is part of another, e.g., department, division, section, branch, and their equivalents in other languages."

The terms *administrative office* and *secretariat* should be considered as evidence that the body is part of another.

United States. *Environmental Protection Agency. Grants Operation Branch*

New Mexico. *Commerce and Industry Dept.*

South Dakota. *Division of Aeronautics*

Alabama. *State Planning Commission*

United States. *Dept. of Housing and Urban Development. Office of Policy Development and Research. Division of Policy Studies*

United States. *Dept. of Defense. Washington Headquarters Services. Directorate for Information Operations and Reports*

New York *(State). Division of the Budget*

United States. *Dept. of Agriculture*

United States. *National Park Service. Midwest Region*

24.18   TYPE 2

AACR2 says: "An agency with a name containing a word that normally implies administrative subordination (e.g., committee, commission), providing the name of the government is required for the identification of the agency."

There are thousands of subordinate bodies in all levels of government, many of which are advisory bodies. A report listing all advisory committees to the United States government is submitted to Congress each year by the President.[4] Advisory committees are established by statute, executive order or memorandum, or agency authority. In 1975, 1,267 committees existed, of which 272 were new and another 233 were terminated. These advisory committees advise executive branch departments and independent agencies (including those in the Executive Office of the President and in the Congress). They are established in relationship to these bodies and receive money and personnel support from them. In most cases they lack even the authority to call a meeting of their own group; instead, the agency establishing them must call the meeting. They must report to the bodies creating them: committees established by Congress may report directly to Congress or to an agency designated by Congress.

A study of most common terms used to describe advisory committees results in the following list: committee, advisory committee, review committee, council, council on, advisory council, board, board of, advisory board, panel, panel on, panel on review of, advisory panel, commission, study section.

There is confusion between commissions, councils, and committees established by Congress as independent agencies (such as Federal Communications Commission, U.S. Commission on Civil Rights, Railroad Retirement Board) and those established primarily to study or advise. The same terms are sometimes used to describe both types of bodies. Advisory committees under the Federal Advisory Committee Act, Public Law 92–463, can only exist for two years and then they must be reestablished. They must

---

4. Federal Advisory Committees. Fourth Annual Report of the President covering calendar year 1975. U.S. General Services Administration. 1976. (For sale by GPO; stock number 040–000–00345–2)

also be listed in the advisory committee report, therefore catalogers can easily establish their status as committee or independent agency.

A good example of the same term used for both types of commission is:

example
The Radio Technical Commission for Aeronautics advises the Federal Communications Commission.

hierarchy
    United States
    Federal Communications Commission
    Radio Technical Commission for Aeronautics

Other examples of advisory committees:

example
Citizens Advisory Committee on Environmental Quality advises the Council on Environmental Quality (an office within the Executive Office of the President)

hierarchy
    United States
    Executive Office of the President
    Council on Environmental Quality
    Citizens Advisory Committee on Environmental Quality

example
Merit Review Board for Hematology advises the Veterans Administration

hierarchy
    United States
    Veterans Administration
    Merit Review Board for Hematology

example
National Study Commission on Records and Documents of Federal Officials advises Congress

hierarchy
    United States Congress
    National Study Commission on Records and Documents of Federal Officials

example
Council on International Economic Policy, created by Presidential memorandum. It is part of the Executive Office of the President just like OMB.

hierarchy
    United States
    Executive Office of the President
    Council on International Economic Policy

There are problems with the examples in AACR2 listed under type 2. The example "United States. Commission on Civil Rights," implying subordination, is not a good one since its name is "U.S. Commission on Civil Rights" and it is listed that way on its publications and in most reference works and manuals. It should be entered as stated in 24.17 under its own name.

Since the Council on International Economic Policy advises the President of the United States and since the Consejo Superior de Investigaciones Cientificas could also be a part of the government of another Spanish-speaking country as well as of Spain, both of these bodies should be qualified.

Council on International Economic Policy *(U.S.)*

Consejo Superior de Investigaciones Cientificas *(Spain)*

The LC rule interpretation says:

> Test a name against this type [24.18, type 2] only if it contains "a word that normally implies administrative subordination." Whether or not a word has such an implication depends on whether it is used commonly in a particular jurisdiction as part of the names of government subdivisions. Use judgment; if in doubt, consider that the word in question does not have such an implication. For names of government bodies whose official language is in English, French, or Spanish, we shall attempt a higher degree of uniformity by making a list of words used within these entities that normally imply administrative subordination. In addition to "committee" and "commission" (cf. the rule), other type 2 words for these languages are as follows:

English

administration	. . . group
administrative . . .	(e.g., work group)
(e.g., administrative office)	office
advisory . . .	panel
(e.g., advisory panel)	secretariat
agency	service
authority	task force
board	working party
bureau	

French

administration	direction
agence	groupe de . . .
bureau	inspection
cabinet	office
comité	secrétariat
commission	service
délégation	

229

Spanish

administración	gabinete
agencia	gerencia
asesoría	grupo de . . .
comisaría	jefatura
comisión	junta
comité	negociado
coordinación	oficina
delegación	secretaria
diputación	secretariado
direccion	servico
directoria	superintendencia
fiscalía	

For bodies with names in English, French, or Spanish, only names containing one or more of the words listed above are to be treated acording to type 2.

If the name passes the test described above, then evaluate it in terms of the second criterion in type 2: "providing the name of the government is required for the identification of the agency." Apply this criterion in the following way: If either the name of the government is stated explicitly or implied in the wording of the name, enter it independently; in all other cases, enter the name subordinately. Apply this interpretation to the names of agencies at any level of government. *Note:* (1) If variant forms in the body's usage create doubt about whether or not the name includes the name of the government (as defined above), do not consider the name of the government as part of the name of the body. (2) In applying the single criterion of "name of government . . . stated explicitly or implied," note the following special decision: "England," "Scotland," and "Wales" imply "Great Britain."

Ivory Coast. *Conseil économique et social*

If, according to type 2 and this interpretation, the body is entered under its own name, add the name of the government as a qualifier unless this name or an understandable surrogate is already present in the body's name (cf. 24.4C).

United States. *Office of the Federal Register*
   x United States. *General Services Administration. National Archives and Records Service. Office of the Federal Register*

United States. *Employment and Training Administration*
   x United States. *Dept. of Labor. Employment and Training Administration*

United States. *Securities and Exchange Commission*

United States. *TMI-2 Lessons Learned Task Force*
   x United States. *Nuclear Regulatory Commission. TMI-2 Lessons Learned*
    Task Force
   x Three Mile Island-2 Lessons Learned Task Force

Québec *(Province). Ministere des affaiers intergovernementales. Service de recherche*

North Carolina. *State Goals and Policy Board*

United States. *National Commission on Digestive Diseases*

United States. *Federal Trade Commission*

United States. *Dept. of Energy. Historian's Office*

United States. *Drug Enforcement Administration. Office of Enforcement*
   x United States. *Dept. of Justice. Drug Enforcement Administration. Office of Enforcement*

Sierra Leone. *Faulkner Commission of Inquiry into the Finance and Administration of the Transport and General Workers Union*

United States. *Head Start Bureau*

United States. *Environmental Protection Agency. Oil and Special Materials Control Division. Marine Protection Branch*

Nigeria. *Office of the President. Dept. of Information*

New York *(N.Y.). Human Resources Administration. Office of Policy and Program Development*

New York *(N.Y.). Human Resources Administration. Office of Policy and Economic Research*

Mexico. *Comisión de Estudios del Territorio Nacional*

United Nations. *Economic Commission for Africa*

United States. *Mississippi River Commission*

United States. *Federal Emergency Management Agency*

24.18   TYPE 3

AACR2 as revised says: "An agency with a name that is general in nature that does no more than indicate a geographic, chronological, or numbered or lettered subdivision of the government or one of its agencies entered subordinately."

    United States. *National Labor Relations Board. Library*
      Name: Library

Illinois. *Bureau of Employment Security. Research and Analysis*
   Name: Research and Analysis

Niger. *Commissariat général au développement. Centre de documentation*
   Name: Centre de documentation

Malaysia. *Royal Customs and Excise Department. Sabah Region*
   Name: Sabah Region

United States. *General Services Administration. Region 5*
   Name: Region 5

United States. *Public Health Service. Region XI*
   Name: Region XI

In case of doubt, do not enter the body subordinately.

Governor's Internship Program
not   Minnesota. *Governor's Internship Program*

National Portrait Gallery *(U.K.)*
not   United Kingdom. *National Portrait Gallery*

Musée des beaux-arts *(Béziers)*
not   Béziers. *Musée des beaux-arts*

The LC rule interpretation says:

If the body is at the national level of government, consider that the name is "general"—and enter it subordinately—in the following cases:

a) the name contains neither very distinctive elements (such as proper nouns or adjectives) nor subject words; e.g.,

Research Center

Library

Technical Laboratory

b) the name consists of a general phrase (cf. explanation immediately above) plus the "national" or "state" (meaning "national") or their equivalents in foreign languages; e.g.,

National Gallery

State Library

c) the name indicates only, or chiefly, the location or a numerical or alphabetical designation. Enter the names of all other national level bodies independently, e.g.,

Population Research Center

Nuclear Energy Library

Technical Laboratory of Oceanographic Research

National Institutes of Health

Corporation for Public Broadcasting

with qualifiers as necessary (cf. RI 24.4C). In case of doubt as to whether the name fits a) – c) above, enter it independently.

If the body is below the national level, and its name does not fall into any other type under 24.18, enter it under the heading for the government unless either the name of the government is stated explicitly or is implied in the wording of the name, or the name contains some other element guaranteeing uniqueness (usually a proper noun or adjective). (If variant forms in the body's usage make it unclear as to whether the name includes the name of the government (as defined above), do not treat the name of the government as part of the name of the body.) In case of doubt as to whether the name of a body below the national level fits the criterion for subordinate entry, enter it subordinately.

If according to these instructions, the body is entered under its own name, generally add the name of the government as a qualifier unless this name or an understandable surrogate is already present in the body's name (cf. RI 24.4C).

24.18   TYPE 4

AACR2 says: "An agency that is a ministry or similar major executive agency (i.e., one that has no other agency above it) as defined by official publications of the government in question."

United States. *Dept. of Labor*

United States. *Community Services Administration*

Great Britain. *Welsh Office*

Victoria. *Ministry of the Arts*

LC rule interpretation says:

Restrict the application of type 4 to major executive agencies of *national* governments.

24.18   TYPE 5

AACR2 says: "Legislative bodies (see also 24.21)."

Australia. *Parliament*

Philippines. *National Assembly*

LC rule interpretation says:

Do not apply 24.18, type 5 to the names of county, regional and district councils in England, Scotland, Wales, and Northern Ireland, since the bodies are primarily administrative rather than legislative. Instead, apply 24.17 or 24.18, type 3 to these names.

24.18 TYPE 6

AACR2 says: ''Courts (see also 24.23).''

> **United States.** *Court of Appeals (9th Circuit)*
>
> **United States.** *District Court (Arizona)*
>
> **United States.** *District Court (District of Columbia)*
>
> **United States.** *District Court (Tennessee : Middle District)*

24.18 TYPE 7

AACR2 says: ''Principal armed services (see also 24.24).''

> **United States.** *Air Force*
>
> **Canada.** *Canadian Army*
>
> **Great Britain.** *Royal Navy*

24.18 TYPE 8

AACR2 says: ''Chiefs of state and heads of government (see also 24.20).''

> **Canada.** *Prime Minister*
>
> **Montana.** *Governor*

24.18 TYPE 9

AACR2 says: ''Embassies, consulates, etc. (see also 24.25).''

> **China.** *Embassy (U.S.)*

24.18 TYPE 10

AACR2 says: ''Delegations to international and intergovernmental bodies (see also 24.26).''

LC rule interpretation says:

> Do not apply 24.18, type 10 to the names of National Unesco Commissions that are agencies of the governments they represent. Instead, apply 24.17 or 24.18, type 2 to the names.

24.19 DIRECT OR INDIRECT SUBHEADING

AACR2 says:

> Enter an agency belonging to one or more of the types listed in 24.18 as a direct subheading of the heading for the government unless the name of the agency has been, or is likely to be, used by another agency under the name of the same government. In that case, add, between the name of the government and the name of the agency, the name of the lowest element in the hierarchy that will distinguish between the agencies.

234

United States. *Dept. of Energy. Division of Data Analysis*
    x United States. *Dept. of Energy. Office of Conservation and Solar Applica-tions. Division of Data Analysis*

United States. *Food and Drug Administration. Medical Library*
    x United States. *Dept. of Health and Human Services*

Public Health Service. *Food and Drug Administration. Medical Library*

United States. *Food Safety and Quality Service*
    x United States. *Dept. of Agriculture. Food Safety and Quality Service*

Connecticut. *State Manpower Services Council*
    x Connecticut. *Labor Dept. State Manpower Services Council*

Organization of American States. *Division of Codification and Legal Integra-tion*
    x Organization of American States. *Dept. of Legal Affairs. Division of Codification and Legal Integration*

United States. *National Fire Safety and Research Office*
    x United States. *Dept. of Commerce. National Fire Prevention and Control Administration. National Fire Safety and Research Office*
    x United States. *National Fire Prevention and Control Administration. National Fire Safety and Research Office*

United States. *Environmental Protection Agency. Oil and Special Materials Control Division. Marine Protection Branch*

Nigeria. *Office of the President. Dept. of Information*

New York (*N.Y.*). *Human Resources Administration. Office of Policy and Economic Research*

Mexico. *Comisión de Estudios del Territorio Nacional*

United Nations. *Economic Commission for Africa*

United States. *Dept. of Defense. Washington Headquarters Services. Director-ate for Information Operations and Reports*

The example "United States. Division of Wildlife Service" used in 24.18, type 1 represents a mistake. The parent body of the division is the U.S. Fish and Wildlife Service, which is established under this name. Therefore the heading for the division must be created according to 24.13, not 24.18, resulting in the following correct form of the heading:

U.S. Fish and Wildlife Service. *Division of Wildlife Service*

LC's rule interpretation says:

> The rules emphasize omission of hierarchy but qualify this emphasis as follows:
>
> (Omit hierarchy) unless the name of the subordinate or related body has been, or is likely to be, used by another body entered under the same higher or related body.
>
> (Rule 24.14 for bodies entered under a higher body other than a jurisdiction)
>
> (Omit hierarchy) unless the name of the agency has been, or is likely to be, used by another agency entered under the same government.
>
> (Rule 24.19 for bodies entered under a jurisdiction)
>
> The words "or is likely to be" will carry a varying import to different catalogers. The statement below indicates the particular import of the words that Library of Congress catalogers should heed.
>
> Two types of names do not need explanation, i.e., in these cases all catalogers reading only the rule and no gloss would reach the same conclusions. These types of names are:

> A) Names of subordinate bodies performing functions common to many higher bodies,* when the name of the subordinate body (exclusive of any names of higher bodies included in its name) is as common sounding as its function:

> Personnel Office
> Archives of the Ministry for Rural Development
> Research and Development Section
> Planning Dept.
> Procurement and Supply Division

> Headings for such subordinate bodies as these obviously could not omit hierarchy.

> B) Names of subordinate bodies performing one or more of the major functions that are unique to the particular higher body (within the same corporate structure):

> Bureau of Libraries, Museums, and Archaeological Services
> (*Under the Dept. of Conservation and Cultural Affairs, which should be omitted from the heading*)

---

*This evaluation of the body's functions indicated in two "obvious" categories is based on the names of the bodies involved, not on any special searching.

Division of Industry and Engineering
Division of Transport
> (*Both under the Ministry of Transport, Industry, and Engineering, which should be omitted from the heading*)

but not Library
> (*Also under the same ministry, but it belongs in category A, and the department must be included in the heading*)

Division of Fisheries
Division of Forestry
Geological Survey
> (*All three are under the Dept. of Conservation, which should be omitted from the heading*)

but not Division of Education and Publicity
> (*Also under the same department but belongs in category A; the department must be included in the heading*)

Names of such subordinate bodies as these obviously could omit hierarchy.

If the name of the body being established does not fit either of the above obvious categories, consider whether or not the name would be appropriate for another subordinate body within the same corporate structure. Common sense will be the best guide, but in some doubtful cases it may be relatively easy to make the decision if an important idea expressed in a word or phrase present in the higher body's name is missing from the name of the body in question.

> **United States.** *Dept. of Housing and Urban Development. Office of Environmental Factors and Public Utilities*

> **International Union for the Conservation of Nature and Natural Resources.** *Commission on Education. North-West Europe Committee*

> **United States.** *Office of Education. Office of Librarians and Learning Resources*

Avoid a very literal approach to this question, however. The name of the body being established may adequately imply the ideas expressed in the higher body's name without actually repeating the words of that name.

> **Pennsylvania. Bureau of Financial Management**
> (*omitted: Office of Administration*)

> **United States.** *Division of Nuclear Power Development*
> (*omitted: Dept. of Energy*)

If still in doubt, retain the higher body in the heading.

> **United States.** *Dept. of Health, Education, and Welfare. Advisory Council on Vocational Education*

24.20 GOVERNMENT OFFICIALS

24.20A Scope

AACR2 says: "Apply rule 24.20 only to officials of countries and other states that have existed in postmedieval times, and to officials of international intergovernmental organizations." This of course would include many of the documents generated by such international organizations as the United Nations, the European Economic Community, the International Development Bank, the Organization of American States, etc. This is an important rule to those who have international collections of documents.

24.20B Heads of state, etc.

United States. *President (1969–1974 : Nixon)*

United States. *President (1977–1981 : Carter)*

24.20C Heads of governments and of international intergovernmental bodies

Kansas City *(Kan.). Mayor*

United Nations. *Secretary General*

24.20D Governors of dependent or occupied territories

Jersey. *Militarischer Befehshaber*

Germany *(Territory under Allied occupation, 1945–1955 : U.S. Zone). Military Governor*

24.20E Other officials

AACR2 says: "The subheading for any other official is that of the ministry or agency that the official represents."

United States. *Dept. of Energy. Office of Energy Technology*
 x United States. *Dept. of Energy. Assistant Secretary for Energy Technology*

United States. *Government Printing Office*
 x United States. *Public Printer*

United States. *General Accounting Office*
 x United States. *Comptroller General*

The LC rule interpretation says:

> If the chief source gives only the name of the official, nevertheless use the name of the ministry or agency that the official represents in the heading. If necessary, determine the latter from reference sources.

24.21 LEGISLATIVE BODIES

24.21A AACR2 says: "If a legislature has more than one chamber, enter each as a subheading of the heading for the legislature."

United States. *Congress. Senate*
not   United States. *Senate*

United States. *Congress. House*
not   United States. *House*[5]

Great Britain. *Parliament. House of Commons*
not   Great Britain. *House of Commons*

New York *(State). Legislature. Assembly*
not   New York *(State). Assembly*

New York *(State). Legislature. Senate*
not   New York *(State). Senate*

24.21B AACR2 says: "Enter committees and other subordinate units (except legislative subcommittees of the U.S. Congress) as subheadings of the legislature or of a particular chamber, as appropriate."

LC rule interpretation says: "Enter a body that presents itself as a subordinate unit of a legislature or a chamber as a subheading of that legislature or chamber, even though the membership of the body is not composed of only members of the legislature or of its staff."

United States. *Congress. House. Select Committee on the Outer Continental Shelf*

United States. *Congress. Joint Committee on Printing*

United States. *Congress. Joint Committee on the Library*

Australia. *Parliament. Joint Committee on Publications*

New York *(State). Legislature. Select Committee on the Economy*

New York *(State). Legislature. Senate. Special Committee on Manpower*
x New York *(State). Special Senate Committee on Manpower*

Washington *(State). Legislature. Legislative Budget Committee*
x Washington *(State). Legislature. Budget Committee*

---

5. LC has stated in rule interpretations that *House* is the conventional name for *House of Representatives* under rule 24.3C1 and that *Great Britain* is the conventional name for *United Kingdom of Great Britain and Northern Ireland*. This decision was made in connection with the British Library which also continues using *Great Britain*. Consequently, it is necessary to ignore the examples in *AACR2* showing *House of Representatives* and *United Kingdom*.

"Establish headings for U.S. state legislative councils according to 24.21B unless the council is staffed entirely by other than members of the legislative body."

> *name:* Colorado Legislative Council
> *heading:* **Colorado.** *General Assembly. Legislative Council*

24.21C AACR2 says: "Enter a legislative subcommittee of the U.S. Congress as a subheading of the committee to which it is subordinate."

> **United States.** *Congress. Committee on House Administration. Subcommittee on Contracts and Printing*

An LC rule interpretation says: "Apply the treatment of legislative subcommittees of the U.S. Congress also to legislative subcommittees of U.S. states."

> **New York** *(State). Legislature. Assembly. Committee on Governmental Operations. Subcommittee on Indian Affairs*

> **New York** *(State). Legislature. Assembly. Committee on Social Services. Subcommittee on Adoption Practices*
> *x* New York *(State). Legislature. Assembly. Subcommittee on Adoption Practices*

LC rule interpretation says: "Also apply 24.21C to other types of bodies subordinate to legislative committees and subcommittees, e.g., task forces, panels."

> **United States.** *Congress. House. Committee on Ways and Means. Subcommittee on Trade. United States – Japan Trade Task Force*

> **California.** *Legislature. Assembly. Subcommittee on Housing Production. Housing Advisory Panel*

LC rule interpretation says: "Make a reference from the name of the subcommittee as a direct subheading of the chamber to which the parent committee belongs if the name of the subcommittee is unique within the legislature."

> **United States.** *Congress. Senate. Committee on Foreign Relations. Subcommittee on Canadian Affairs*
> *x* United States. *Congress. Senate. Subcommittee on Canadian Affairs*

24.21D AACR2 says: "If successive legislatures are numbered consecutively, add the ordinal number and the year or years to the heading for the particular legislature or one of its chambers."

> **Great Britain.** *Parliament (1697–1699). House of Commons*

24.22 ———

24.23 COURTS

LC rule interpretation says:

> In the absence of a rule for formulating headings for the prosecuting

attorneys of jurisdictions, apply the principle of a conventionalized heading used in 24.23 for the heading for the court with which the attorneys are closely associated:

1) Enter under the heading for appropriate jurisdiction. Note that in the states of the United States prosecuting attorneys are agents of the states as a whole, not agents of a particular county as a publication may suggest.
2) Use a conventional name for the office, e.g., "Attorney," "District Attorney."
3) Add as a parenthetical qualifier the name of the particular area served.

United States. *Attorney (District of Columbia)*

United States. *Attorney (Illinois : Northern District)*

New Mexico. *District Attorney (2nd Judicial District)*

Wisconsin. *District Attorney (Milwaukee County)*

24.24   ARMED FORCES

24.24A   Armed forces at the national level

AACR2 says: "Enter a principal service of the armed forces of a government as a direct subheading of the name of the government."

Great Britain. *Royal Navy*

Canada. *Canadian Army*

AACR2 continues: "Enter a component branch, command district, or military unit, large or small, as a direct subheading of the heading for the principal service of which it is a part."

United States. *Army. Corps of Engineers*

United States. *Air Force. Thunderbirds*

AACR2 continues: "If the component branch, etc., is numbered, follow the style of numbering found in the names (spelled out, roman numerals, or arabic numerals) and place the numbering after the name."

United States. *Army. Infantry Regiment, 350th*

United States. *Army. Airborne Division, 101st*

AACR2 further says: "If the name of such a component branch, etc., contains but does not begin with the name or an indication of the name of the principal service, omit the name or indication of the name unless objectionable distortion would result."

United States. *Defense Mapping Agency*

United States. *Army Map Service*

LC rule interpretation says:

For forms for component branches, command districts, and military units of military services define "component branch, command district, or military unit" as an agency which constitutes:

1) A unit subject to combat service or an administrative unit over such units, e.g.,

> commands
> corps
> fleets
> general staffs
> military districts
> regiments or divisions of infantry, etc.

2) A unit which serves as a direct support unit to category 1, e.g.,

> corps of engineers
> legal units, e.g., judge advocate general
> materiel command
> medical corps
> military police
> transport services

This means treating the following types of bodies under the general rules:

> research agencies, e.g., laboratories, research centers, institutes,
>   experiment stations, museums
> schools, e.g., service academies, Air University
> musical groups, e.g., military bands, choirs, etc.
> armories, arsenals
> base hospitals, other hospitals

Treat forts, bases, camps, airfields, etc., as jurisdictions (see RI 23.4B).

Fighting units of the U.S. Civil War present a special problem because they come to the attention of the cataloger primarily via "casual" publications such as diaries, personal histories or regiments, etc., rather than official documents. These publications show an extreme variety of designations for the regiments and other units and so do not constitue a proper AACR2 source of a name on which to base the heading. Furthermore, a library catalog that contains very many headings of this nature quickly sees a real need to standardize the file of headings somewhat. For these reasons, the Library of Congress has issued the following rule interpretation:

When establishing either Union or Confederate fighting units of the U.S. Civil War consult reference works (e.g., *The Union Army* (Madison, Wis. : Federal Pub. Co., 1908)).

If the unit is one of a numbered sequence, use a uniform designation of the number in the heading for each unit in the sequence. Make the normal cross references required by designations found and also make a reference from a standardized form beginning with the state name as shown below (only this reference is illustrated):

UNION UNITS
(title page: Journal History of the Twenty-ninth Ohio Veteran Volunteers)

United States. *Army. Ohio Infantry Regiment, 29th (1861–1865)*
  x Ohio Infantry, 29th Regiment *(1861–1865)*

(title page: History of the Forty-eighth Ohio Vet. Vol. Inf.)

United States. *Army. Ohio Infantry Regiment, 48th (1861–1865)*
  x Ohio Infantry, 48th regiment *(1861–1865)*

(title page: Annals of the Sixth Pennsylvania Cavalry)

United States. *Army. Pennsylvania Cavalry Regiment, 6th (1861–1865)*
  x Pennsylvania Cavalry, 6th Regiment *(1861–1865)*

(title page: the Seventh Pennsylvania Veteran Volunteer Cavalry)

United States. *Army. Pennsylvania Cavalry Regiment, 7th (1861–1865)*
  x Pennsylvania Cavalry, 7th Regiment *(1861–1865)*

N.B. Because of the high incidence of conflicts for Union units, a date qualifier (for the duration of the unit) is added routinely. Normally there is no such problem of conflict with Confederate units.

CONFEDERATE UNITS
(title page: Old Nineteenth Tennessee Regiment, C.S.A.)

Confederate States of America. *Army. Tennessee Infantry Regiment, 19th*
  x Tennessee Infantry, 19th Regiment

(title page: History of the First Regiment, Alabama Volunteer Infantry, C.S.A.)

Confederate States of America. *Army. Alabama Infantry Regiment, 1st*
  x Alabama Infantry, 1st Regiment

NUMBERED U.S. MILITARY UNITS
If a component branch, command unit, or military unit of a United States military service is numbered, use arabic ordinal numerals in the heading. If the form of numbering found on the item being cataloged differs from the form used in the heading, make a reference from the found form, in the order that matches the heading.

source: Sixth Fleet

heading: **United States.** *Navy. Fleet, 6th*
  x United States. *Navy. Fleet, Sixth*

24.24B ———

24.25 ———

24.26 DELEGATIONS TO INTERNATIONAL AND INTERGOVERNMENTAL BODIES

LC has issued the following guidelines:

> When entering the body subordinate to the government according to this rule, omit the name of the government or abbreviation of the name of the government in noun form unless such an omission would result in an objectionable distortion (cf. 24.18).

> When the delegation is to a meeting, add number, date, and place of the meeting in a conventionalized manner to the end of the heading according to 24.7. Use a sequence of commas to connect the data elements, i.e., do not treat these elements as AACR2 qualifiers but as part of the cataloger's construction of the name (even if otherwise the name is not being constructed).

> > *in source:* Gobierno de Ecuador . . . Segunda Delegacion a la Quinta Conferencia Panamericana de Bellas Artes Tenida a Lima 5– 10 mayo 1949
> > *heading:* **Ecuador.** *Segunda Delegacion a la Conferencia Panamericana de Bellas Artes, 5th, 1949, Lima, Peru*

> > *in source:* Indonesia . . . Delegation to the Sixth Conference of the Council of South Asian Ministers of Education . . . Manila, 1965
> > *heading:* **Indonesia.** *Delegation to the Conference of the Council of South Asian Ministers of Education, 6th, 1965, Manila, Philippines*

> When a serial entry is being prepared, follow the usual practice of omitting number, date, and place when appropriate. In monograph cataloging, normally formulate the heading to include number, date, and place, even though theoretically it would be proper to omit these elements, so that the one name authority record would stand for all such delegations. Generally make a separate name authority record in each case.

24.27 ———

Index

Compiled by Carol R. Kelm

Index

Index